COLLEGE TEACHING ABROAD

A Handbook of Strategies for Successful Cross-Cultural Exchanges

Pamela Gale George

North Carolina Central University

Allyn and Bacon
Boston • London • Toronto • Sydney • Tokyo • Singapore

Associate Publisher: Stephen D. Dragin
Editorial Assistant: Mary Visco
Cover Administrator: Solar Script, Inc.
Manufacturing Buyer: Megan Cochran
Production Coordinator: Solar Script, Inc.
Editorial-Production Service: Michael Bass & Associates

Library of Congress Cataloging-in-Publication Data

George, Pamela.
    College teaching abroad: a handbook of strategies for successful
cross-cultural exchanges/Pamela Gale George.
        p.   cm.
    Includes bibliographical references and index.
    ISBN 0-205-15767-X
        1. Educational exchanges—United States—Handbooks, manuals, etc.
    2. College teachers—United States—Handbooks, manuals, etc.
    3. Teachers, Foreign—Employment.   I. Title
    LB2283.G46   1994
    370.19´63—dc20   93-50164

Printed in the United States of America
10 9 8 7 6 5 4 3 2 1   98 97 96 95 94

COLLEGE TEACHING ABROAD

Contents

Foreword

For the twelve years that I served as executive director of the Council for International Exchange of Scholars, I was part of an elaborate and careful process for sending U.S. faculty abroad to teach. I witnessed the pride of selection, the excitement of moving to another culture, and the eagerness to do abroad what one did well at home . . . teach college students. I know from hundreds, no thousands, of conversations, visits to many foreign institutions, and reports that the transition is probably more difficult than ever imagined when the plan to teach abroad was set in motion.

American professors cannot easily transplant their teaching styles and methods to their foreign classrooms. Why is it so difficult when these professors have been invited to teach and the invitation is based upon their experience and reputation? Why is it that what works so well in their home classrooms often fails abroad?

As any of us moves abroad the "otherness" is readily apparent and we soon learn the joy of discovering another culture, understanding it, and appreciating it. We see ourselves as Americans all the more clearly when we look at our own cultures through the mirror of another culture. The transition for someone teaching abroad is even more profound. Not only do professors reflect their own cultures in daily life and routine, but also in how they teach in their classrooms. For many the disjuncture between teaching abroad and at their home institutions is a profound and frustrating adjustment. One learns that students and classrooms are not the same the world over and that the culture of the classroom is as important and as pervasive as the culture of the country. How well a professor teaches abroad often makes all the difference in the personal enjoyment and professional satisfaction of the foreign experience.

As I read *College Teaching Abroad,* I felt keenly the frustration as well as the fulfillment that so many faculty described. How confusing it is to be invited for an overseas assignment because one is good at teaching at home and then to find that the transfer of those lauded skills and teaching style is not understood and not accepted. The joy of this book is the sharing of experiences and insights faculty have gained in struggling with teaching in a foreign classroom and the many exciting approaches they have developed to adjust their teaching to a new and different workplace. One can read this book and feel encouraged that transition, adjustment, success and, yes, a good deal of satisfaction, is possible.

The great value of *College Teaching Abroad* is in its practical advice combined with the subtle and ever-so-true cultural insights. It is a wonderful road map that helps the visiting professor read the signals, as well as provide encouragement to develop new strategies to reach a new audience. The book also describes the joy of discovery professors can experience from testing and changing and adapting teaching methods.

Pamela George has experienced firsthand so much of what this book is about. Her journeys abroad and those of countless other professors bring important lessons, insights, and encouragement for those who will follow.

Cassandra Pyle
Founding Executive Director
Council for the International Exchange of Scholars
Washington, D.C.

Introduction

If you are one of the thousands of American professors who leave each year for universities around the world to participate in academic exchanges which involve teaching and lecturing across cultures, *College Teaching Abroad* is written for you. Or if you plan for a future international assignment as part of your professional experience, this book will help you dream practically. But it is also written for those administrators, sponsors, funders, and colleagues who believe professors participating in academic exchanges can take their skills, lecture notes and slide shows and transfer them with little or no modification to a new learning setting half-a-world away. This belief has contributed to an astonishing neglect of discussion on the actual process of how American professors teach and how host country students learn.

This book does not assert that instructional strategies from the United States are ineffective or that they should be arbitrarily discarded in intercultural academic work. Rather, it suggests that methods and techniques successful for teaching American college students are not sufficient to meet the challenges of university teaching across cultures.

For those readers who will soon be working in an intercultural situation, this book describes what American professors who managed effective academic exchanges abroad experienced and learned:

- *to observe the cultures of their classrooms* and academic workplaces;
- *to modify their teaching methods,* hewed in the American university tradition, to fit the new instructional demands;
- *to structure thoughtful learning environments* to maximize student comprehension and participation; and
- *to practice flexibility and patience* with their students and colleagues.

By collecting the lessons of American professors who have taught in cross-cultural contexts around the world, I have tried to expand the discussion of strategies for effectively managing cross-cultural academic exchanges and for competently teaching students whose language and cultural perspectives differ from our own. By synthesizing these observations, I have sought to dispel the complacency implied by the belief that university teaching across cultures occurs like a "holiday task." It does not.

The first theme of this book is that *university teaching strategies can not be implemented on their intrinsic merits alone.* These strategies have a cultural context which must be considered if they are to be effective. Variables such as the perceptions of the professor, the performance or behavioral expectations of students and patterns of teacher-student interaction are examples of variables examined in their cultural contexts.

The second theme is that *university worklives and workplaces in other cultures often demand distinctive professional management strategies.* We American professors understandably seek manageable teaching assignments and the promise of relief from the logistical pressures of maneuvering complex academic settings. However, the tendency when we go abroad may be to apply familiar methods, based in U.S. pedagogic and business traditions, for achieving this manageability. We often lack knowledge of more culturally appropriate alternatives. We soon learn we need to reconsider and modify these methods for academic exchanges to be constructive.

A third theme is that *good planning, effective lecturing, sound instruction, and meaningful evaluation in a cross-cultural context require reflection, direction, and practice.* In the cross-cultural setting, these do not happen incidentally or accidentally. This work draws on many observations from American professors abroad whose instructional practices, language usages and evaluation strategies did and did not produce desired positive results. Good teachers learn from both.

For those readers who would like to pursue international teaching and research opportunities, but who do not yet have assignments, this book provides information on sources of fellowships, scholarships, professional development training, and travel grants. See appendix A—Resources for Higher Education Faculty Exchanges.

For readers who already have assignments to specific countries or regions or for those who have specific geographic interests, see appendix B—Planning Resources for Faculty Exchanges by Region.

For readers who are in the midst of teaching across cultures and need resources for advising host country undergraduate and graduate students, appendix C—Resources for Advising Foreign Students on Study in the U.S.A. provides an annotated list of current and useful materials.

For those readers who will teach at colleges and universities abroad and who will return to the United States, this book addresses the needs to readjust to American academic life and to integrate the international experience. Appendix D—Resources for Affiliations and Linkages upon Reentry to the U.S.A. provides contacts and resources for that readjustment and integration.

Acknowledgments

College Teaching Abroad was crafted to be a substantive, readable, functional, insightful, and enjoyable guide to college and university teaching across cultures. But it has been made more substantive by the real voices of the more than 700 U.S. and foreign professors and students whose individual stories and perspectives are shared here. It has been made more readable by the thoughtful editing of Steve Dragin, David Austin, Mary Ann Sagaria, and Al Bailey. It has been made more functional by the technical assistance of Richard Ward, Lee Mayfield, Mary Johnson, Vimala Rajendran, Joy Barron and Sonny Snead. It has been made more insightful by the wisdom of Cassie Pyle and David Adams. And the crafting of it was made considerably more enjoyable by the presence of Kemen and JamJam. To all of these colleagues, family, and friends, I say thank you.

Concept Map

1

EXAMINING THE CULTURE
OF THE CLASSROOM

*La lafoia i le alogalu . . . Take care to be cast on the land
side of the reef [overcoming all difficulties].*
—SAMOAN PROVERB

Teaching across cultures may profoundly change the way we think about teaching, the relationship between teaching and learning, and the learning process itself. We are at a threshold of understanding how effective professors in the cross-cultural context identify the behavioral complexities of students, colleagues, and classrooms, how they modify their familiar teaching methods to fit the new teaching demands, and how they transcend the limits of their own culture. The lives and work of the successful teachers whose voices are shared in these pages verify that these skills of identification, modification, and transcendence in college teaching across cultures are practiced and possible.

RESEARCHING COLLEGE TEACHING ABROAD

This year, approximately 50,000 American academics will participate in more than two hundred programs facilitating international exchanges. In addition to government programs, there are numerous organizations in the United States, not including individual universities' international programs, which support American faculty participation in university teaching across cultures.

Since the launching of the Fulbright program in 1946, U.S. government programs through the United States Information Agency (USIA) and the Department of Education (DOE), have supported the participation of more than 100,000 American academics in scholarly exchanges (Board of Foreign Scholars, 1987). In 1993, the U.S. Fulbright program alone sponsored more than 1,000 American academics abroad (CIES, 1994).

American professors' experiences abroad, which document this book, are collected from twenty-six countries—Australia, Bangladesh, Brazil, Chile, China, Czechoslovakia, Egypt, Hong Kong, Hungary, Indonesia, Israel, Ireland, Japan, Korea, Malawi, Malaysia, Mexico, New Zealand, Nigeria, Pakistan, Poland, Portugal, Nepal, Norway, Thailand, and Turkey. The data, observations, interpretations, and quotation materials are drawn from four major sources:

1. Interviews conducted with American professors during (or immediately following) their academic exchange experiences from 1986–1993. The eighty-seven professors interviewed were chosen for representation of age, gender, assignment location, family constellation, home-institution, sponsoring agency, and discipline.

2. Documentary video footage (sixty-four hours) of U.S. Fulbright professors shot on locations in Indonesia, Hong Kong, Malaysia, China, and Thailand collected by the United States Information Agency's University Teaching Across Cultures Project from 1988–1990.

3. Interviews with seventy-two English-speaking host colleagues and students in Southeast Asia who were surveyed for information and perceptions of the efficacy of teaching methods of foreign visiting professors. Additionally, conversations regarding effective cross-cultural teaching were recorded with students in classes of American professors teaching in the Peoples Republic of China.

4. Reports from 529 American professors participating in academic exchanges from twenty-three countries during 1986–1992. The Council for the International Exchange of Scholars (CIES) provided access to the documents of those who received U.S. government support from USIA's Fulbright program.

Added to these data sources were my own teaching, teacher-training, and research experiences across cultures. I have spent twenty-five years as an educator in cross-cultural settings. As a novice teacher in Germany, I struggled with teaching in the native language. As a Peace Corps teacher and UNESCO teacher-trainer in Western Samoa, I learned to be a scholar of the cultural context of my students' learning and thinking. As a Fulbright Professor of Educational Psychology in Thailand, I witnessed the academic benefits of cooperative learning methodologies used with college students and of cooperation among faculty.

As director of the University Teaching Across Cultures Video Project sponsored by USIA, I spent three years documenting the worklives of American Fulbright professors in Indonesia, Malaysia, China, and Thailand. Modeling some of my teaching techniques on the most effective ones I videoed, I modified my instruction to become a better professor than I had ever been. Through research assignments in the PRC, the Philippines, and the University of Hong Kong, I experienced the difficulties of managing academic work outside the classroom. Finally, for the last seventeen years, I have been a graduate professor of educational psychology and research at a historically black university in North Carolina.

In this challenging culturally diverse environment, I have learned that the lessons from academic exchanges abroad have powerful implications for building the capacities of professors to work more effectively in multicultural university environments.

Combining the perceptions, observations, opinions, criticisms, and wisdom of nearly 700 people into this book was to explore again that dynamic synergism which happens at the interface of cultures in a learning setting. Many voices speak some aspect of the whole truth. Each perspective is only one facet of the many-colored beachball; each observation is only one small tile in the vast mosaic. My perspective as an Anglo-American, Southern, female professor academically socialized at large state universities in the 1960s and currently a professor in a school of education in a comprehensive university in a state system in the American South will be evident. I have drawn deeply from the Asia and Pacific regions and focused somewhat less on other regions. I have utilized many university work experiences of professors in developing and nonindustrialized countries. These perspectives are simply those that I know best and to which I have had the most access. But each of these viewpoints has been intentionally broadened in this book by adding diversity of region, discipline, type of U.S. university represented, type of host institution represented, age, gender, and ethnicity.

The risks in writing such a book are that a single observation is presented as a generalization or that in focusing on the small tile, the big picture in the mosaic is missed entirely. Even with the best attempts to avoid oversimplifications and myopia, both will inevitably occur as we expand and reshape our understanding of university teaching across cultures.

No one should interpret this book to suggest that "American teaching methods or institutional practices are best." Nor should they interpret it to suggest that effective methods or practices used in U.S. classrooms or faculty lounges are necessarily ineffective or inappropriate in the cross-cultural context. Rather, you are encouraged to hold the position that methods and techniques successful for teaching American college students and doing business in the U.S. academic context are insufficient to meet the challenges of university work across cultures.

In reporting this information, I took care to relate observations that were illustrative of more than one professor's comments or reports. Unique trials and triumphs, despite the entertaining nature of the stories many embodied, were omitted because they were not representative. The use of the term "American" in the text refers only to the United States, unless otherwise specified. "Western" is used to refer to professors from European backgrounds or who teach in the "American" or "European" tradition and may include Canadians, Australians, etc. "Cross-cultural" contexts are those in which academics from the United States teach in countries, cultures or in languages which are not their native ones.

By agreement with sponsoring agencies who provided access to participants and their documents, identifying information for most professors and/or their host institutions was omitted or muted. This was done to allow for optimal candor on the part of the U.S. academics, to minimize any perception of insult or offense on the part of host institutions, and to encourage readers to identify with generic situations rather than to dismiss them as unique circumstances at specific institutions. Exceptions were made, and professors were identified, when previously published material or documentaries assured the professors' observations were a part of public record.

ACKNOWLEDGING A CLASSROOM CULTURE

For professors who are new to cross-cultural teaching, the awareness of the new classroom as a microcosm of the larger culture, and at the same time a subculture which must be analyzed and understood as itself, can be astounding. The strengths of American professors involved in academic exchanges predictably are their knowledge of the subject matter and their skills for obtaining more information and material in their disciplines. Furey (1986) argues that American professors are often so concerned with the teaching of this material and these skills that they overlook the values, attitudes and norms of behavior of the classroom where this teaching will take place (Furey, 1986). To provide effective instruction in a cross-cultural setting, a teacher must consider pedagogical, linguistic, and psychological factors related to learning within, not only the larger cultural context, but also in the subculture of the new classroom. This book is aimed at the teacher who wants to and will consider those factors.

It is not maintained that you should adopt the teaching norms or student expectations of the host country. Nor is it suggested that a comparison of American teaching methods or student behaviors in the new setting will ensure efficacy or win you favor with your host colleagues. It is, however, argued that reflecting on the nature of a classroom's culture can aid in modifying classroom materials and practices to suit the new cross-cultural situation and can help in anticipating sources of conflict which could undermine effectiveness.

Some American professors argue that "classrooms are classrooms," that "university education has universal features which supersede cultural settings," or that the only difference is "English is not their mother-tongue." Their arguments are supported by the fact that Western thought on education has had a pervasive influence on universities around the world. Indeed, the structures and functions of academia look very similar at first glance. While there are many similarities, Furey (1986) and Fieg (1989) assert that in numerous respects classrooms across societies are quite dissimilar.

The frameworks used here to investigate cultural characteristics of classrooms were developed in part for the purpose of training Fulbright professors teaching in East Asian and Southeast Asian countries and cultures, but universal attributes are focused upon here. The categories are drawn from three sources: reports of scholars teaching abroad deposited with the Council for the International Exchange of Scholars (CIES), my own experience training Fulbright and other government-sponsored professors to and from Asian countries, and the perceptive documentation of Patricia Furey (1986) and her colleagues at the University of Pittsburgh in their work with ESL/EFL teacher training. These frameworks consist of three areas of concern: Perceptions of the Teacher, Performance Expectations, and Teacher-Student Interaction.

Regarding Perceptions of the Teacher

Those who have taught in more than one culture often report being astounded at differences in perceptions of the teacher's role and in attitudes toward them as teachers. Even those who have been informed of these differences before they begin teaching often report surprise at the extent these attitudes influence student behavior in and out of the classroom and at the often immutable nature of these perceptions. An overview of the framework of Perceptions of the Teacher is adapted from Furey (1986) and is shown in Figure 1-1.

Social Distance

Rules of Deference. Differences in status and prestige of teachers present many sources of consternation for professors in cross-cultural situations. Classrooms vary widely in their norms of verbal and nonverbal demonstrations of deference and reflect these broader cultural differences in status and prestige shown the teacher. In societies where teachers have traditionally been guardians of sacred bodies of knowledge, Furey posits that they are treated with greater formality and status (1986).

Sometimes American professors initially respond favorably to this deference which they call "respect" or "politeness." Sometimes they define this distance as "awe," "reverence for authority," or "deferential behavior." In Hungary, it was

---

A. **Social Distance Between Student and Teacher**
   1. Rules of deference
   2. Rules of propriety
   3. Rules of privacy

B. **Rights and Obligations of the Teacher**
   1. Role as parent/state surrogate:
      a. Degree of authority
      b. Degree teacher dominates class activities
   2. Role as mentor:
      a. Teacher as sage/scholar
      b. Teacher as counselor/advisor
      c. Teacher as tutor
      d. Teacher as patron

FIGURE 1-1   Perceptions of the Teacher

Source: Adapted from Patricia R. Furey, A framework for Cross-Cultural Analysis of Teaching Methods, in Byrd, P. (1986). *Teaching Across Cultures in the University ESL Program,* p. 20. Used with permission of the National Association of Foreign Student Affairs.

reported by one American professor, "In the provincial universities, students are so polite they even stand when I enter the room." Fulbright professor Al Bailey described a similar experience with this nonverbal deference in China:

> *Chinese students give a great deal of respect to their professors in a more formal sense. In my first term the custom was for the students to stand when I came into the classroom and then there would be an exchange of bows on my part and theirs. This struck me like something of the old European way. We did that for the first term, then I said we could dispense with that custom.*

Another American professor to Thailand observed a *wai khruu* ceremony:

> *Today, Thai students paid homage to their professors. It was a symbolic celebration which, after teaching American students for fifteen years, I found astonishing. In a large room students crawled up, in the 'kowtowing' manner of supplication, and gave beautiful floral offerings to their professors. Their choral chants asked for blessings and expressed gratitude. Their speeches asked forgiveness for any disrespect or non-fulfillment of expectation. They promised to work diligently.*

Regarding the often discussed deferential behavior of Asian students, a professor to Japan expressed, "As a Fulbright lecturer, I was treated with a great deal of respect, concern, and probably too much deference from the students. Knowing how much respect is accorded to professors in Japan, one of my [Japanese] colleagues at the University of Oregon warned me before my departure that it might be necessary to 'deprogram' me upon my return."

But after the initial enjoyment of the deference accorded them, many professors see deference as a cultural difference in social distance, formality, and status. An American professor of textile design in Brazil addressed this difference:

> *Respect for the instructor's opinion was so great that students offered no argument or opposing opinions. I felt this lack of free exchange between faculty and students inhibited students' ability to express their ideas about their own work as well as the work of their peers.*

American literature professor Bill Slaughter conveyed his experience with student deference and his frustration with it in China:

> *The teacher is the authority figure — they give me deference and respect, because I am the teacher. Not because I've earned it, but because I am who I am— their teacher. I would much rather have their live presences and their voices in the classroom than I would that kind of deference and respect.*

A law professor shared, "Because deference also conveniently keeps people apart and uninvolved with each other, I discovered upon my return from Japan to the

U.S. that I happily traded most of that deference for the opportunity to get closer to students."

In a different cultural situation, however, the social distance between student and teacher is not as far as some would like. An American geographer in Mexico found his students "are not bashful at all about seeking my advice. They hang around my departmental office." While he praised his students' strong sense of community as "far friendlier than any academic community in the U.S.," he noted, "It does place enormous time demands on the professor."

Rules of Propriety.   In interviews with students and professors in host institutions, we often heard students comment on American professors as "very informal in class." Arab and Asian students were surprised at the informal way American teachers dress and sit in the classroom. "Sometimes they sit on the table or put their feet on chairs. Our teachers don't do this. They are generally more formal in class," stated a Pakistani student.

One example of a major difference in concern for propriety exists between Western and Thai academics. Thais care more for the orderliness of how actions are done than Westerners. Fieg (1989) argues that Thais, unlike Americans, seem to care "more for the way things look than the way things are." In Thai classrooms, this priority shows up in student work that is always *riaproi* (tidy, orderly), but not necessarily accurate. One Western professor criticized her students' particularly neat and colorful papers of poorly executed work as "Thais will guild rust." Debates, especially among Westerners, over the value in crosscultural classrooms of "polite speech" and of "uncomplaining compliance with propriety and bureaucratic minutia" abound.

One way to begin to reflect on the differences in social distance between you, the professor, and students in your classes is to ask yourself some questions about distance:

1. What are your forms of address?
   - With what names do students address you in class? out of class?
   - With what names do you address students in class? out of class?
2. What are the students' visitation patterns?
   - Do they (often, sometimes, rarely, never) visit?
   - Do these visits take place in your (office, class, cafe, home)?
   - Are the visits (by appointment, by invitation, unannounced)?

Rules of Privacy.   The level of personal disclosure in an academic setting is another area of classroom culture difference. I recall my teaching experience in Germany, where the level of personal disclosure in the workplace was so limited that I was stunned to learn my host professor in an adjoining office and the professor across the hall were man and wife and married for more than a decade. While often a matter of personal comfort, the nature and quantity of factual information and personal opinion that is appropriate for teachers and students to ask about or reveal is a cultural phenomenon. Declaring her position on personal privacy in the academic setting, a Chinese graduate student from Szechuan University commented about her Fulbright professor, "If I will tell something true to him, he first must tell something true to me."

Rights and Obligations of the Teacher

The roles of university teachers across cultures vary along two continua. First is the degree to which the teacher is perceived as the authority figure who serves in the stead of the parent or the state. The second continuum along which the rights and obligations of the teacher vary is the degree to which the teacher is viewed as a mentor.

Teacher as Authority Figure. In many universities across Asia, teachers are seen as having great authority to control exclusively what happens in a classroom. A Korean student is far less likely to challenge or even question a professor than is his Mexican counterpart. A Fulbright professor to Japan noted, "Because Japanese students invest so much authority in their professors, it is beyond their imagination to interrupt, speak to or ask a questions of me in class."

Furey argues that in societies where there is a high degree of teacher authority and direction students may have a low tolerance for ambiguity in directions and assignments and may have difficulty with activities requiring student choice and initiative. Participating in group problem-solving activities or choosing a topic for a thesis may be very difficult for students from cultures where schooling is primarily a matter of receiving knowledge that a teacher dispenses.

Teacher as Mentor. Cultures vary in their regard for the professor as a mentor (i.e. a counselor, guide, guru or tutor) of a select few students. The wide range of duties (beyond their roles as scholar/teachers) assigned university professors reflects this variability. In Scandinavian countries where teachers are more likely viewed as scholars, a professor teaches a comparatively light load (which may even decrease by rank to one course biannually with minimal administrative responsibilities) reserving his or her time for scholarly pursuits and mentoring a few young scholars. A Thai or Japanese professor's role, however, often includes serving as the favorite or special teacher, tutor or mentor to students who will return for special favors many times and even years after graduation.

Examining Performance Expectations

For the purposes of illustrating differences in students' expectations of performance across cultures, four areas are included in this framework in Figure 1-2. They are Competitive vs. Cooperative Orientation, Attitudes About Time, views of the "Appropriate" Workload, and the Purpose of Performance.

Competitive versus Cooperative Orientation

The American university educational process reflects and reinforces Western culture's competitive structure in which students work to outperform their classmates and faculty work to outperform their colleagues. In this paradigm, students

Competitive vs. Cooperative Orientation
- Degree of and rewards for student competition or cooperation
- Degree of privacy about work and achievement
- Role of external exams

Attitudes about Time
- Presence of and adherence to schedules, deadlines, planning
- Views of punctuality and speed

"Appropriate" Workloads
- Views of *"hard vs. easy"* and *"work vs. play"*
- Degree of *"compartmentalization"* of work
- Standards for course loads

Purposes of Performance
- Fulfillment of personal aims
- Fulfillment of social aims for:
  - national development
  - modernization
  - skilled manpower
  - cultural preservation

FIGURE 1-2   Performance Expectations

usually work alone, strive to perform better than others, and celebrate their own success and other's nonsuccess. Professors usually limit the rewards (e.g., they give less than 20 percent of the students A's) or grade "on a curve" from best to worst performance. Both students and teachers have a sense of "privacy" about assignments, tests, and academic achievements.

In contrast, many cultures value more harmonious interaction with one's social group and collective work. Avoidance of shame or "loss-of-face" is paramount. This cooperative orientation impacts extensively on students' classroom behavior. Students may exhibit great aversion to verbal expression in class and to "standing apart" from the group. A student from a culture with a cooperative orientation may feel extreme shame when called on to demonstrate something for which he is ill prepared or to answer from reading she has not done. Conversely, a student may experience ridicule from peers when she answers correctly from readings she *has* done. A pedagogical method common in the United States, such as Socratic questioning, may embody more inherent risks for loss-of-face than you might initially surmise.

Privacy in cooperatively oriented cultures is usually not as sacrosanct as in more competitive Western cultures and presents problems for Western professors when students share work or "borrow" the work of others. For example, an American professor in Malaysia exclaimed her astonishment at students' reading her comments on other students' written work and "not seeing that as a violation of their privacy."

Individual ownership of work differs for competitively and cooperatively oriented cultures and this difference presents some of the most challenging differences in the classroom. A Fulbright professor to Turkey complained:

Midway thorough the 2nd semester, a number of my first year students were found to be plagiarizing. Even though the university has a 'code of conduct' about plagiarism, much of that is ignored by the faculty members whose response was one of chagrin but leniency.

Another reported that a Korean student apologized for not handing in his work because he had "to write a report for a friend." Yet another described his student work situation in Thailand as a "homework cartel" where students in varying degrees of discretion work together to get assignments done.

There are more complexities to this discussion of competitive and cooperative orientation. Standardized testing, often encouraged by the exportations of the U.S. psychometric industry, has fueled much individual competition for university admission and placement. This emphasis on external exams may shape the curriculum and the motivations of students toward your subject matter and lesson strategies. Additionally, it would be naive to conclude that some group-oriented cultures, such as Japan, where a student must "establish" himself or herself in a group for study, matriculation, and employment, have no competitive orientation. Yet the manifestation of competition in the classroom may be different than in the United States.

One of the ways to begin to reflect on these differences in competitive v. cooperative orientation and how they will affect your teaching is to ask yourself:

1. How important is it to me that a student's work handed in to me is his or her own?

2. How do I react to a student in class who answers a question remarkably well? Or who (from his answer) clearly has not read the material?

3. What if I have to tailor course material toward a certifying or external exam? Would doing so require modifications of my content or strategies, or compromise my personal politics or patience?

Attitudes about Time

Punctuality and speed are rewarded in American classrooms. Professors expect assignments by deadlines and exercise their authority to lower grades for belated work. They often reward speed as much as accuracy in classroom responses and assignment completion. Professors from such varied cultures as Nepal, Czechoslovakia, Ireland, New Zealand, Poland, Brazil, Japan, Israel, Yugoslavia, and Malaysia complained of students who were "woefully unpunctual," who "sauntered into class moons after the semester began," and who handed in work "up to twenty years late."

Schedules, time lines and calendars are obviously highly valued in American academic culture. University classes usually begin on (and final exams are administered on) the official and published dates. Students generally get to class on time and few allowances are made for those who do not. The features of time, which American professors have come to expect, contrast markedly with cultures which have different attitudes and practices of time. One harried Fulbrighter to Pakistan lamented, "The academic calendar here is not very fixed. Heck, it's not fixed at all."

Thai academics trained in the West have a proud affinity for planning and "five year plans" are common in Thailand. But from my experience as a Fulbright professor, close examination of these plans in the university context reveals they are rarely adhered to. Western professors who expect to develop a new graduate curriculum, complete a study, implement a marked change in university policy, or even get through the course material they had planned in a specific time frame are usually frustrated. Many examples of the problems confronted by American professors teaching in cross-cultural situations where time, schedules, deadlines, time lines, etc. are viewed differently are discussed in more detail in the Chapter 6 section on Anticipating Potential Conflicts and in the Chapter 11 section on Evaluating In-Class and Out-of-Class Assignments.

"Appropriate" Workload

Views of what constitutes an appropriate workload for a single academic assignment, a bibliography of out-of-class reading, or a set of thesis requirements are part of the larger culture's attitude toward work. Differences in views of work vary considerably across cultures. American academics are rewarded for a "seriousness of purpose," "*hard* work" and "getting down to business"—a sharp difference from the Indonesian way which prefers "*light* work" and a fluid mode, for example. American professors may stick with tedious, dull research tasks for hours on end and criticize their host colleagues for lengthy lunch breaks. American professors often will work on only one task at a time, while Koreans may juggle many.

According to an American linguist to Thailand, John Paul Fieg, it is the American tendency to compartmentalize work. An American physics professor illustrated the difference by saying, "Thais work at play and play at work." Fieg supports this cultural observation by adding that Thais use similar terms to describe work and play (1980). For example, work can be *sanuk* (fun) or not. If something is sanuk, it is absorbing, interesting, and worth doing. The term *len* (to play) is used to refer to serious activities such as academic research, political lobby and business investment.

Differences in expectations about an appropriate workload has decided implications for the classroom. For example, it was reported by professors from many countries and cultures that students they taught "did not have the practice of preparing for class, doing the assigned readings, or doing homework." From Nepal, a University of Idaho instructor lamented, "Undergraduates are unfamiliar with the demands of university work." In Brazil, an American literature professor from Brigham Young University observed that his graduate students were not as productive as undergraduates in American universities, but, he added, "Thankfully, I did not bring the same expectations to Brazil." Another to Thailand commented, "The idea that broad or deep reading outside of class should supplement lectures was not accepted or appreciated. An average of fifteen pages per week was tolerated and thirty pages was far too much."

Professors of some students, some classes, some programs, and some countries reported different experiences. In New Zealand, it was noted that graduate students were "comparably trained as in America but expect higher work demands and are more highly motivated." Some professors found that students' expectations were not the cause of their limited performance, but rather it was their other demands placed on them. Professor Mary Rose Shaughnessy of Chicago State found in China "undergraduate students take twenty to twenty-four hours of classes a week, so they cannot spend much time preparing" (1987). A Fulbrighter reported, "Almost all my Brazilian students worked full time or part time, so my normal assignments could not be done." From Monterrey, Mexico, an American Studies professor offered:

> *After one entire semester I began to understand the source of problems in my teaching was that Mexican students are badly overworked and are in class more than 25 hours per week. Additionally, they usually work at least 20 hours per week. They have little time to read, write and study and are not in the habit of doing so.*

A Fulbrighter to Eastern Europe concurred, "Students in Prague are bright, dedicated, but very, very busy! They take a lot of classes. Even under the new reforms, they spend close to 30–36 hours per week in class." Another to Eastern Europe said, "Hungarian students, while not usually working, with these all-around shortages have enormous family responsibilities." It is commonly reported by professors on exchange teaching assignments in Japan that students are enormously burdened with out-of-class responsibilities especially with "time-consuming obligations to their clubs."

Some international education watchers argue that the perception of difference between American and other students' view of appropriate workload may depend on the population one teaches in America. American educators, they contend, still hold to the concept of the American student as the 18- to 22-year-old, full-time liberal arts student with a leisurely four-year window for "cafeteria-style learning." U.S. demographic shifts show otherwise. For example, according to the National Education Association (NEA, 1992, 1993), students in America are increasingly older, attend part-time, work while going to school, and take considerably more than four years to finish college.

Asking the following questions of yourself may help you troubleshoot your own expectations of an appropriate workload and how they may differ from your hosts':

1. What have you traditionally assumed was an appropriate amount of reading (# of pages) to expect graduate/undergraduate students to read in your class in one week?

2. If you provide a reading list in your syllabus, do you expect students to read these recommended readings? For class discussion? For exams?

3. How much time do you expect a graduate/undergraduate student to pre-

pare for a class (with assigned readings, recommended readings and out-of-class assignments)?

4. How do you recognize and reward compliance? What is your reaction to a student's noncompliance?

Purpose of Performance

One final illustration of differences in performance expectations is variations on the purpose of performance. This topic is, of course, a small part of the larger discussion of differences in the goals and objectives of university education across cultures. Clearly, students wish *to further their own personal objectives* by influencing or demanding certain performance expectations in the classroom. These personal objectives may or may not reflect their cultural or national objectives. Reports of four American professors in Israel illustrate the differences in personal performance objectives:

- *Israeli students are more mature and responsible than American students, but they are also more self-directed in ways that dismay us American teachers.*
- *Almost all of them are veterans; most have jobs; many have families; very few of them think of themselves as full-time college students in the manner of American liberal-arts students.*
- *Their attitude toward both the material in their courses and the circumstances under which courses are conducted are severely pragmatic. They have little interest in the acquisition of knowledge for its own sake and scant patience with a pedagogical agenda that does not correspond to their own."*
- *Teaching them can be exceptionally rewarding here once you get over the idea that they are looking for something different from the 'adventures in learning' commonly offered by American colleges.*

Another, sometimes competing, purpose of performance is *to promote national development.* Many third-World countries hold this purpose as the major role of the university. Ideals of education as development of free intellect, as the nurturing of universalistic morality, or as the acquisition of accurate and well-documented information are, in this view, subordinated to the national interest. In Southeast Asia, for example, higher education is a central part of national plans for economic development. In this scheme, the university should be politically and economically "modern" (though this has many interpretations). It is often with this objective in mind that Western professors are sought to teach in universities in developing countries. Students may flock to the classes of Western professors for this exposure to "modern" ways. One Fulbright professor to Turkey remarked that the only obvious credential for his popularity was his "growing up in modern America."

Related to this aim of fostering national development is the purpose *to produce skilled manpower.* In places where there is a shortage of qualified and trained personnel and a university education is aimed at filling positions. Higher education is, in this view, responsible for the production of entrepreneurs, managers, government officials, and teachers. When students see their university stint as a "paycheck education," or directly related to a particular job pre-determined for them, they may have different levels of commitment to different courses of study. American literature professor Peter Beidler articulated a dilemma when faced in China with the conflict between students' objectives and the national objective:

> My graduate students were to become teachers, but they were not at all convinced that they wanted to be the teacher they were almost destined to become. It came clear to me that I had to do some work in pedagogy, in the experience of teaching...In a sense, I turned my courses into a scientific laboratory in the technique of teaching.

Another objective of university education held in some countries, for example, is *to preserve traditional culture*. Teaching in Thailand, for example, means working in a workplace where instruction, research, and consultation must take into account the clash between the more fundamental conflict between Western and traditional political and economic systems—a conflict which, as social change progresses, affects daily activities and interests of students (George, 1987). I recall Prasong, a graduate student I trained at the University of ChiangMai in Thailand, who each afternoon rode his motor bike down from the mountain where, as the village teacher and only educated member of his Blue Mao hill tribe, he chose to live and teach grades K–6 with no electricity, running water or roads. Each day on this forty kilometer journey he crossed a veritable millennium. For Prasong and the thousands like him can there be education for economic progress which embraces capitalist development with traditional values? Can there be university education which draws from empirical research and scientific technologies for which these students hold so much pride—yet which is responsive to spiritual and cultural beliefs for which they hold so much affection?

In traditional cultures, contradictions between economic or cultural values and educational ideologies may cause ambivalence, frustration, and disjuncture between aspiration and reality within the academic community and among the students we teach. Balanced and empathetic understanding of the effects of the clash of Western and traditional values on your students my cause some anxiety for you about what constitutes correct conduct as you teach about progress in the United States or lend your imprimatur to changes in your host country.

Observing Teacher-Student Interaction

> I would say, 'What about this?' And then I'd wait. I'd sit there and sip my tea...Nothing. Then I'd call on somebody, 'Chung, what do you think?' He would look down at this book . . . [silence] . . . [silence]. I have no experience with this — the experience of calling on a student and the ability of that student to outwait me! (A Syracuse University Professor, China)

The third area of consideration in an analysis of classroom culture is the area of teacher-student interactions. A few areas of interaction (of which there are hundreds) are described here, and a broader scheme is provided in Figure 1-3.

Amount of Student Participation

Norms for student participation in the classroom vary considerably across cultures and are probably the most discussed attribute of classroom culture. An entire section in Chapter Eight of this text is devoted to Encouraging Student Participation and, as such, reflects the American value of this interaction pattern. The amount of participation expected by teachers and by students may differ. The conditions under which participation and silence exists may differ. Modes of solicitation of student participation surely differ. To think about your comfort with silence and its implications in your classroom ask yourself:

1. When I ask a student a question and she is slow to respond, how much time do I allow her to answer?
2. If the time passes and she still does not answer, what do I usually do?

Gesture Patterns

My first awareness of the enormity of difference in the use of gesture in a classroom was as a Peace Corps teacher in Western Samoa where students acknowledged the

---

Amount of Student Participation

- Amount of participation, delivered, valued
- Types of solicitations for participation

Gesture Patterns

Appropriateness of Topics

- What kinds of topics can/cannot be discussed?
- Who generates the topics?

Praising and Criticizing

Attention-Getting Devices

Verbal Interaction Patterns

- How are seats arranged?
- How flexible is this arrangement?
- What is the correct distance between teacher and student

Humor and Joking

Physical Interaction

FIGURE 1-3 Teacher-Student Interaction

affirmative not by nodding or saying "yes," but by silently lifting their eyebrows in a manner similar to our gesture of surprise. This expression took years to translate "yes" to me. I wondered how I must have moved about that was equally as obtuse to Samoan students. A Fulbright professor to Thailand shared his observation of gesture differences:

> *Thai body motions are restrained. Professors stand almost still as they lecture from the front of the class. With overheads, they use tiny pointers on the projector rather than pointing motions or highlighting gestures. They rarely move to different quarters of the room. They quietly emphasize their points with restatement. By contrast, I must appear like Phil Donahue brandishing his probing mike. They must think I prance around and wave my arms with exaggerated gesticulation. Do I motion to my main points wildly on the screen or board as my volume punctuates them?*

John Paul Fieg admonishes professors who point or gesture with their feet in Thailand where the head is sacred and the feet profane (Fieg 1980, 1989). Furey (1986) reminds us that one of the most common classroom gestures teachers use in the United States to beckon students to the front of the room—the palm held upward with fingers moving toward the body—is, in some parts of the world, a motion reserved only for animals. Other professors remind us of the reserved uses of the left hand in some cultures and encourage instructors to pay particular attention to their ambidextrous gesturing. The list of possible misunderstandings in this category is well beyond the scope of this text, but the few mentioned here serve as illustrations. If you have a videotape of yourself teaching, you might review it again in light of this discussion and think about these questions:

1. Do I move my (hands, arms, body, location) demonstrably during lectures? to illustrate, punctuate, and/or infatuate?
2. How do my students nonverbally register agreement, readiness, confusion, or comprehension?
3. How do I solicit student responses nonverbally?

Appropriateness of Topics

My observations in the classrooms of many Western professors abroad have taught me that American teachers employ deliberately provocative topics and provoke conflicts often as part of their pedagogical repertoire, just as they do in American classrooms where students are often quite habituated to topics of sex, drugs, violence and to public debate. Some American academics argued like John Dewey that "conflict is the gadfly of thought." Occasionally, the professors' tactics I observed seemed sensitive to the new classroom atmosphere and interaction patterns—but sometimes they did not.

Experience soon teaches that students in some cultures will discuss a rape in a Faulkner story more easily than in another. Yet some will be made uncomfortable by a discussion of the leftist leaning of Friere's pedagogical methods with farmers in Latin America. A colleague of mine worked with one group of young Chinese professors preparing for doctoral study in the United States who quietly resisted participation in a simulation exercise on academic debate using the topic of the legalization of marijuana.

I am not contending that controversy or debate should be avoided or that interesting topics should be rejected because someone is made uncomfortable by them. Indeed, the Chapter 9 section on Teaching for Critical Thinking encourages the use of controversy as a teaching device. However, you can expect that your experience with American students has probably not sensitized you sufficiently to the appropriateness of topics in the cross-cultural classroom. In thinking about this ask yourself:

1. Have I ever deliberately chosen a provocative example, reading, or discussion topic to teach a concept or process? What is an example?
2. Did I know if any student was embarrassed, angered, threatened or made anxious by the topic? If so, how did I find out?

Humor and Joking

In Malaysia "students laugh often and easily," Indonesian students "bring rather positive dispositions to the classroom," and Mexican students "have a *joie de vivre* which can be used in teaching" reported American professors who tried humor and laughter in their classrooms as ways to teach and build rapport with students. But one Fulbright professor observed that when he threw jokes into his lectures, he got no response at all. His interpretation was that his students "were startled that so august a professor would mix jokes and serious content."

One of the ways we recognize humor is through giggles and laughter, but another instructor warned that laughter is "not always joyful. . . . My students sometimes use giggles to communicate 'no,' 'I don't know,' 'I didn't prepare that,' 'please pass me,' or 'that makes me feel uncomfortable.'" Clearly, humor is in the eyes of the beholder as this story from Thailand attests:

> *A student handed me a letter and bowed politely. The writing was in Thai, which I had not yet learned to read. I looked up and jokingly asked if it were a love letter. The young man's face blushed visibly. As the translation ricochetted around, the class began to laugh. The letter invited me to a reception the class had planned in my honor. The young man did not make eye contact with me for weeks. Joking with a class is risky business.*

Physical Interaction

Another kind of interaction important to examine is physical or touching behavior in classrooms, which will vary with cultures, subcultures, ages and genders of the students and teachers and with levels of social awareness and sensitivity toward forms of physical abuse. American campuses with their flattened sense of social hierarchy are places where students and professors can be seen exchanging hugs and friendly slaps on the back. But in recent years, with heightened awareness of sexual harassment on campus, some American professors have become more guarded about touching. It may be useful to ask yourself some questions about when, where, and under what conditions you touch students:

1. Do I touch (male, female) students (upon meeting, upon greeting, to get his/her attention, to emphasize a point, and/or to give praise)?
2. Was any student embarrassed, threatened or made anxious by my touching? If so, how did I find out?

Other topics codified in Figure 1-3 are discussed in more detail in other sections of this text. For example, giving and receiving praise and criticism is discussed in the section on Anticipating Potential Conflicts in Chapter 6 and again in Chapter 11, Evaluating Student Performance. American college professors carry to their intercultural teaching many other perceptions of the role of the teacher, expectations of student behavior and performance, and patterns of teacher-student interaction. These reflect our cultural, geographical and experiential norms. It may be useful, as you plan for intercultural teaching, to examine your own perceptions, expectations, and patterns of interaction.

Currently, limited systematic comparative analyses exist which allow us to examine teaching methods and classroom practices across cultures, but that is changing. The ESL/EFL community with its extensive experience with foreign students and adult immigrants is growing. University classrooms in America are annually becoming more multicultural. We now have more than forty years of government-sponsored Fulbright and other similar grants programs sending American teachers abroad and bringing foreign scholars to the United States. Your efforts to analyze your teaching experience across cultures and to make systematic comparisons of methods and practices are an important part of this ongoing research.

Concept Map

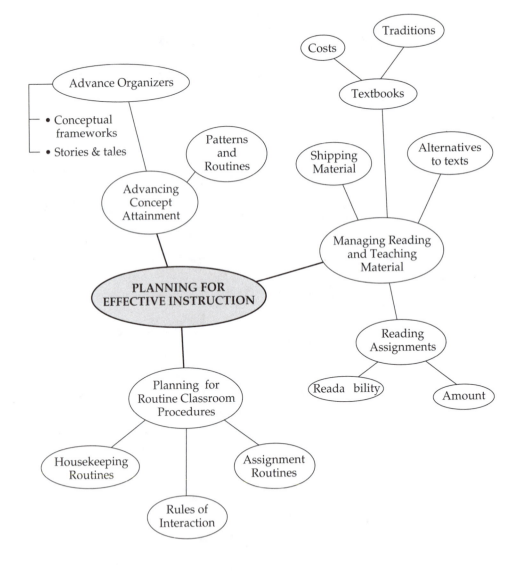

2

PLANNING FOR EFFECTIVE CLASSROOM INSTRUCTION

*How do I start teaching a class . . . Where do I fit
in? . . . How far at the beginning do I begin? . . .
How do I deal with the language barrier? . . .
Even when some speak English, what about all
those subtleties? . . . How will I know if they
understand me?*
—A VIRGINIA TECH PROFESSOR, INDONESIA

This chapter is about planning for successful university teaching across cultures. It focuses on planning for students' concept attainment when normal conventions of language in the new classroom do not easily convey intended meaning. It discusses the management of reading and teaching materials where cultural norms and university support systems are dissimilar from your own. It is about getting ready and beginning what, for many, proves to be a "most unforgettable," "absolutely rejuvenating," and "unbelievably challenging" teaching experience.

This chapter is not about making lesson plans or writing learning objectives. While both of those functions are important for effective teaching, this text assumes readers are skilled in those functions. It is another assumption of this text that professors who are curious, energetic and committed enough to consider and execute the challenging sojourn of cross-cultural teaching, plan to follow principles of good university teaching in their work. Chickering and Gamson (1987) found that effective professors plan to:

1. Encourage contact with students;
2. Communicate high expectations for performance;
3. Accommodate diverse talents and ways of learning;
4. Strengthen cooperation among students;

5. Facilitate active learning; and
6. Give prompt and useful feedback;

To the Chickering and Gamson list, we will add and discuss several more essential areas of planning for the university professor abroad:

7. Advance Concept Attainment;
8. Plan for Classroom Procedures
9. Manage Reading and Teaching Materials; and
10. Structure Learning Environments (Chapter Four).

ADVANCING CONCEPT ATTAINMENT

It has been my experience researching "best practices" in teaching university students in America that good planning evidences a rhythm. That rhythm, as Whitehead described in the 1920s, seems to be characterized first by "romance," then "precision," then "generalization." Initially, a motivated instructor must "romance" his or her students—engaging them and delighting them with excitement and joy about the topic at hand. Good opening lectures and media presentations can often do this. But then there is a need for the development of "precision"—studying the subject matter in detailed fashion and reading for data and examples. Socratic questioning, guided practice, self-directed reading, and exercises are done here. Then a well-planned instructor works for "generalization" —mastering of details and promoting comprehension of the whole. Case studies and strategies for critical thinking are used to promote this phase.

Behavioral norms vary, therefore, "romancing" students across cultures needs to be approached differently. Where students may keep emotions on a very even keel or suspect teachers of being ideologues of the state or feign excessive deference, instructional planning requires more concerted strategies. The several strategies discussed here are not new or unique to cross-cultural settings, but are perhaps more fundamentally necessary in this difficult teaching situation.

Using Advance Organizers

Advance organizers are devices (e.g. models, outlines, schema, diagrams, time lines, etc.) given to students prior to the material to be learned. Experienced educational psychologists such as Ausubel posit that these devices provide stable cognitive structures in which the new knowledge can be subsumed (1960). The use of advance organizers is helpful when:

1. students have no relevant information to which they relate the new learning; and
2. when relevant cognitive structures are present but are not likely to be recognized as relevant by the learner.

Both of these cases are evident in abundance when you are teaching in a cross-cultural classroom. In these cases, advance organizers provide students with general information sets that help cue them to key ideas and organize these ideas in relationship to one another.

Western professors teaching in cross-cultural situations have found advance organizers effective and, in many cases, essential as anchors for students to comprehend the material covered in class. An American professor in Malaysia reported that his students "clearly want to understand the objective of each class and each assignment, but they will not ask me directly." Advance organizers he and others have used include:

1. Announcing the lesson or lecture topics and subtopics to be covered in detail
2. Summarizing the main points of a lecture, reading, or lesson *before* delivering them
3. Preparing outlines of lectures, lessons and reading for students to follow as they listen, discuss, read or write
4. Creating exact models for students to follow in analysis, problem-solving and writing

For other examples of how other professors have used advance organizers to promote concept attainment, see Figure 2-1.

Conceptual Framework. Students in cultures where learning has been based primarily on rote memorization of facts delivered by the teacher in lecture format will need more concrete guidelines and supports to do activities than you are accustomed to providing American students. Ausubel argued that we can teach new information to students only if they can "anchor" it to a previously constructed conceptual framework.

Fulbright law professor, Sharon Hom, whose text on *American Legal Education Methodology in China* (1989) is the first text on legal teaching in China, found her students' performance vastly improved when she provided detailed frameworks for their learning. Her classroom was ceiling to floor wall-chart paper and poster board with "analytical frameworks, structural frameworks, theoretical, and conceptual frameworks." She described the reason:

> *When I introduce an idea and they aren't getting it, maybe they need a specific outline saying, 'This is the conceptual framework for categories of law...This is an explicit framework for the 'negligence' area of the law...This is the analytical model for how to brief a case. You have to give them models.*

One Western professor in Thailand told of an experiment he conducted with his classes at Chulalongkorn University. Using as his dependent measures short mini-quizzes and the quality of class notes students took following three types of presentations, he proceeded to search for the method that promoted the best com-

Advance Organizers as Outlines

- *Historical concepts:* A "time line" or "histogram" of world events puts a discussion of contemporary East-West international relations in sequence and context.
- *Geographical comparisons:* An outline map of the United States and Mexico supports a discussion of immigration policy and information.
- *Sociological research methods:* A skeletal outline of the lecture material (to which students can add their own thoughts and examples) supports memory for major methods.

Advance Organizers as Overviews

- *Literary constructs:* Mark Twain used the "river journey" as a framework for his novels; Shakespeare used the concept of "natural order" as a basis for his plays.
- *Historical concepts:* American values were shaped by pioneer views that "nature was to be conquered."

Advance Organizers as Key Examples or Models

- *Legal writing:* A model brief is presented with all the elements exhibited for students to replicate.
- *Social science research:* A short executive summary of a research report emphasizing key findings and recommendations serves as a model for final orals.
- *Model processes:* An example of classifying an insect uses a taxonomic chart which the student can use to classify similar and different genus and species.

FIGURE 2-1   Guidelines: Examples of Advance Organizers to Promote Concept Attainment

prehension. First, he lectured, but gave them no written outline of the material. In In his second trial, he lectured and gave them a framework outline. Third, he lectured and gave them exact notes of the lecture. He found that the best performance on the quizzes and the best class notes were attained with the lecture that used a framework outline. He posited that this advance organizer encouraged them to take their own notes, to add points and to "practice" thinking about the material. The second best method was the lecture with notes fully written out. He noted, however, their class notes were usually just Thai translations (Frankel, 1987).

A science professor, who carefully observed students' notes and note-taking as a way to determine if there was concept attainment, recounted, "I tell them they should listen to what I am saying, try to understand it and then take notes in their own language. The important thing is for *them* to make that transformation into *their* notes—some can and some cannot."

These examples illustrate that "advance organizers" are more than professors' outlines. They are conceptual frameworks on which a student can "plug in" his or her existing knowledge. Your students will need to fit their own experiences, which are both personal and culturally relevant, onto this framework. In planning an "advance organizer," it is best to design the framework and develop the hierarchy of information. Then you can present general material first, move on to specific material, and differentiate progressively as you go. Each piece of material presented will be related to what has been presented before.

In practice the "advance organizer," as a working conceptual framework, is the reference point you use to plan lectures and class activities. Instructional activities can be tied to the framework by:

1. Requiring students to look at the "larger picture" in the framework as they give examples or describe differences.
2. Having students formulate the framework in their own vocabulary or language.
3. Asking students to describe how information relates to their own personal or cultural experience.
4. Restating the framework in subsequent lessons.
5. Soliciting a summarization of the main points of the material.
6. Asking students to show how new material fits into the framework.

These classroom activities are not easy to execute even among students with whom we share language and cultural context. But without the aid of a thoughtful conceptual framework serving as the basis for a lesson or lecture, the likelihood that you can promote much learning in the cross-cultural context is scant. One Fulbright professor in Southeast Asia warned that the "American example" or "in my country" has only "limited novelty value and then the perspective must return to that of the student's for him to learn what we are trying to teach." An economist from San Diego State described his experience of building conceptual frameworks relevant to students' needs and experience in Malaysia:

> *My students' main interest is to find out how to* use *forecasting and modelling for public policy analysis, not in theoretical foundations. I have to make a radical departure from my usual teaching methods, because those practical applications need to fit their mind set and be relevant to issues in developing countries, not applications from American textbooks.*

Tales, Stories and Parables. I grew up in a huge Southern kinship network where my family paid homage to ancestors with tales spanning generations. That may be why I so identify with peoples in the world who teach using stories and parables. I enjoy and value in teaching the use of a good story—one that stretches, exaggerates, makes larger than life, freezes moments, names events, takes students outside the present, entertains, makes order, chastises and instructs.

American history professors, who perhaps have keener ears than many of us for stories that live on, reported that legends and parables were a galvanizing way to plan for and organize a class in a cross-cultural setting. Many countries and cultures are so full of working proverbs and illustrative legends and stories that the Western professor can find many illustrations of major concepts, propositions, generalizations, principles and theses useful for forming a central "anchor" or advance organizer. Of course, reading the folk tales, literature and history of your host country is the best way to begin this process before you go, but learning as much of the language as you can and using colleagues and students as "key informants" are other effective ways of building your repertoire of good stories.

In cultures where tales, stories and parables are fundamental to the teaching process, you have the luxury to suspend accuracy (for which we are all held so accountable in our work in the United States) and let the stories illustrate your points. When the skillful "talking chief" in Samoa teaches, he tells the story, not the way it happened, but the way he wants his students to remember it. Suspending accuracy and creating situational stories which illustrate main points is a familiar advance organizer to many students who will remember and conceptualize the essential ideas.

Using Recurrence of Patterns and Ritual of Routine

Recurrence of Patterns. When language barriers interfere with communicating concepts, it is likely that use of recurrence and patterning become more important than usual to facilitate concept attainment. In a 1920s classic experiment on learning, students were taught a series of traditional Mandarin Chinese characters. The characters were different in most respects, but each had embedded in it a symbol that all the characters had in common (Hull, 1920). For example, in the characters in Figure 2-2, each character represents something made from wood, therefore, the symbol for wood appears in each character:

In studying the conditions which facilitated the memory for the characters and the conceptualization that the common element made these characters constitute a set, it was concluded that:

1. Teaching the characters from simplest to most complex construction was not enough;
2. Teaching the symbol for wood in isolation and relying on students to conceptualize the commonality in the set was not enough;
3. But presenting the entire set of characters, one at a time with the common element emphasized (redrawn in red), facilitated the conceptualization.

The fact that students need things spelled out and repeated following a familiar set of patterns and routines is not a startling revelation to contemporary college teachers, but the extent of the need to plan for patterns to occur and reoccur

椅	牀	架	木	林
Chair	Bed	Frame	Tree	Forest

FIGURE 2-2   Recurrent Themes for Promoting Concept Attainment

Adapted from: Hull, C. L. (1920). Quantitative aspects of the evolution of concepts. *Psychological monographs,* No. 123, Washington, D.C.: American Psychological Association. (Material in the public domain).

in lectures and in class activities across cultures may be. American history professor Richard Burg, a two-time Fulbright professor to Pakistan and Indonesia, stated, "I have to spend much more time than I normally would using the chalk board, spelling things out, illustrating my points . . . things I wouldn't bother to do in an American classroom."

American professors emphasized again and again the need to identify one main point, one theme, one law, in one class and repeat it, restate it, go over it and repeat it again—using the "red color over the common element" method as Hull did. A biologist in Indonesia reiterated the need for recurrence:

> *Fortunately the subject I'm dealing with is describing the morphology of things, so I can draw lots of pictures on the board and label them. Then I give them a detailed outline of what I am talking about using the same labels. The same outline is then projected up with transparencies.*

Concept attainment in this laboratory setting seems to be a function of conscious planning for the use of recurrence and patterning.

Ritual of Routine.   Additionally, the simple act of routine, or as one professor said, "doing the same thing over and over until you get it," seems to facilitate concept attainment. As with patterning, the ritual of routine must be similarly planned for in class. In a situation where language allows much misunderstanding, students will often perform in ritualistic routines, despite your wishes and intentions to the contrary. Some American professors reported that they get the best performance from students after they taught them to use *one* framework for analyzing a problem or worked with them over and over using *one* model. For example, law professors in China found that if they used one model for briefing a case, rather than allowing students to choose from many alternatives, students' briefing performance improved. The "trial and error" method of American pedagogy often encourages us to toss a technique which does not produce the results we desire and opt for a new one. Experience with ritual and pattern in cross-cultural settings would suggest otherwise. Effective professors find a scheme for analysis or a model for abstracting readings or a routine of classroom questioning and stick to it to get its "ritualistic" benefits when verbal explanations fail.

PLANNING FOR ROUTINE CLASSROOM PROCEDURES

Early in your teaching assignment it may be necessary to plan for, discuss and establish some class procedures in the new intercultural classroom that you have long taken for granted in your American classroom. The first of these might be to decide *how you and students will be expected to enter and leave the room.* In Chapter One, Professor Al Bailey of Madonna University in Michigan described his Chinese students' standing and exchanging bows when he came into the room. I too found similar confusion in Thailand when late students were not certain if they could enter the class after it had begun and, if they did so, were they to apologize and *wai* their polite gestures and bows? It seemed to me unnecessarily deferential, not to mention disruptive. Some issues to consider may be:

- How will student enter the classroom generally?
- If they are late, under what conditions will they enter?
- May students leave the classroom early? during class?
- How is the class dismissed?

Another set of procedures which may need specifying for students in intercultural situations is *how students participate in class.* A broader discussion of how to facilitate student participation can be found in Chapter 8, but an initial discussion with students about participation procedures may allay some of their fears about how to participate in discussions and question/answer sessions with you. Some considerations are:

- Do students need permission from the teacher to speak?
- How do students follow or interrupt another speaker?
- How should students respond who do/or do not know the answer?
- Will participation be evaluated?

A third area of classroom procedures which might need clarification will be *communicating, collecting and returning assignments.* Some professors found preparing an "assignment sheet" with directions and stated expectations minimized confusion associated with oral instructions. Some, like Sharon Hom, a professor of law in China, gave sample assignments and found, for better or worse, that students followed the expected model very literally. Other considerations include:

- When specifically is the assignment due?
- Are there penalties for lateness?
- Are there penalties for English errors?
- Is collective work allowed, forbidden, encouraged?

- In what form is the work expected? Typed, hand-written, highlighted, illustrated? (You think I jest?)
- What is the procedure for queries on the assignment?
- Will revisions be allowed? How many?

Figure 2-3 provides a set of questions to use in Planning for Classroom Routines in cross-cultural settings.

MANAGING READING AND TEACHING MATERIALS

The Chinese have a high regard for the printed word. Printed matter is rare and very few people have had access to libraries. One colleague reported to me that she had read the English novel Jane Eyre *(the only English book available to her in her youth) thirteen times. (A University of Hawaii professor, China)*

Planning for Texts and Book Use

It is commonly reported that teaching across cultures is, as one professor put it, "teaching from scratch!" The lack of availability of texts and teaching materials

---

A. **Discuss how you and students will be expected to enter and leave the room.**

- How will student enter the classroom generally?
- If they are late, under what conditions will they enter?
- May students leave the classroom early? during class?
- How is the class dismissed?

B. **Identify ways and procedures for students to participate in class.**

- Do students need permission from the teacher to speak?
- How do students follow or interrupt another speaker?
- How should students respond who do/or do not know the answer to a question?
- Will participation be evaluated?

C. **Detail how assignments will be communicated, collected, and returned.**

- Consider "assignment sheets" with directions and expectations;
- When specifically is the assignment due?
- Are there penalties for lateness or English errors?
- Is collective work allowed, forbidden, encouraged?
- In what form is the work expected? Typed, hand-written?
- What is the procedure for queries on the assignment?
- Will revisions be allowed? How many?

FIGURE 2-3   Guidelines: Planning for Routine Classroom Procedures

is usually the impetus for this definition. Some visiting professors report, even when material is available, that undergraduate and graduate students at their universities do not have a tradition of out-of-class reading and have read little related literature in their field of study. The explanations for the observation that students have never developed the habit or discipline of professional reading vary—"Because texts are unavailable and expensive"; "Because there are too few related scholarly journals and texts written in their languages;" or "Because class readings are often not assigned or expected." What ever may be the reasons for limited reading among your students, the experiences of many American professor abroad indicate that you may be in a situation of teaching courses without texts or with books that are neither on-target, current or comprehensible to the average student.

A brief examination of the problems surrounding texts and their availability and use is worth some attention, not only for its utility in planning, but also for the small window on cultural differences it provides. American professors reported extensively on two major problems they encountered—*limited availability and high costs of texts* and *few traditions of assigned reading.*

Availability and Cost of Texts. American professors reported the following as affecting the availability of texts: slow distribution systems, political bias and censorship, exorbitant costs, retentive library policies, students' "hording" materials, etc. One Fulbrighter to Ireland remarked on the problem of *slow distribution*:

> *No one should ever come to Ireland assuming books can be ordered for a course! First, it goes against the grain of the way things are done, and second, books take forever to get here from suppliers. . . . I could swim the Irish Channel quicker than books come from the U.K.—my books arrived five months late—and the bookstore did not think that was unusual!*

From countries with disparate resources like Norway, Nepal, Pakistan, New Zealand, and Mexico, the stories were similar— "It was hard to order (and took a long time to receive) books for my class;" "Books arrived half way into the semester;" and "We lacked appropriate, affordable textbooks whose supply was dependable, even in the capital city." A Fulbright professor to Japan reported, "I have been hard pressed to find adequate texts and reference material here. My own textbook, published by the world's largest house, took two months to get through customs from Singapore."

The problem of availability of texts is difficult in many fields in many countries, but for literature professors, whose primary objective may be to have students read and react to textual material which can be delivered no other way, the problem is serious. An American literature professor with a two-year assignment to Czechoslovakia related:

> *The second year, I used practically all of my book allowance to buy enough copies of each volume. This allowed me the unprecedented luxury of lending each student*

for the entire semester a book that could be taken home, lived with, written in, read and re-read. Lest this reaction seem excessive, it should be mentioned that the usual situation is either to hand out and re-collect material in each class or to ask about fifteen students to share three copies of a novel!

Another factor affecting availability of texts is *state policy or censorship*. One example is from China:

Without a doubt the biggest hindrance to effective teaching in China is the paucity of texts. . . . There are a few anthologies of selected readings in English and American literature published in China that have brief introductory comments on periods and authors as well as some footnotes in Chinese. I found these books far from satisfactory due to the nature of the selections, which are usually only excerpts obviously made with a strong political bias (Leonard, 1986).

But even if the distribution systems were in place and speedy and the governments and universities enlightened, the *costs of books*, especially English language or U.S. press editions, are often prohibitive. Caroline Alexander related her experience in Malawi:

The difficulty in obtaining textbooks was an ongoing problem. Each student received an allowance of fifty kwacha *[about forty-five dollars] for a semester's worth of books. As these were usually sold at unsubsidized Western prices, it was impossible for students to meet the basic needs of more than one course. Instead there was heavy use of the photocopy machines (Alexander, 1991).*

An American History professor to New Zealand complained, "Books costs here are very erratic and expensive and students are on a very limited budget." From Ireland, "American books were outrageous. I purchased them myself (ouch!) and put them on reserve." Another from Pakistan offered, "I suggested students buy a book subsidized by a U.S. government program, but they said the cost [$4.00] was far too prohibitive. When tuition is only $1.00 per year, that attitude is understandable."

Skidmore professor Bruce Ronda saw lack of availability of texts another way: "My approach to American studies became eclectic and experimental; I am not above dabbling shamelessly in fields far distant from my home turf (of history). The absence in China of texts in many collateral fields—art history, psychology, sociology, political science—forced me to become a sort of renaissance person" (1986).

Few Traditions of Assigned Reading. Different customs, expectations, and traditions of reading in preparation for class or of reading in association with out-of-class assignments impact on availability and utility of texts. A Fulbright professor to Ireland claimed, "Students typically do not purchase books, and no specific texts are assigned. Rather extensive reading lists are handed out and the students are expected to 'graze' among them." "My students do not have the custom of using texts," reiterated a Fulbrighter to Pakistan. An archeologist in Israel complained, "Students don't read much, especially if assigned in English." Professors to Thailand reported that students did not have the practice of "preparing for class, doing the assigned readings or doing homework." A geographer to Mexico summarized a "double whammy" of availability and custom: "The lack of books in the absence of a tradition of reading is a serious problem!"

Host professors' low expectations have a major role in students' noncompliance with the visiting professors' expectation of preparatory reading, some American professors argue. "Readings are assigned, but Japanese professor do not seem to expect that most students will do it, and so cover the same ground in class. "The professor," one Chinese graduate student said, "is our 'library' ".

One sees the complexities and contradictions of availability and tradition in a society like China where texts have been valued, vilified, heralded, censored, avoided and memorized. One professor in China reported, "While a few students were outstanding exceptions, many seemed unable or unwilling to read extensively. Low English language ability and the inordinate amount of time Chinese students spend in the classroom may account for this." But Joyce Fuller of Queens College countered, "In the Chinese tradition, a text is worth going over again and again until all possible meaning has been exhausted, until every nuance of structure and lexis is understood, and perhaps until it is committed to memory." Indeed it is not uncommon on a Chinese campus to see students sitting under trees or walking around campus, book in hand, reciting over and over, as if they are memorizing lines in a play.

Maps and Graphic Materials. In the 1970s I worked on a UNESCO project to regionalize social science curricula in the South Pacific and train teachers there to teach geography. I remember a graphic irony of that work—the islands where I was based fell into the "gutter-binding" of the world atlas and were not even visible. An instructor to Ireland warned that many students will not have a "mental map of the world," so you must use maps when you talk about global problems and events.

A Fulbright professor to Mexico reminded others of the importance of maps and graphic materials when he advised, "For any comparative subject matter, bring an atlas, a wall map of the United States, and outline photocopied maps for student notebooks. I am convinced that the spatial dimension in understanding the world, the United States and Mexico's relationship to both is fundamental."

Determining Amount and Readability of Assignments

Among Thai students, the idea that broad and deep reading outside of class should supplement lectures was not accepted or appreciated. (George, 1987)

Amount of Reading. James Thorson, a Fulbright professor in the former Yugoslavia, paralleled my own experience in Thailand where graduate students tolerated fifteen pages of assigned reading per week, but would mutiny at twenty pages. He misjudged assignments:

> *I found very quickly that I had grossly overestimated the amount of reading that I could assign with any reasonable expectation that it might get done. I suspect that my experience along these lines has been replicated by hundreds, if not thousands, of Fulbrighters over the past forty years (1987).*

Another from Japan, "I assigned about fifteen pages a week which proved demanding . . . roughly half of the students did all of the work." An international studies professor in Mexico concurred: "At first, I gave heavy reading assignments, and the students had trouble keeping up."

A professor of American studies in Jerusalem cut back not only on his readings, but on his entire course syllabus, "I'd originally planned to teach about 120 short stories over the year. My chairperson, without asking me, dropped most of the second half of my syllabus leaving about seventy stories and ending my historical survey with Hemingway. At first, I was miffed, but now I'm glad she did so . . . I'd seriously overestimated the ability of students to keep up with readings in English."

Some professors feel that not only are these practices of nonreading and narrowing of scope hurtful to students' grasp of the content, but it dampens their *own* interest. A teacher of American literature in Turkey disliked the pace with which he had to cover reading material, "Instead of giving reading assignments, we read from photocopies of text materials together in class discussing the material one paragraph at a time. In the beginning, I thought this methods would be manageable, but the class went slowly. Although most of the material was understood, it proved to be very boring for me."

Readability of Assigned Material. It may be necessary to determine if textual material planned for students in this cross-cultural setting is appropriate in terms of readability. Judging vocabulary and grammatic complexity of material is difficult for most of us who are not linguists or reading specialists. But some of these specialists' techniques might aid your task. One of the most common informal measures of readability, used by EFL/ESL instructors and reported to be useful by American professor abroad, is the Cloze procedure (Borsuth, 1972). The procedure, which has reasonable validity and reliability for an informal procedure, can be used with almost all instructional material. The professor selects a passage from the proposed reading or text and eliminates every fifth word and replaces the word with a standard blank space. The reading is then given to the students who fill in each blank with the word they think was deleted—including, for example, both articles and key nouns. The response is scored as correct if it matches the deleted word (or reasonable synonym of it). Misspellings are disregarded.

Criteria for determining acceptable mastery of the material vary. Some argue that supplying ninety percent of the deletions is necessary at the instructional level; others argue that seventy-five percent (or even sixty percent with non-native speakers) is adequate. Whether you should use the class average to determine the figure or some other statistic varies as well. Whether or not you can definitively interpret this aggregated data using a "cloze" procedure, you may be able to get some insight into the difficulty of the reading materials and their consequent utility in your classes.

Some Fulbright professors in Japan found that "high interest, low vocabulary" materials, such as those used in American high schools, served as excellent introductory materials for their courses. They explained, "Materials used in senior high schools in the United States tend to use simpler English, to define terms, and to cover a lot of ground in a few pages. In class you can elaborate, follow interesting tangents, offer your own professional interpretation or explanation and supply the cultural background." Another added, "Normal American texts are well beyond my Japanese students' skills. For third- and fourth-year students, I excerpted from simple texts written for junior college level."

Planning for Alternatives to Texts

To teach a course successfully without a text requires thoughtful planning and searching for appropriate articles, chapters or handouts for each class. Because it is not uncommon to have only a vague idea of the general area of your course assignment, no "fail safe" forethought on texts and materials is possible. University of Tennessee professor Fran Trusty advised, "Bring as many single books as you possibly can . . . brand new books in as many subjects as you might be called on to work with . . . and bring copies of articles and chapters generally across your field."

By far the most common practice of providing "texts" to students where there are none available is photocopying them. "Photocopying is the world's new 'cottage industry' " said an instructor to Eastern Europe where the "neighborhood copy stand" is as ubiquitous as it is all over Asia. American professors, who have been schooled in the legality of copyrights (or know first hand the problems for authors and presses of the misuse of the photocopier), often have mixed feelings about photocopied materials and texts. One American professor in Asia lamented, "My text, my very own text, was pirated and copied in Hong Kong and sold for a quarter of the price charged in the United States. Now I can't make a penny on those sales and I wrote the damn thing!" But another professor's point of view was more common: "The only way a student can possibly have a book of his own to take home, write in, read and reread is if he can afford it. My text costs forty dollars U.S. and a photocopy of it here costs $4.00. The local 'copy hut' will even bind it for that."

Another way some professors deal with teaching without texts is to prepare textual material of their own. This varies from the compendium of articles in a "course packet" to authorship of a curriculum or text. San Diego State economist Hari Singh developed a "case study manual" and explained, "There was no textbook available for this course, so I had to start thinking about applications and developing cases which could really interest them in a meaningful way." One Japan Fulbrighter created a book for his students of his typed lecture notes. A professor to New Zealand advised future instructors to bring "large numbers of reprints in your field for the book binderies at the university to put together . . ." and he added, "Because I didn't know exactly what my course assignment would be, I chose general articles from several different subspecialties." Occasionally, a professor will write his or her own text. One professor to Nepal explained, "There were no adequate materials, so I wrote the textbook and called it *Basic University English.*"

In short, as you plan for reading and teaching materials, consider taking materials that are already short, easily reproducible, modifiable, and flexible. Guidelines for Preparing Materials for Teaching Abroad are provided in Figure 2-4. Additional resources for planning for college and university teaching abroad in various regions of the world are available in appendix B—"Planning Resources for Faculty Exchanges by Region.

A. **Take class notes, syllabi, bibliographies, overheads, cases, and problems for classes you expect to teach.**

- Be sure to pack these essential notes in your *accompanying baggage* as international post is too unpredictable.
- Make *copies* of these class notes to leave at your home institution in case of loss.

B. **Plan for the contingency of teaching introductory or generic courses.**

- Bring a few recent *introductory texts* in your field.
- Consult with stateside professors of introductory courses for syllabi, bibliographies, and other teaching material.

C. **Bring supplemental reading materials.**

- "High interest, low vocabulary" materials for students with limited English proficiency;
- A *community college or high school text* in your field;
- *Readers* as sources of articles and short readings in both your generic and specific fields;
- *Abstract compendiums* on research or issues in your field (often published by professional organizations);

D. **Send sets of recent professional journals and desk copies of texts.**

- Multiple copies of journals and unused desk copies make excellent donation to departmental library collections and gifts to colleagues (by sea mail).
- Publishers and their local "book reps" may donate books to this cause (and even pay postage).

FIGURE 2-4   Guidelines: Preparing Materials for Teaching Abroad

Shipping Books and Teaching Materials

Because rules, regulations, procedures, postal services, and luck vary so greatly among all the world's teaching assignments abroad, this section is *not* about "how to ship your rare and beloved copy of Keats' poems without risk to Inner Mongolia." It is rather to help you troubleshoot that peril. One of my fellow Fulbright professors to Thailand was caught in the classic "Catch 22" on her shipment of teaching materials. In one of her shipped boxes she packed her marriage license, a document then required for a work permit if accompanied by a spouse. Her boxes were being held by the post office until she had the permit. But to get the permit she needed the marriage license, which was in the box in the post office.

Sometimes your U.S. grant and sponsoring organizations, if you have one, will facilitate shipping of some books and teaching material. Using those services may work without a hitch and save you time and money. However, an enormous amount of anecdotal evidence exists to support the suggestion that these services should be viewed as "backup" support and not your primary method of arriving on location with adequate and manageable teaching materials. Problems exist with both the timing and the reliability of both inter-country and intra-country shipping systems.

The reports on shipping materials read like annals of disappointment. A recent Fulbrighter to Poland wrote, "Out of six shipments of books, I have received only two (4 months later). One semester has gone by with me using only the materials I brought." Another from Hungary reported, "Shipments of materials arrived irregularly from six weeks to eighteen weeks, but blessedly all arrived! Next time, I'll bring all teaching materials with me." "Some of my book shipments did not arrive until after the semester started. In fact, (four months later), one of my shipments is still enroute!" optimistically remarked another who taught in Czechoslovakia.

It seems luck plays a significant role in the arrival of teaching materials through the shipping routes. "Boxes I sent surface mail two months ahead to Japan arrived at my doorstep without difficulty, though worse for wear (for example, without square corners)," said one lucky professor. Another to China shared her secret, "I carried my most important teaching materials and shipped the rest by surface mail in small boxes (about ten pounds each). My personal good luck charm with shipped boxes of books overseas is to paint each box red!"

Concept Map

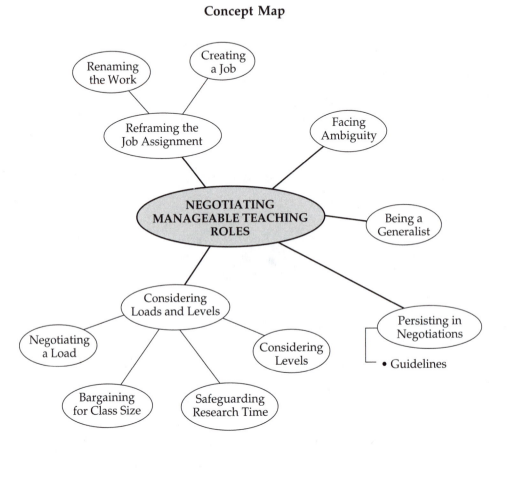

3

NEGOTIATING MANAGEABLE TEACHING ROLES

If I had not heard so often before coming that this is typical—you don't learn until the last minute what they want you to do, and that's not what you can do, and when you try to do what they've asked, you discover all sorts of barriers in your way. If I hadn't realized that, I'm not sure what I would have done— fallen on my sword?
—A UNIVERSITY OF SOUTH CAROLINA PROFESSOR, THAILAND

Negotiating a manageable teaching role in a cross-cultural setting exposes deeply rooted differences in cultural values. American professors are accustomed to receiving a proposal for their work and teaching load, possibly presenting one or more counter proposals, and reaching a final agreement (usually in writing) before the work has begun. Precision, directness, and a fondness for agreements written down characterize the negotiation from a Western perspective.

However, in some countries and cultures, intangible factors of human relationships, status, social reciprocities, and a myriad other customs often overshadow the systematic "efficiency" of Western negotiation. Of primary importance in some settings is the establishment of a personal relationship with the new instructor before any definite agreements are reached. The pace is slow. Details and a more informal embodiment of agreements will come, if they do, later. American professors should not be naïve and believe that this, or other styles of negotiating is not thoughtful or intentional. The "let's wait and see" attitude of negotiation, common in some Asian countries and manifested in the common practice of not negotiating course assignments until after the professor arrives, for example, may be the academic supervisor's way of balancing off your potential discomfort with his or her potential regret.

FACING AMBIGUITY

One of the first difficulties in negotiating a manageable teaching role is facing ambiguity. The American penchant for fair and timely contractual negotiations, which spell out the fine details of expectations, requirements, time-frames, and compensations, did *not* characterize most of the situations we observed.

Limited or No Prior Notice

Many instructors either never received prior and specific documentation of their course requirements and teaching loads before departure or these were found, upon arrival, not to be what they expected. They related a profusion of frustrations. In her early negotiations prior to leaving for Mexico, a professor from DePaul University communicated several times by telephone with her Mexican dean. "After these consultations, it was decided that I would teach two courses at the Law School, approved in a letter," she said. "After my arrival I found out that the Law School was not at all interested in the proposed courses. So much for formal letters of invitation!" Another professor lamented:

> *After receiving a letter telling me what I was to teach and after purchasing textbooks for those courses, when I arrived in Turkey I was told that someone else was teaching those courses. We arrived at an agreement, but there were no materials for the courses to be offered, which put me into dire straits for a few weeks while I tried to develop materials.*

A professor to Turkey found upon arrival, "The faculty had no exact plans for my functioning." Another professor in Thailand related, "When I arrived in the country I was assigned a course which was not in my areas of expertise. But the former dean who agreed to my hiring had 'requested' it." Still another announced with exasperation that, unknown to her, she had been "assigned by her dean to teach several classes for every professor in the department [even though the content was not altogether appropriate] just to 'be fair.' " A Fulbrighter to Ireland faced this common ambiguity:

> *My memoranda clarifying my assignment with administrators had gone permanently unanswered. When I wondered out loud why I had not been able to negotiate a job description before this assignment began, I was told, 'We Irish are a "face-to-face" country.'*

Because so many professors related the information that their courses "were not determined until they arrived," we discussed this practice of belated negotiation with several host university administrators. A dean at Chulalongkorn, one of the major universities in Thailand, who had extensive experience dealing with foreign professors, argued that from her (and the Thai) perspective, "We like to know first the people with whom we are negotiating." Another offered, *"cha pen kan-naan pen khun"* ("taking a long time is [to our] advantage.")

Mismatch of Expectations

Chris Silver of Virginia Tech, puzzled by the expectations of his Indonesian university, remarked:

> *I wonder, what are they looking for? What is it that I am expected to do? They're looking for something special. I told them what I could do, but I don't think they're looking for that.*

A professor of special education to Czechoslovakia was disappointed to learn upon arrival to his assignment that he was not to be given his own class "because of my inadequacies in Czech—yet, from the beginning, the university had been informed that I did not speak Czech." A professor from Malaysia recalled, "The courses and work that I was assigned had nothing to do with the stated Fulbright assignment. At the beginning of the semester here in Malaysia, it was very confusing how the course selections were made for me. I was never consulted about what I could do or how I could best help the program." A contract professor in China advised:

> *Don't count on an assignment tailored to your particular areas of expertise. It is wise, of course, to correspond with your host institution regarding the courses you will teach, but you may not succeed in pinning them down in advance. And even if you do, things may have changed by the time you arrive on the scene. Consider bringing a bit of everything in the way of teaching materials.*

Professors with Fulbright Fellowships to Latin America sometimes concurred with this mismatch. A visiting professor from Brazil offered, "The official information from San Paulo said I would teach three 2-hour classes per week, when in fact, I teach four classes 3 to 4 hours per week." Another stated, "Much beyond my control, I did not instruct in the material I was fully prepared to teach. Upon my arrival in Brazil, it became clear that my host lost interest in having me instruct in this area." From Mexico, an Arizona State professor related her story: "Due to scheduling changes, my anticipated grad seminar, for which I had done the most preparation, did not materialize." Another professor to Mexico conveyed:

> *In my [appointment] letter, I was even requested to serve as interim chair of the department. The current chair, temporarily in that position, wished to be relieved of those duties in order to pursue other interests. Upon my arrival in country, I found my service as chair (a job I had declined) to be a* fait accompli.

"The posted position sought an attorney to assist in the establishment of a legal clinic," explained a professor on assignment in Pakistan, "but upon my arrival I discovered that neither the Law School nor the Bar Association had considered this prospect at all."   A two-time Fulbrighter professor to Pakistan and then to Indonesia, Richard Burg summed up his latest job, "I am not doing exactly what I thought I would be doing; in fact I am not doing exactly what the (host institution) thought I would be doing either."

BEING A GENERALIST

An old medical school adage states that the difference between the generalist and the specialist is that the specialist learns more and more about less and less until he knows a lot about nothing and the generalist learns less and less about more and more until she know nothing about a lot.   In teaching situations abroad, American professors often are required to stretch beyond their fields of expertise to the general content of their disciplines, for some this stretch begins in the negotiation process.   This process is illustrated by correspondence from a dean at a university in Malawi to Caroline Alexander (1991), an American professor en route to teach there. The correspondence reveals some hosts' expectations that American professors can be "generalists" when teaching across cultures:

> *Please excuse the brief note. . . . I thought that you would wish to know that the Appointments Committee has agreed to offer you a lectureship as from October 1st. This will mainly involve the teaching of Latin here. . . . I am afraid the salaries here do not compare to those in America, but you will find the cost of living relatively cheap. . . . Considerable interest was also expressed in your athletic prowess, and it was hoped you might help the College coach in this area. I don't suppose you also play a musical instrument? We are in great need of a bassoonist.*

Alexander continued with the negotiations for some weeks only to find that she was expected to teach Latin *and* establish a Department of Classics at the university, as well.

Responding to this call to be a "generalist," it is common for American professors who teach abroad to "teach courses outside their specialty," "teach out-of-field," "teach a smattering of classes across the curriculum," "teach English 'by default,'" and almost always, "paint with a far broader brush than I ever expected to in my field."

PERSISTING IN NEGOTIATIONS

A Thai proverb says slowness is achievement *(cha pen kan)*. Slow persistence is called for in some negotiation processes across cultures. As Lehigh professor Peter Beidler in China said, "My first letter from the university stated, 'We've lined up these five courses for you.' I wrote back than I can't teach those five courses.' [Me thinking the load was too heavy; Me thinking I've never taught these courses before; Me trying to be polite]. We negotiated that down to three courses." He added, "But when I got here, there weren't enough students for those courses, so I agreed to two other courses, both brand new for me." Another professor offered:

> *Before I arrived in Mexico, I received an ambiguous letter describing my teaching assignment. I deduced that the teaching load would be eighteen hours per week. I wrote back that this seemed excessive (even though I knew it was the standard). I argued that there were other important things for me to do, like helping with problems of institutional development, and collaborating with host professors on significant research projects. After much back and forth, my alternatives seemed to satisfy them.*

A Purdue University professor on an exchange program to New Zealand recounted his negotiation, "My teaching assignment was changed at the last minute because the one instructor teaching in my field resigned just before the meeting of the first class of the year. The course I was to have taught was canceled." As an alternative idea, this professor negotiated to be the chief research consultant for the faculty. He explained, "My teaching subsequently consisted of offering a series of eight open research seminars for students and staff and advising students on their M.A. theses." Another University of South Carolina professor who was being shared between two programs in Thailand reported, "Five days before I left, I received a letter from one of the chairpersons listing the five courses that I would teach. The expectation was that I would teach a great number of hours like the other contract teachers, which I couldn't if I was also to teach in another department and also do the research I had contracted for. [After much negotiation] . . I now teach two courses in English literature, but courses like literary theory I have never taught before!"

Sometimes it seems, even with the best of plans and persistence, that the "other side" wins. One professor to Czechoslovakia said, "I demanded a contract before I began teaching . . and got a two-page detailed contract. But, I found out later, they buffaloed me! They didn't honor it and they knew that I didn't have much recourse." In another case, two law professor had negotiated with the Fulbright program in Turkey to share one grant. They recounted, "My wife and I were awarded one position between us, but were informed upon arrival by Turkish administrators that 'bureaucratic obstacles' made our sharing one position impossible. We were told it would 'derail the Turkish mind.'" They both ended up teaching full loads.

A professor to Thailand who was not able to renegotiate his courses shared this: "I now spend hordes of time reading Aristotle to teach a required course on literary theory to graduate students that no one on the faculty wants to teach; I told them I am not competent to teach it, but they said I had to! It requires me to study Aristotle more than I did even when I was in graduate school." Another professor to Mexico related a similar story: "I agreed to teach a course for which

I was not really qualified. I could have refused, but in the interest of collegiality, I did not. This was not an efficient use of my time—I spent most of my time studying for this course."

Reports on negotiations of manageable teaching roles identify *patience* and *flexibility* as the keys to successful negotiations. The American professor who is flexible will bend with the situation. For example, he may teach a course off-target from his preparation and interest one semester, but get to teach his favorite course the following semester, which was not planned. Another professor may agree to write a proposal for a graduate curriculum in trade for professional writing time she almost never has at her home university. Professors who are flexible and willing to live with job uncertainty experience less frustration with the job definition.

CONSIDERING LOADS AND LEVELS

Negotiating a Teaching Load

One of the most difficult considerations in negotiations is the teaching load. The norms of your host colleagues may be different from your experience, or they may seem inscrutable. What is important to keep in mind is that teaching across language and cultural barriers is, obviously, more difficult than teaching in your home institution where you do not experience as much modification and acculturation. Loads at home and in the new situation rarely are equivalent. For example, Iizawa reports that Fulbright professors to Japan argue for smaller than average teaching loads (1991): "Linguistic and cultural barriers make teaching more difficult and put more of a burden on preparing for class. Moreover, these difficult teaching responsibilities often keep professors from carrying out their [other] professional commitments."

There is sometimes a criticism raised that an institution "did not really want a well-established scholar," but rather someone to "cover a certain number of unstaffed courses." Or a teaching load is "appropriate to an *instructor* at an American university, but not a *full professor*." Even when teaching loads seemed initially manageable, sometimes they become otherwise. For example, one Fulbrighter to Norway argued:

> *I did not ask anyone what a six-hour teaching load represents in Norway, as compared to what it means in America. I arrived in Norway believing that a six-hour teaching load would represent a modest level of teaching responsibility, but I have come to feel I was mistaken. Six hours here is the full load normally carried by junior level faculty.*

A foreign expert in TEFL composition explained her negotiation dilemma in China: "One professor teaches one or two courses while some other professors teach four or five courses. It seems so unfair. It is not meant to be unfair, because each contract is individually negotiated." Other visiting professors to Western Europe report varying loads and demands. Some said that their instructional duties required more time than they had anticipated and, as a consequence, they had less time for their own research. Others say their teaching loads were light (in keeping with rank as is typical of European universities) and they had "ample time for research and scholarly writing."

Carol Chapman, a veteran foreign expert with ARCO China, Inc. in the Peoples Republic of China (PRC), describes the issues in a typical university contract negotiation for teachers of English in the PRC. It is similar to what foreign professors who negotiate their own situations report from their experience:

> *Teaching loads generally run from twelve to eighteen contact hours per week and classes are scheduled Monday through Saturday, so you may have a longer than usual teaching week. In addition to teaching, you may be expected to assist colleagues with lesson preparations. Almost certainly, you'll be asked to prepare or edit teaching materials or to make English language recordings. And you'll be called upon to give supplementary slide shows and lectures. . . . If you are presented with too onerous a load, you can probably negotiate a change in your assignment. Don't agree to something intolerable to oblige your hosts, for it is better to negotiate a manageable assignment from the start than to find yourself bogged down and exhausted later on.*

Bargaining for Class Size

Some professors advise that the most important negotiating point in some assignments is class size. For example, teachers of composition (e.g., creative writing, legal writing, and literature), languages (e.g. TEFL, TESL, and other foreign languages), graduate research classes, and equipment-based courses (e.g., film production, natural sciences, and computer science) need to take special precautions to assure a manageable class size. Neither the tradition of smaller class sizes nor a commitment to "learning by doing" (both valued in the American educational tradition) exist in some cultures to support your bargaining.

Reports abound from professors who did not negotiate manageable enrollments. A professor of film production in Pakistan said, "Class sizes of forty were huge and not workable for production work." An American literature professor to Nepal, whose teaching was based on papers, bemoaned his enrollments: "Students were enthusiastic and attendance was excellent, however, fifty students in one class is not realistic." From New Zealand, a professor reported facing seventy students per class—"three times more per class than I am used to in my home institution." Another stated, "I was given far too many courses [six] and far too many students [425] to be able to enjoy my work or interact with my students as personally and effectively as I would have liked." From Japan a Fulbrighter complained, "Not only were my classes larger than I anticipated, but I meet [with students] only once a week. I do not like seeing students for less than two hours with attendance not required and no test or grades. I was never consulted before decisions were made about my classes."

TEFL, TESL and other English language instructors told many stories of oner-ous class sizes. A professor of TESL reported, from Turkey, "It is impossible to attend to 410 students. Unfortunately, I am beginning to behave as many of my Turkish colleagues do—sigh, shrug my shoulder, expect half of my students to fail, and leave them to their fate." Typically in Eastern Europe, these instructors served large numbers of students in classes up to 150. From China, a TEFL com-position professor described her situation, "The university wanted me to have three classes (each with twenty-five students). I thought I couldn't teach compo-sition to seventy-five students and get to know them all. So we negotiated and compromised with two classes . . . just the right amount of work for me to handle."

Larger than expected enrollments can put both a burden on you and your resources as this professor of American History, teaching a course on North Ameri-can Indians in New Zealand, described, "I prepared a course for the twenty graduate students I was told to expect. I had more than double that enrollment . . with the resultant shortage of texts, inadequate space, and a strain on library resources." One Fulbrighter related a method to alleviate some of the burden that did not work as well as hoped:

> *My Japanese co-teacher, upon finding that we had 250 students enrolled in a class on international law, attempted to cut down the enrollment on the first day by requiring the students to write a one-page essay in English about why they wanted to take the course. The next class period 330 students submitted essays!*

Considering Levels

Another issue in negotiation is whether a visiting professor should teach under-graduate level or only graduate level courses in a cross-cultural setting, espe-cially given the problem of students' English proficiency. The Fulbright program has been struggling with this issue since its inception more than forty years ago. Typical of this debate were professors to Nepal who expressed a reluctance to teach undergraduates who were "woefully unprepared for the rigors of univer-sity work," and those from Czechoslovakia, who declared, "Undergraduates did not understand half of what was said in class." But a professor to Turkey argued the other position, "Some think foreign visitors should only teach upper level graduate courses. I'm not convinced. I am a small college teacher and take un-dergraduate education rather seriously. I believe the beginning courses both in Turkish and American universities need the best teachers."

To further complicate the consideration of level, graduate classes and law school classes in all the situations we examined seemed to have enrollments more manageable than undergraduate classes. Graduate classes ranged from 5–25, with about fifteen being the average enrollment. An additional question raised by some senior Fulbright faculty is whether experienced, senior American fac-ulty on academic exchanges should be teaching students at all. It is argued by some that the primary and most effective function of these senior participants is to do staff development work and train faculties in new research, clinical or pedagogical techniques in their disciplines.

Safeguarding Research Time

The safeguarding of research time was one area routinely reported as a disappointment in negotiating manageable teaching roles. The difficulty centered on how professors' roles are viewed in the culture (discussed in the section Perception of the Teacher) and on the norms that exist there for teaching loads, levels, and class sizes. A Fulbright professor to Mexico offered the typical sentiment: "Course preparations and consultations with students have taken much more time than I had anticipated and have left me with little time for my own research and writing." A professor to both Sri Lanka and Nepal advised, "It is important for any professor planning to do any research to guard the research aspect. The tendency is for research time to be eaten up by increasing requests for lecturers, thesis advising, etc." "My hosts view foreign teachers merely as warm bodies to alleviate overcrowded conditions," complained an American professor to the Middle East. He argued for careful negotiation to safeguard research time. He added, "My professional activities were limited to teaching overcrowded classes, grading multitudes of essays, and filling out forms just like my overworked colleagues. I have little time for my own research and writing." Guidelines for Negotiating a Manageable Teaching Cross-Cultural Role are listed in Figure 3-1.

REFRAMING THE JOB ASSIGNMENT

My job was so completely undefined . . . and that turned out to be good. What it meant was I defined my own job. The description was very vague, but in a way that's an ideal situation for anyone to come into, because you can make it anything you want. (A Coe College professor, Thailand)

Renaming the Work

CUNY law professor Sharon Hom told of negotiating to spend her second year in China training young law teachers. Her administrators conceptualized this work as her "lecturing to rooms full of young teachers just as is done with law students." She spent an inordinate amount of time trying to explain to them her contrasting ideas. When she was faced with their befuddled but tacit approval, she negotiated to "do *something* with the young teachers," which they then endorsed.

Some foreign professors assigned to teach courses out-of-field suggest that one be flexible. "Regardless of course names, it seems you are welcome to teach any subject matter you believe will be beneficial and interesting to the students," said one professor. Another advised, "Choose to teach what you know, regardless

1) Be prepared for limited prior notice of your exact teaching assignment.

- Expect limited or no prior notice in the case of:
  a) exact course names or content;
  b) numbers of students expected;
  c) courses for subsequent semesters;
  d) teaching roles for accompanying spouses;
- Try phone and fax queries and proposals.
- Recognize that contracts are often unfamiliar American-style conventions and are rarely binding in cross-cultural contexts.

2) Expect that a previously negotiated role might change upon arrival.

- Be prepared with proposals for how your talents, interests, and expertise might benefit the host institution.

3) Be a "generalist."

- Be prepared to teach more general content than specific content, regardless of the specifics of your agreements.
- Take introductory texts and materials from your field.

4) Negotiate for preparation and research time when possible.

- Linguistic and cultural considerations means intercultural classes require more preparation than in the United States.

5) Negotiate for smaller class sizes when possible.

- Smaller class sizes may be more valuable to you (especially in traditions of large classes) than a course load reduction.

6) Use the "3 P's" of negotiation—Patience, Politeness and Persistence.

FIGURE 3-1   Guidelines: Manageable Cross-Cultural Teaching Role

of the assignment."   A professor to Poland advised negotiating with students directly about course content, even schedules. "I've found if you're unhappy with your schedule, the best thing to do is work out a new time with the students." A Fulbright professor to Egypt presented his solution. "I was told I would be teaching in a graduate program, but there was no such program. I was misinformed about the content of a course. Another foreign professor told me to keep it and transform it into something different. I did, happily."

Creating the Job

"My Irish hosts did not have a specific idea of what they wanted me to accomplish or how to coordinate my efforts to meet their goals—they viewed this as giving me a great deal of freedom, but initially I was forlorn. The good news was it required that I be a self-starter, looking for opportunities and asking lots questions," said a Fulbright professor who subsequently created a successful series of four short-term graduate seminars. From Nigeria, an American instructor (who set up a first-ever American-style simulation courtroom training program after his legal seminars did not materialize as planned) advised:

> *If one accepts an assignment in a developing country like Nigeria, one will probably not have detailed information regarding the teaching assignment prior to leaving the United States. But, I remained open to suggestions and responsive to on-going changes and a wide variety of excellent opportunities for professional development opened to me.*

A geography professor found little was expected of him in his assignment in Norway, so he took advantage of the time to write a textbook. Syracuse law professor Peter Bell said of his early negotiations in China, "The Law School here doesn't know what to do with me. It is like I am this big white elephant. I am not a great go-getter or initiator, but it is real important to initiate things here. . . . I started making suggestions to the Dean, 'Here are ways you could use me — I can do "this" and I can do "that."' At first, he'd say, 'That sounds good, that sounds good,' but nothing ever happened." Bell persisted, collaborated with other professors, and eventually shaped a meaningful assignment for himself.

University of Tennessee professor Fran Trusty described his job as an evolution. "When I first came I had a very explicit job description, but my role has evolved into something that was not contemplated in the job description. It requires a great deal of flexibility, spontaneity, creativity. . . and it evolves gradually as faculty gets to know me."

Concept Map

4

STRUCTURING LEARNING ENVIRONMENTS

Even experienced professors who have taught the subject for twenty years at home, when they come here, materials, resources, libraries, student-levels are all unknowns.—A SUNY PROFESSOR, ISRAEL

Before the actual instructional strategies are chosen for teaching in your new setting, some consideration of the structure of the learning environment is necessary. Because of so many exigencies, you often will not be in as much control of the structural variables as you would be in your home institution. For example, initially you may not have a cooperative co-teacher or a quiet classroom with chairs unbolted from the floor. But you may be able to manipulate *some* environmental variables to support your new learning setting. Classroom structural considerations discussed here: Team-Teaching with Host Professors to build on the strengths American and host colleagues bring to the classroom and each other; Setting Up Cooperative Learning Systems to capitalize on the strong tendency for cooperative work already established in some cultures and subcultures; Teaching Large Classes to troubleshoot one of the common difficulties of teaching abroad; and Working in Environments Where Resources Are Limited to examine limitations on space, materials, and other resources that affect teaching.

TEAM-TEACHING WITH HOST PROFESSORS

University teaching across cultures is a situation which lends itself well to the process of team-teaching. The new setting calls on a variety of talents and expertise and often demands translation and focus on culture-specific issues beyond the capabilities of American professors unfamiliar with the cross-cultural context. When the team-teaching process works well, it enriches the teaching experience for the American professor and the host colleague, and enhances the learning experience for students. A public health professor to Brazil commented that her "most effective technique, by far, was team-teaching with a coworker." An American University professor of business who team-taught an undergraduate course in entrepreneurship with his New Zealand counterpart recounted, "Students and faculty seemed pleasantly surprised by and intrigued with this new teaching method. . . . We both endeavored to attend all classes, and some days we were able to teach in a true team-like manner."

There are many functions of teaching as a team in cross-cultural settings. The first is a very practical one—when you first arrive in country, *problems with the unfamiliarity of the language, culture, or work assignment are lessened by a host colleague's early leadership in the class.* Often the course assignment or content is not exactly what the Western professor had expected to teach, and appropriate materials and readings are not prepared upon arrival. Collaborating with a colleague eases the burden of initial teaching problems. A Fulbright professor to Ireland negotiated with a "colleague of a friend" at his university before his arrival to "co-teach two courses with me in psychology." He explained, "I agreed that if he would help me teach mine, I would help him teach his....In the first month when I was in a daze, I knew I had been smart to make this arrangement."

A second function of teaching as a team is that *it makes effective use of different professional talents and interests of the participating professors.* "Teaming" allows differentiation in course content and instructional strategies which can build on your and your co-teacher's strengths. As a Fulbright professor, I team-taught a graduate seminar on evaluation methodologies with a Thai professor trained in England. This host colleague brought research from systems around the work using the British models and I contributed ideas from the United States. I provided examples for classwork and my host professor reshaped them into the Thai context. Another variation on this theme is when two or more foreign professors team up in a classroom, such as one I observed in China. Two American law professors who taught the joint seminar described it: "Every Monday night we talked about one different subject in American law. Some one of us has more experience with, others are better handled by the other one. It's turned out to be a marvelous arrangement. In addition to students, faculty and visitors who have no affiliation with the Law School come, make comments and discuss."

A third function of team-teaching is that *host colleagues can translate English into the host language for those students who need extra language support.* (For further discussion of this function, see Employing Translators and Translations in Chapter 9.)

Another function of team-teaching, articulated by Desretta McAllister, North Carolina Central University professor and Fulbrighter to Jamaica, is that *it offers the presence of a "second grader" or "external evaluator,"* commonly found in British-style higher education traditions such as those in Jamaica and India. The host professor's assessment will be essential where it is expected that papers and exams be graded by at least two evaluators, or where problems or language are culture-specific.

A fifth function of team-teaching is that *it provides in-service education and training opportunities for the co-teachers.* Often, American professors with their repertoire of alternative pedagogical techniques, and host professors, with their capabilities to be "key informants" on the culture of the classroom and the broader society, serve as models for each other. "Shoulder-to-shoulder" team-teaching is one of the most effective in-service training experiences a teacher could provide or receive.

One Fulbright professor to Thailand, who teamed with a host colleague, extolled the relationship. "Both I and my colleague agreed that it was one of our fondest courses in our collective forty years of teaching experience." Figure 4-1 provides additional ideas and guidelines for Team Teaching with a Host Professor.

There are limitations to the ideal. One American professor, self-described as a "horse for a single harness," found it difficult to work cooperatively on a professional level with host colleagues whose "teaching and work styles differed significantly." In a case where the course and the coworker was assigned prior to

---

1) **Identify a potential collaborator.**

- Because team-teaching may be an unfamiliar concept, don't wait for a potentially cooperative host to approach you.
- Junior faculty may be eager collaborators.
- Offer to co-teach another professor's class in trade.

2) **Recognize the value of teaming.**

- Your cultural/language incompetencies can be ameliorated.
- Translation supports are built in for students without proficient English.
- Teaming with junior faculty provides some staff development.
- "Second readers" and alternative student evaluation methods can be employed.

3) **Troubleshoot potential difficulties with collaborators.**

- Expect teaching and workstyle differences.
- Avoid role imbalances, e.g., one lectures, the other translates; one preps lectures, the other gives, etc.
- Think of ways to minimize status conflicts, e.g., Ph.D./M.A.; professor/instructor; male/female; mature/young, etc.

4) **Establish a planning time with collaborator before every class.**

- Collaboratively determine the how, when, where of planning.
- Avoid collaborative planning on *your* territory.
- Rotate jobs and roles (e.g., lecturer, discussion facilitator, translator, materials preparer, class questioner, student reviewer, and grader) each time, when possible.
- Determine what to do in case of teacher absence.

FIGURE 4-1   Guidelines: Team-Teaching with a Host Professor

the American professor's arrival, the Fulbrighter "did all the lecturing, but the content, syllabus and evaluation were determined by the host." In another case, a visiting professor "wrote all the hosts' lectures, which the host subsequently delivered to the class." In one incident, the American professor reported, "The host professor viewed me as his opportunity for a lightened teaching load and he was absent frequently, did not find time for collaborative planning and sometimes suggested, at the last minute, that I do the class alone, because I 'could do it so well.' "

In some locations, another limitation is the potential for a conflict of status. In some countries, Ph.Ds visit and M.A.s host; lecturers visit and translators host. Age and gender complicate the ideal even more. Given these perils, team-teaching may not work for every course in every semester. Establishing a true team spirit is difficult, even under ideal conditions. Nonetheless, team-teaching's many functions make it an alternative worthy of consideration.

SETTING UP COOPERATIVE LEARNING SYSTEMS

> *To answer the question of what is the most effective method of teaching, the best answer is that it depends on the student, the content and the teacher. But the next best answer is 'students teaching other students'. (McKeachie, 1986)*

In a definitive work based on forty years of college teaching, Wilbert McKeachie identified another important classroom structure to employ in cross-cultural classrooms: cooperative learning. Cooperative learning organizes students in small groups so to maximize the learning process. After receiving instructions from the teacher, students work through an assignment until all group members understand it and the task is completed. Usually there is some group incentive for individual effort. The instructor's role is being a "guide on the side."

Cooperative learning is suggested as a structural alternative for cross-cultural situations because it capitalizes on a common practice in many cultures and classrooms—students working cooperatively in groups on assignments, translations, explanations, note-taking, and even tests. In Japan, an American Fulbright professor figured "if you can't beat 'em, join 'em":

> *I co-opt students' tendency toward 'schooling behavior' for pedagogical purposes. Each class already has informal cooperative learning groups, each with a spokesperson who is the* yonensei *(senior member). So I use that tendency and set up a system where these groups compete with each other to come up with an answer to the day's questions.*

The preference for cooperative environments among some populations may be related to their preference for different participation structures. Research with Athabaskan and Warm Springs Indians (Gage & Berliner, 1991), Polynesian-Americans, Asian-Americans, African-American undergraduates (George, 1994) and Mexican-American children (Kagan, et.al., 1985) supports the contention that some students prefer and achieve better in cooperative structures and tend to avoid competitive structures. Another hypothesis for why cooperative structures might be successful is that some cultures or subcultures have experiences of poverty or resource limitations that cause them to rely on family, friends, or "the group" more than others without those limitations. For example, Samoan students often work at home without adult supervision and rely on peers to help them with assignments. These students commonly learn more effectively when teachers stress student cooperation and minimize competition.

Yet, among university students, the tendency toward collective work in some cultures has been described by Western professors as "anathema to the integrity of real learning" or is viewed as "insurmountable cultural differences." An American professor in Thailand called this tendency toward cooperative work a "homework cartel." A professor in Malaysia reported with disapproval that students read her comments on other students' written work. Professors in every country we investigated questioned that the work they were reviewing was indeed a student's own.

In response to some cultural tendencies toward collective effort and to the American professors' struggles to understand and often to thwart them, another paradigm is suggested. This paradigm asks you to jointly create the learning setting with students who are actively constructing their own knowledge while you work to develop their competencies to do so. Mounting evidence on the efficacy of cooperative learning across disciplines, and some observations of its successful practice in China and Thailand, suggests it is a promising territory to explore.

Defining a Cooperative Class Structure

In order for a class structure to be cooperative, some basic elements are essential (Johnson, Johnson, & Holubec, 1990). The first element is *interdependence*. Student activities are linked in ways that one student cannot succeed unless the other members of the group succeed. The instructor may require that group members agree on the answer and the strategy for solving each problem. Roles are assigned to aid interdependence. Additionally, the instructor arranges for each group to assign roles to its members. Johnson, Johnson and Smith (1991) describe one professor's method:

> *A professor in his Introductory Astronomy class at the University of Minnesota randomly assigns students to groups of four. Each group member is assigned one of the following roles:* recorder *(who records the group's work by writing out the steps necessary for solving each problem);* checker *(who makes sure that all the members can explain how to solve each problem correctly);* encourager *(who makes sure each member participates in the discussion and sharing); and* elaborator *(who relates this new activity or learning to past learning). [p.3:3-4]*

Additional roles might include *reader, researcher, runner* (one who gathers materials for the groups and communicates with other learning groups); *accuracy coach, summarizer, translator* (one who has strong English skills); or *"rappateur"* (one who makes restatements in the native language).

A second element of a cooperative learning structure is *face-to-face instructional interaction*, which exists when students help, assist, encourage, and support each others efforts to learn. Students orally explain to each other how to solve problems, teach their knowledge to each other, and tutor each other on concepts and strategies being learned. Examples of this element include Peer-Tutors or Drill & Review Dyads. Instructors must provide time, knee-to-knee seating arrangements, good instructions, and constant back-up support for this interaction to work.

The third element is *individual accountability*. Students are not allowed to "hitch-hike" on the work of others or meet the criteria of an assignment without substantive effort on their part. Some instructors using cooperative learning methods give partial weight to individual assignments done within the group setting and partial weight to the group's outcome. Students soon learn who needs the most assistance in completing the assignment. Other instructors give individual tests and randomly assign one student's grade to represent the efforts of the entire group. Additionally, student ratings of a group member's performance or effort may be one measure of individual accountability.

Another element of cooperative learning is some *group incentive*. There is usually a benefit to a group's successful completion of a task. The currency of the setting may be a group grade (e.g., in addition to his own grade based on his individual performance, a student may receive the collective grade of the group).

Organizing Cooperative Learning Arrangements

Pre-instructional Decisions. Before you can set up a cooperative learning structure, you will need to make some pre-instructional decisions. According to Johnson, Johnson and Smith (1991), common decisions involve group size, student assignment method, room arrangement, and role designations. To help make these decisions, answer the following questions:

1. *Should students be assigned to groups heterogeneously or homogeneously (based on some ability or attribute)?* The rule-of-thumb is heterogenous as possible, because more elaborative thinking and more frequent giving and receiving of explanations seem to occur in heterogeneous groups. In cross-cultural settings, group assignment must take into consideration English facility (where English is the medium of instruction) and whether the role of *translator* can be covered in each group.

2. *Should students be placed in groups randomly or using some other method?* Random assignment seems to work best overall. In the United States, students complain less about their learning partners. Student-selected groups tend to be more homogeneous. In cultures where statistical randomization is not a common prac-

tice, to enhance your credibility you might consider handling this randomizing task in full purview of students in class.

   3.   *How long should the same groups stay together?* Some instructors like to keep a learning group together all semester. Others only until the end of a specific task. The best advice is long enough for them to be successful. Breaking up groups that are having trouble is often counterproductive, since resolving problems by collaborating with each other is part of the learning task.

Room Arrangements.   Room arrangement sends out a symbolic message. Students need to be facing each other. Sharon Hom, the Fulbright law professor in China who experimented with a variety of classroom groupings, found that Chinese students had never been face-to-face with each other in instructional interaction and the new arrangement took some getting used to. At first, she said uncomfortable students would continuously crane their neck to find her, hoping that she would be the "voice of authority" telling them the answer.

   Besides students facing each other, the instructor needs a clear access lane to every group. Within each group, students need equal access to task materials. Groups need to be far enough apart so that they do not interfere with each other's learning, but close enough to model appropriate group process.

Specifying Effective Group Behaviors.   A professor who wants to use cooperative learning arrangements can not assume that students understand and have in their repertoire of classroom interaction skills the group behaviors necessary to make cooperative activities work. They need to be specified and practiced. Each student, according to Johnson, Johnson and Smith (1991), needs to be able to do the following:

   1. Explain how to get or "how I got" an answer.
   2. Ask each member how the new information related to what was previously learned or worked on.
   3. Check to make sure everyone understands the material or agrees on the answer.
   4. Listen to what other group members are saying.
   5. Change his or her mind, but only after logical persuasion, not majority vote.
   6. Criticize ideas, not people.

Choosing Among Cooperative Procedures

Those instructors who are experienced with using cooperative learning arrangements assert that any material can be learned and all activities can be structured using cooperative learning procedures. Described here are a few examples of pedagogical processes that foster cooperative learning—Peer-tutoring, Collaborative Answering, and Peer Editing.

Peer-Tutoring. With peer-tutoring, each student is assigned a learning partner randomly or by designation (based on competency, age, or seniority, for example). The Drill-Review Dyad is an example of peer-tutoring whereby the goal is for both members to understand the main points of content or the procedures for solving a problem. Usually, the first student relates the information or works the problem and the second student checks the work or the information;Then the roles are reversed for the next set. Drill-Review Dyads in my undergraduate classes have learning partners review class lecture notes during the last ten minutes of each class. One student is the "recaller" and the other the "listener." Roles are reversed every other assignment. Students are trained to detect and correct errors and omissions in the notes and to judge the importance of the ideas presented.

Another example of peer-tutoring is the Read-and-Explain Pair. Both students read a segment, and one person summarizes the content to the other. They agree on the summary, meaning, or questions raised by the segment. They move on and repeat, exchanging roles. This technique may be useful in classes where students often do not read assigned material outside of class, as one Fulbright professor to Japan described:

> *I use teams with one partner reading and summarizing a sentence or two from the readings to the other. . . . It works, but it simply takes an incredible amount of time. However, when I realized that we all found these experiences to be fun as well as useful, I worried less and less about the amount of material I could cover.*

The individual accountability of both these peer-tutoring procedures is that one group member will be randomly chosen to explain the meaning of a segment of reading, or one member's notes, chosen at random, will be reviewed by the teacher.

Collaborative Answering. The cooperative technique in this category, most commonly used with university students, is Simultaneous Explanation Pairs or Think-Pair-Share. In Think-Pair-Share, a method attributed to Frank Lyman (1991), a student listens to a teacher-posed question, takes time to think and formulate his own answer, listens to his assigned partner's answer, reformulates a combination or chooses the best of the two answers, and shares the collective response with the whole group. Individual accountability comes when the person who delivers the collective response or explains how the pair decided on its answer is chosen randomly.

Peer Editing. Cooperative learning can be used in composition, thesis writing, case analysis, and other writing tasks where specific criteria are set by the teacher. All group members must verify that each member's composition is written in accordance with the criteria. The group incentive for this task is that each member is given a first score for the total number of "perfect" sections on all the collectively edited papers in the group. The individual accountability in peer-editing is that of a second score on the quality of the individual composition after the rewrite. The greatest difficulty in implementing peer editing activities in cross-cultural classrooms, according to American professors who tried them, is overcoming students' reluctance to criticize each other's work.

TEACHING LARGE CLASSES

Some college professors teaching abroad are assigned large classes. While it may seem reasonable to some instructors to lecture 310 international economics students in Japan or 470 history students in Turkey (the largest classes reported), most American professors abroad strongly preferred to work with (and tried to negotiate for) smaller groups. TESL and TEFL instructors teaching English were often assigned unworkably large classes (made more difficult by many auditing or "informal" listeners coming to class to "improve their English with a native speaker and expert language teacher.")

The story of Sabina and Anthony Carlen, both of whom taught computer applications and TEFL at a college on the Malaysian-Thai border, is instructive. Each were initially assigned four classes of fifty students each—from their account unworkable numbers for language training and computer laboratory work (there were only twenty computers). Their solutions to the problems of each managing the learning of two hundred students may serve as models for others with similar numbers.

First, because the Carlens felt strongly that student achievement increases as class size decreases, they tried to *negotiate with the administrators to reduce the class sizes*. They felt that twenty students should be the maximum in such classes where intensive practice and instruction is necessary. But this was a developing institution in a developing country with limited resources and much demand. The administrators agreed to forty students per class. (Tales of other professors' enrollment negotiations can be found in the section in Chapter 3).

Secondly, the Carlens sought *to increase one-to-one instruction with help* by hiring some graduate students as teaching assistants. They offered them the prevailing wage for such work, though the couple felt the wage was far too little for the services rendered. Initially, the Carlens hired four assistants (one for each class), but found that the assistants "volunteered" time in their unassigned classes. Working with the assistants required additional classtime each week for training, but both agreed the extra time was well spent. The graduate students provided one-to-one instruction, served as small group facilitators for discussion and problem-solving, acted as translators when concepts and professional jargon in English were difficult for students, monitored individual assignments, and helped with grading. (A further discussion of a similar "staff-extension" idea developed by Sharon Hom for training young law teachers in China can be found in the Chapter 7 section on Training Students for Teaching.)

The Carlens's third strategy, was *to use student learning partnerships*. A kind of cooperative learning structure discussed earlier in this chapter, learning partnerships pairs students either by random, ability, demographics or choice assignment, and allows them to work together. The partners are held accountable for the partnership's performance *and* their own individual performance. Sabina Carlen, the computer instructor, paired each dyad with one computer where she and her graduate student taught one of the partners a practice; he in-turn taught his partner the practice.

Anthony Carlen, the TEFL instructor, used the partnership idea by assigning dialogues and peer-tutoring activities to partners. Review other cooperative strategies used with small groups and learning partnerships in the section on Setting Cooperative Learning Systems with the idea of adapting them to larger classes.

WORKING IN ENVIRONMENTS WHERE RESOURCES ARE LIMITED

Resource allocations to universities involved in exchange programs are described using many comparisons. The international education literature is full of comparisons of institutions—North vs. South, First World vs. Third World, Capital vs. Provincial, Urban vs. Rural, Open vs. Closed, Many Foreign Faculty vs. Few Foreign Faculty, or Colonial vs. Independent. Regardless of these explanatory paradigms for the disparities and variations in educational resources, many of the professors whose work we observed operated, during their exchanges, with far fewer material resources than they were accustomed to in typical American universities. In many assignments in developing countries, libraries, labs, classrooms, equipment, offices, and budgets were extremely modest and often were created like "stone soup." Even in first-world institutions, custom, tradition, or budgetary constraints limited access to resources for even the most prestigious scholars.

For some American professors, exposure to different priorities and procedures in the uses and allocations of resources requires adjustment. One professor found the permission system a hurdle and said, "Being at the primo institution in Poland, I have equipment available, but every use, however, must first be approved by the dean, who is often difficult to find." Another to Malawi (Alexander, 1991) found budget priorities inscrutable:

> *The sight of students 'researching' through odd volumes of an old set of the* Encyclopedia Britannica *was common . . . a nest egg for library books had initially been pledged by the university offices, but the promised funds were never released . . . one of the first lessons as an administrator was that the term 'budgeting' referred to a kind of Platonic Form, the apprehension of which is both the highest desirable good and, for most mortals, a practical impossibility. In general, the funds for library books, slides, maps—anything but the most basic operating costs—had to be solicited from sources outside the university, or the country.*

A Fulbrighter to Hungary lamented the time-consuming nature of managing classroom chores where resources are limited. "It takes three times as long to do anything in Hungary over what you are used to." A professor to Turkey vented frustration over limited resources with this story:

> *My lecture was scheduled for the late afternoon. The electricity had gone off on the campus that day and halfway through my presentation it was too dark to read the handouts! I remembered that this class had some group work planned, so we moved to do it. But it became impossible when I realized that the rows of benches on which the students sat were bolted to the floor. What can you do except be patient and maintain a sense of humor?*

Another economics professor to Malaysia expressed similar sentiments in relation to his planned research. He remarked:

> *I realized that I was not going to be able to continue the kind of research I was doing in San Diego. Some of my programs for research were shelved for the simple reason that I could not find the back-up resources and support I needed to continue it. So coming here, I really had to start up fresh research assignments which were suitable to the resources available. Now that can be a tremendous handicap!*

Sparse Office Space

> *Space is so limited, I share a 7' x 9' office with a Czech colleague, half taken up by a desk of which I have half! (A University of Georgia professor, Czechoslovakia)*

Many professors had no university-based offices for professional duties. Even those with offices rarely had the space, privacy, equipment, or telephones to which they were accustomed. Over time, like the professor to Hungary who shared an office with five colleagues, American professors abroad who did have office space began to feel fortunate, "because most faculty did not." In Mexico, where "a constant problem is shortage of office space," one Fulbright professor said, "Because of the shortage of space, only the director has a private office and all the other staff share three offices. I was lucky to get a desk in a small room shared by five other colleagues." The value of even the most modest office space becomes intensified in scarcity, as an instructor to Poland explained: "When there was a classroom crunch, as for two of my classes, I had to teach in my office cubicle, which had no blackboard. One class ended up with nineteen people in it!"

In contrast, some professors in some locations are assigned comfortable office space, as was an instructor to Nepal who praised his "spacious office with access to the departmental library." Two others in Japan described their good fortune to have climate control. One reported, "I got a fairly spacious office (with air conditioning—oh wow!), which I shared with a research assistant." The other described his space: "My office was located in the field house complete with swimming pool and year-round temperature control." Tone Carlen, a professor to Czechoslovakia who got an office, reported a darker trade-off. "Unlike many visiting professors, I got an office. In fact, I got the biggest office in my department, even with a private bathroom. But, when I needed things that meant much more toward effective teaching, it seemed that they said, 'Now that we gave you our best office how could you ask for more?'"

Limited office space had an impact on the amount of time professors spent on campus and available to students and each other. "I meet with my graduate students whose theses I advise in empty classrooms (when we can find them), but I don't have my reference books or access to my files there—I consider it a real handicap," offered a professor to Indonesia. Another to Mexico explained, "I shared an office that did not have room for books or a secure place for a computer or printer. Consequently, I did not spend much office time on campus." Professors to China, who rarely have offices and often maintain office space in their apartments, complained that they feel "isolated from students who do not have easy access to them holed away in the foreign expert living quarters." One American literature professor to Indonesia reported, "There is no office here for faculty use and no faculty here regularly except for the director or assistant director of the program. When the faculty and students float in and out, to walk in one day and figure out how to get started is very difficult."

Scant Support Services

Another resource limitation in many assignments is scant support services. From Norway, an American professor reported, "The biggest adjustment that I have had to make in two Fulbrights has been the nearly complete lack of secretarial assistance. This is not horrible, but it changes what you must do and the planning necessary to accomplish your writing and preparation of materials." A professor to Pakistan puzzled at the question of support service and answered, "What support services?" Professors to Japan report the availability of office staff "for chores like photocopying, supplying audio-visual equipment for class, ordering books, and making phone calls," but a general unavailability of secretarial assistance.

In addition to the limited availability of support services, occasionally the rules about what is appropriate to request are enigmatic. A professor to Malaysia reported that there were secretaries in his school but "they had very strict boundaries on their work. It seemed they would type a test, but they would not type anything related to research." He explained, "If I tell them it is a student assignment and not research, it gets done routinely." Additionally, even when support staff is willing to do clerical work, secretaries may not read or type well in English.

Meager Materials and Equipment

Although a few professors reported material and equipment in abundance, like the Fulbright professor to Japan who found ample access to "a gym, pool, bookstore, mainframe, Bitnet, telephone, fax service, post, photocopying, and audio-visual equipment," most did not. In both Third World and First World institutions, many American professors reported that materials and equipment were heavily used and quickly depleted.

With regard to photocopying, the common theme seemed to be, "With the copy machine, already at mid-year the paper is gone and there is no money to purchase more." An instructor to Czechoslovakia recounted, "More than anything else, I have seriously missed the Xerox machine—aware as I am how much of teaching depends upon duplicating." Another remarked:

> *Copies here are done by carbon paper [not even dittos]. I used a substantial part of my monthly salary on Xeroxing for my classes at a local vendor at a relatively high price. Occasionally, the department would copy my stuff, but the administrators [who held the key to the machine] would never copy materials for a regular Czechoslovakian professor.*

From Mexico, an American instructor remarked, "The Xerox copier is out off and on. Few people can fix it. Fax is limited to a single machine in the Chancellor's office. Mimeograph, Thermofax and ditto machines are not easy to come by." Another resourceful Fulbright professor to Hungary found, "Photocopying is not the answer! Toner is frequently out, paper has to be provided by the teacher, and photocopying at shops in town is not reimbursed. Because of the scarcity [of supplies], people will not necessarily share information about where to obtain certain goods. I had to buy paper in Vienna!" From Turkey, another reported, "Although my faculty associates had told me before I left the United States, that a Xerox machine would be available and that making copies would be 'no problem,' the story changed once the machine belonging to my department broke down."

Typing and word-processing became difficult for American professors abroad who did not have personal equipment. "All I had to use was an old manual typewriter the institution loaned me, when they just got their second electric typewriter," reported an American professor to Brazil. From Malaysia, another said, "I asked for a typewriter for when I came in July, but this proved to be an impossible request." Another to Israel remarked, "I wasn't able to get regular access to a word processor. My department provided me with a Selectric typewriter, but English language typing elements were in short supply." From Indonesia, Fulbrighter reported, "The department I'm teaching in has one computer and one typewriter. But this is a *Masters'* level graduate program." From Pakistan, it was remarked, "Word processors [and manuals to help you use them] were essentially nonexistent." Another to Turkey lamented, "Even if I could type, which I can't, stationary and secretarial materials [which Americans take for granted] are very limited."

Access to phones and fax machines was also problematic. Electronic mail, available in some First-World institutions, was not generally or predictably available to faculty. One exasperated professor in Malaysia said:

I asked for a phone in July; received a phone cord in November, a phone body in December, and a dial tone in mid-January. But this phone goes only to an internal switchboard operator, who upon hearing English, hangs up immediately. In other words, the phone is not useful.

An instructor to Mexico reported, "Faxes are available, but not for personal use. Communicating with one's home institution often or correcting grad students' work at the home institution was considered 'personal work,' so I had to keep it to a minimum." Mary Ann Sagaria dealt with this problem by purchasing a fax machine for her house in Indonesia so that she was able to communicate with her U.S. institution with some privacy. This arrangement enabled her to take advantage of limited telephone lines when they were available—day or night (Sagaria, 1993).

Limited Library Resources

One of the resources most taken for granted by American university professors is a large, up-to-date library to which they have access. Whether they are assigned to Third-World or First-World countries, most American professors reported limitations to the availability of or access to teaching and research materials in libraries. Here is a sample of the observations on library resources:

- *In the university library holdings, books are not catalogued. Journals are absent and inappropriate foreign journals are being purchased. (Turkey)*
- *The library is inadequate for MA level work and poorly organized. The departmental library has a catalog, but no periodicals, and is open only one hour a day in care of a junior faculty member, not a librarian. (Korea)*
- *Pakistani library resources are antiquated; the books are outdated and the selection is limited. For example, a 1976 book [in 1990] was the newest resource for both my courses.*
- *In Nepal, the main university library is rather useless, but the British Council library and the Fulbright donation mini-libraries are decent resources for English teaching.*
- *Libraries are inadequate for students to write term papers, e.g., the university had only 60,000 volumes. In my own field of political science, no books had ever been ordered. (Brazil)*
- *The library is very limited in terms of journals and books. The university is not very well stocked in terms of material for research, so I geared my research on the Malaysian economy to the available local resources. My research agenda has changed tremendously, just to suit the local environment. (Malaysia)*
- *Archeology libraries in Mexico— gaps!*
- *Materials in libraries are very limited and out of date. . . . There are few current materials available even in Spanish. . . . Students are often unwilling to share scarce materials and books are not returned for use during the semester. (Chile)*

- *The library university-wide is hopelessly outdated and inconvenient for use by faculty and students. (Norway)*
- *In Nepal, theft of books is the biggest impediment to library research.*
- *Selection and classification of text are quite different than our American systems? British? European? Uniquely Irish?*
- *The latest book in my field of linguistics in the library was published in 1979! (Poland)*
- *Libraries close at 9:00 p.m. and on the weekends. What's a scholar to do? (Portugal)*
- *Even a well-stocked New Zealand university library is not likely to be as complete in a professor's field as the one he or she left behind. . . . My first order of business was to survey available resources and to request needed items. With a bit of luck, they should be obtained [or at least located] before it is time to return home.*
- *Japanese library holding are reportedly the best in Asia, but availability of books depends upon a field. I have had difficulty obtaining books from libraries where I have access. Books are often in another professor's or another department's collection where access is difficult.*
- *Because of the scarcity, students horde their academic materials, making it difficult to provide general access to them at a library. For example, there is no closed, reserve-type service. (Hungary)*
- *Research library facilities available to me are nonexistent. The library here is an Islamic library on topics I don't deal with. I brought a small library, but if I had known what I would be teaching, I would have made my selection differently. But I muddle through. (Indonesia)*
- *European government research institutes have libraries and archives which are excellent with incredibly helpful staffs and adequate holdings and are better resourced than the universities. (Norway)*
- *Japanese library facilities in terms of journals and books are great. The problem is access. Library hours are short. Many times I found it necessary to trace books to professors' 'private' collections [checked out for years].*
- *In Israel, library holdings and equipment are in high demand. More than once I had to get to the library at 6:30 a.m. to see a film for my class.*
- *In American literature there is a fair collection on primary sources, but the secondary collection is pretty dismal. (Indonesia)*
- *Most of my department's books remain locked up and unusable, either in the official library room where books are stored in boxes or 'being catalogued' at a snail's pace by a retired faculty member. (Czechoslovakia)*

An American biology professor to Indonesia recounted a story which well illustrates the relationship of general education resources and library resources in some locations:

One of the big disadvantages of working in Indonesia is that you can't get library materials. They haven't had the money to build the collections we are used to. They are building a new library building well suited to the climate. At the dedication of this building, the rector, who was very proud of this building, made the point that it is easier to build buildings than it is to get the supply money for materials. He noted that the shelves were almost empty. He said that if he spent all of the monies he had in the university budget for library materials and all kinds of supplies just for library materials, 'it would take us fifty years to get our library to the minimum level it would take for accreditation in the United States.'

Finite Faculty Resources

One of the major resource limitations faced by some American professors abroad is the dearth of host faculty rewards and the excessive demand on limited faculty resources. One of the obvious ways this manifests itself is in low university faculty salaries. From Turkey it was reported that host faculty members are not paid for any noninstructional duties. One Fulbright professor explained the implications:

Teaching salaries require a minimum of twelve hours per week—anything above that is overtime, but overtime pay is only given for classroom hours teaching. As a result, it is a very difficult to get teachers to organize committees or do extra work outside of class hours—e.g., testing, planning, committees. It is difficult to work with teachers who feel they aren't paid for the time they put in.

Many host faculty members in some countries work several jobs. "A typical Mexican professor teaches four classes and a 'couple more' at another university to try to make ends meet." In Thailand, one instructor reported, "My host colleague and the Associate Dean run a student laundry on the side, much diminishing their energy for academic work." Concurring from his experience in Nepal, another professor said, "Outside work by faculty [the common way to make additional money to supplement low university salaries] distracted faculty from promoting their courses and tending well to their students."

The absence of research and scholarly pursuits are also results of limitations on resources. An excellent discussion of the dearth of scholarly work at some institutions and many of the underlying reasons for it is available in *Decline and Renewal* (1986) by Craufurd Goodwin and Michael Nacht. A San Diego State economist remarked on this dearth of research:

The difficulty about research work at my university in Malaysia is that there are no scholars to share research ideas. You are isolated in terms of your analysis and do not have anyone to talk to and find out if you are on the right track. There is no intellectual interaction going on.

From Pakistan, a Fulbright professor remarked, "My colleagues' research here mostly consists of consultative reports commissioned from government agencies for extra income. Because their refuge is local knowledge [which they see me and other foreigners lacking], they rarely communicate with me about research ideas or formulate them in professional terms." Another American instructor to China found a similar "lack of common ground" concerning research pursuits, and remarked, "My colleagues' professional contact with the international scholarly community doing research is through visitors doing research here, and the occasional chance to attend a conference overseas which is often largely ceremonial. My colleagues don't do research or appreciate mine."

Concept Map

5

LECTURING EFFECTIVELY
IN CROSS-CULTURAL SETTINGS

*Acaan phuut can lahp ling—the professor talks until even
the monkey goes to sleep.*—THAI PROVERB

Despite admonitions from learning theorists and even their students, American
university professors remain drawn to lecturing. Like the ancient Greek sailors
seduced by promises of ecstasy in the Sirens' call, the attraction of sharing knowledge with adoring audiences is irresistible to many, and lecturing remains the
practice of choice for almost all university classroom instructors around the world.
Professors interviewed for this study concurred that their host colleagues thought
"lecturing synonymous with teaching" and often asked them, "How was your
lecture?" rather than "How did your teaching go?" Even the Fulbright Commissions, the administering agencies of the United States' flagship academic exchange
program, give grants for senior "lecturers."

Students also often see lecturing as "synonymous with teaching." In describing lecturing as teaching, one of my Thai graduate students summarized his observations of university classroom instruction in Thailand as "large numbers of
young students eager for knowledge gathered together to listen to a person of
great wisdom lecture in his discipline and, as a result, to become enlightened."
For good or ill, the lecture mode remains the primary instructional method "expected" by students and colleagues in the cross-cultural university setting. In
part due to these expectations, lecturing will undoubtedly be included in your
inter-cultural teaching repertoire.

Additionally, more innovative methods of teaching may not be equally practiced with certain subjects and certain class sizes typical in teaching abroad. As
Al Bailey, director of the Office of International Programs at Madonna University
argues, "Breaking students into small circles is fine in a small class, but will not
work in a class of 125, which is what I found in teaching abroad" (Bailey, 1993).

IDENTIFYING PROBLEMS IN LECTURING ACROSS CULTURES

Because lectures are essentially verbal and students rarely interact with the teacher to alter, refine, or pace the message, using them exclusively for students for whom English is a foreign or second language presents obvious problems. A lecturer in Eastern Europe recounted that when he had finished his first day of lecturing, he was met by some students after class who proudly offered, "We understood a little at the beginning." This statement identifies the first problem with lecturing when used as your only or primary teaching method—*student attention, comprehension and memory decrease as the lecture proceeds.* Penner in his summary of decades of research on lecturing (1984) described some well-known data gathered at the University of Reading in England on student attention during lectures in five-minute segments. Students entered the classroom and settled in for five minutes, listened attentively for five minutes, remained inattentive for the bulk of the lecture and revived at the concluding five minutes of the lecture. The key point here is that only a small portion of total lecture time can be used effectively for learning.

The second major problem with using lecturing as your sole or primary teaching method is that *lecturing reinforces passive listening and discourages the practice of critical thinking* by students. McKeachie and Kulik in their survey of effective college teaching (1975) found lecturing to be superior for promoting learning of factual information, but student discussion superior for promoting critical thinking. Agreeing with these researchers, Johnson, Johnson and Smith (1991) argued that when students need to analyze, synthesize, or integrate knowledge being studied, when material is complex or abstract, or when long-term retention is desired, lecturing is not the most effective method. One Fulbright professor to New Zealand reported:

> *I never lecture in America. I abhor lecturing. Here everybody expects me to be this 'great lecturer,' but I don't believe that students learn anything when I get up and pontificate to them on ideas. They have to manipulate those ideas, talk about them, chew them, make them their own or reject them . . then they learn. New Zealand students too!*

That lecturing is most effective for teaching factual information and less effective than class discussion for teaching higher-level cognitive processes was strongly supported by the practitioners of the discussion method we observed. An example of the impact this dialogue is having upon the international college-teaching scene was a 1988 conference at Szechuan University in China with U.S. Fulbright and Chinese professors discussing Teaching American Literature and History. They examined alternatives to lecturing such as discussion methods and other participatory teaching techniques, and their applications for the Chinese university classroom. The prevailing theme was, "If I tell you a story, you will write it down and forget it. If you tell me a story, you will not write it down, but you will not forget it."

The third problem with using the the lecture method as the sole pedagogical technique is that *lecturing does not model for future teachers in cross cultural settings other effective pedagogical strategies*—and many of your students, especially in developing countries, will become teachers. Enthusiasm for providing a repertoire of teaching strategies in a new classroom may be dampened when students report they prefer lectures or achieve better with lecture formats with which they are familiar. Students who need a lot of structure and guidance or who have a low tolerance for ambiguity (which describes many of the students in cross-cultural situations taught in English) often prefer lectures. Their preferences can be broadened, however, with exposure to other strategies. An example of American professors calling attention to the need for modeling different pedagogical strategies was the 1989 Legal Teaching Conference at Wuhan University in China. At Wuhan, U.S. Fulbright and Chinese professors discussed, experimented with, and adapted for China some legal teaching methods involving group problem-solving and case-analysis commonly used in the United States (Hom, 1989).

The fourth and most often acknowledged problem with using lecturing as a primary teaching tool is that *students in cross-cultural situations where English is a second or foreign language often have difficulty with comprehension of lecture material.* Faced with these difficulties, they often learn material incorrectly and take notes incompletely (if at all). In order to make lessons work, you have to check the accuracy and completeness of students' comprehension often, and while lecturing it is difficult to do this checking. Some American professors said they knew students understood their lectures because "their eyes indicated it," because "they laughed at jokes," or because "they took copious notes." But we observed others who had, at first, relied on the same cues, but were then alert to check students' notebooks where they found "nothing more than the lecture title written down just as it had been written on the board."

PLANNING A STRUCTURE FOR EFFECTIVE LECTURES

After considering the major problems with lecturing as the sole or primary pedagogical practice, it may be concluded that alternative teaching strategies interwoven with lecturing would provide a much more effective composite strategy. Planning for effective lecturing involves both preparing to use lectures effectively and planning to supplement them with other more participatory techniques.

Knowing When to Lecture

A veteran colleague related his story of a recent experience lecturing in Finland at a major research institute. He started with a focus question as his "advance organizer." He then gave a fifteen minute lecture, convinced that a short lecture on the latest research supporting his topic would be useful. When he finished the short lecture, he asked students to prepare a summary of the main points. One student raised his hand and asked, "Professor, what did you say between 'Here's the research' and 'Your task is to create a summary?'" The student got a big laugh, but when the professor checked notes at the break, he found students indeed "didn't know what I was talking about."

There has been considerable research on the efficacy of lectures with university students, but for our purposes in this discussion, the useful question is not, "Is lecturing better or worse than other alternative teaching methods?" but rather "For what purposes is the lecture method appropriate?" From the research it may be concluded:

> Using the lecture method is appropriate *when content material is not available elsewhere*. For example, when text material is unavailable, inaccessible or too complicated for students to learn on their own, lecturing is useful (Pascal, 1983). Additionally, when the idea to be presented is a model or set of procedures you have developed yourself, lecturing serves the students.

> Using the lecture method is more appropriate than alternatives *when you must communicate a large body of factual material to many students* in a short period of time (McKeachie and Kulik, 1975).

> Using the lecture method is appropriate *when introducing content material to students whose motivation or interest is limited*. Here, stories, anecdotes, humor and skillful delivery serve as a motivator.

Planning a Lecture Structure

Effective lecturing in a cross-cultural setting needs more planning than we have ever given that task. The old method of "Tell them what you're going to say, say it, and then tell them what you've said" is not adequate for students who need extra cognitive supports to hear, process, and retain information. For example, it is not sufficient to merely introduce a topic. To give an effective lecture in the cross-cultural situation you must supplement your introduction in several ways:

> Use *advance organizers* by providing for students some outline, model, or list of how the lecture is organized. Discussed more broadly in the section on Advancing Concept Attainment in Chapter 2, advance organizers are especially useful to students coping with new information or processing information in a second language. The simplest advance organizer is an *outline* (with the title, main points, and key terms defined).

> Provide *motivational cues* by identifying why the material is useful, difficult, or current. The grabber for many American students is, "This will be on the test."

> Indicate the *relevance of the lecture material* to the students' country and situation. The novelty of being different, exotic, American, or modern will soon wear off and personal or cultural relevance must be there instead. A biologist to Indonesia gave an example. "In my field of biology, at first, I used specimens from the United State, but I immediately found I needed to put them in

the context of the Indonesian situation. I very quickly had to learn as much as I could about Indonesian flora and land use for teaching my material."

Two frameworks for planning lectures are provided which might be useful to assure that lectures have a structured conceptual framework. The first was developed for use in training new professors in Southeast Asia, and the second grows out of the problem-solving and critical-thinking literature (Chaffe, 1988). The first is the *Thesis-Centered* lecture mode. This mode usually has one main thesis or generalization which is stated in the beginning by the lecturer. Figure 5-1 displays the progression.

Over and over again professors reported that undergraduate and graduate students had difficulty understanding and remembering lecture material. Social science professors whose lectures are full of many complicated theses might remember the old advice on lectures—"It's not how many points one can make in an hour, but rather how much a listener can tell his wife about it at breakfast the next morning." In a case in Malaysia where one professor's key points were carefully delivered, he regretted that "graduate students were able to restate the main idea of the lecture less than 50 percent of the time." Because these students were reported to be bright and motivated, one must conclude that, with the stress of processing information across the language barrier from English to Bahasa Malaysia or Tagalog or Norwegian (and from academic language to personal or

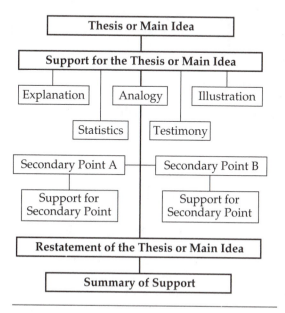

FIGURE 5-1   Thesis-Centered Lecture Model

functional language), you will lose students' attention and comprehension more than half the time. Perhaps this "loss" can serve to reinforce the suggestion of the model to focus on only a few key points which are restated often and summarized in the end.

The body of the lecture provides students with material to support the main point. There are several types of support one can choose, but it is recommended that all be used, because students seem to need this repetition and restatement and repetition again:

> An *explanation* clarifies and defines the main point. It is advisable to restate the point in both English and the students' language by planning to use a colleague or facile student to restate in this way.
>
> An *analogy* points out similarities between something known (a familiar and culturally relevant idea, concept, or practice) and something unknown (presumably the main idea). Rhetorical questions, which might be considered unsophisticated in a U.S. classroom, for example, may be useful in a Nepali class. What is obvious to American students may not be obvious in your new setting.
>
> An *illustration* is a factual or hypothetical example of a main point. In cultures full of proverbs and illustrative legends and stories, the use of cases or stories is good educational practice.
>
> Various *statistics and other factual data* should be used to strengthen the main point and support the thesis of the lecture. In U.S. educational settings, the facts are usually presented early in a presentation and often may serve only as supporting evidence. Statistical data may be less appreciated and often less culturally relevant in other educational settings.
>
> And finally, *testimony* is additional support for the main point. Here first-hand observers greatly enhance students' attention and memory (and perhaps your credibility). You can plan for this testimony by asking students or colleagues beforehand to offer their observations on a point.

The conclusion of this model is the restatement of the **thesis** and **summary of support** for the thesis. This restatement and summation may be more important for students in cross-cultural settings than for their American counterparts. This difference may be partly explained by the new students' slow, methodical, note-taking and translating—often far behind the lecturer's closing point.

Another model for planning carefully structured lectures is the **Problem-Solving** lecture mode. This method, and its variations, have reportedly been used effectively by many U.S. Fulbright lecturers. This problem-solving mode leads students from a problem to solutions and allows students to discover the solutions to problems before the instructor points them out.

First you need to start with a problem that is culturally relevant and meaningful to students. "Start with a problem for which students feel a need for a solution," suggested one lecturer who wove evidence and examples leading to his conclusion so that "most students discovered the solution before it's pointed out." While it takes more planning and skill to execute this second plan, it can be as structured and orderly as the first model and can produce higher thought processes. The conceptual model for the lecture can be seen in Figure 5-2.

RELATING LECTURE MATERIAL
TO THE CULTURAL CONTEXT

There are many days in China when I feel like a walking footnote. Nevermore so than when we are discussing a short story, like Nathaniel Hawthorne's Young Goodman Brown *and I am trying to explain concepts such as sin, guilt, and salvation. Ideas that it seems we take in with our mother's milk are not, after all, universally comprehended. (Leonard, l986)*

Finding the image, the term, the metaphor, or the story to serve as a concrete example of an abstract idea, while at the same time trying bridging cultural canyons, is challenging. "It isn't easy to make material relevant when none of the examples or quotations that come to mind are familiar and when all of my references are hopelessly out of context," insisted one professor of American litera-

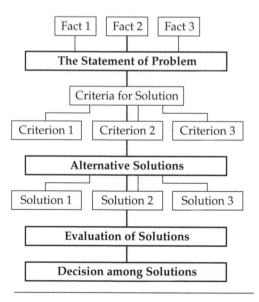

FIGURE 5-2   Problem-Solving Lecture Model

ture. I have observed lecturers in cross-cultural settings who used material that almost no one in the audience understood. A mixture of sympathy at their naïvete and empathy that I had made the same mistakes many time described my reaction. Sometimes the mismatch of the chosen image for the audience was all too obvious. For example, one august American lecturer opened his talk at a university in Buddhist Thailand with a lengthy story about "St. Peter and the Pearly Gates." Another U.S. professor, whose specialty was "Volunteerism in America" delivered a lecture on this topic on tour around China. After his lecture a graduate student in history, who spoke fluent English and served as a translator for a Fulbright professor, asked me, "What is volunteerism?"—an absolutely incomprehensible notion which his lecture had not illuminated. Images from American culture, such as "freeways," "tax-exempt status," "adolescence," or "salvation" (Leonard's example), may not be as universal as some American lecturers assume.

There were two themes running through responses to our queries of how to make lectures relevant and meaningful. The first was that *many professors were surprised at how much general information they could not assume among their students.* Fulbright professor Al Bailey described his Chinese students:

> *Chinese students have a certain provincialism, an ethnocentrism [we call it Middle Kingdom Syndrome]. It makes it rather difficult to draw on a Chinese student to compare his life in China with his travels in Taiwan, his views of Japan, or his readings about the Hawaiian islands. My American students, with those opportunities and their exposure to television and movies, can make that comparison.*

Medford Wilson of Winthrop College related a common observation of Chinese students, "One surprise was that my students knew almost nothing about the world beyond China. At the southern tip of Hainan, China's southernmost island, there is a large rock with the ancient Chinese characters 'End of the World' carved in it. This line encapsulates the traditional Chinese world view still prevalent when my students received their education" (1986). Another professor reported a similar observation far from China, "Israeli students were not as widely read or experienced as American students. I had to lecture on international relations at the most introductory level."

A second response theme to questions about planning for relevant lectures was that *professors felt they needed "crash courses" in the cultures and related disciplines* within those cultural contexts in order to teach their own courses well. Many had made concerted efforts to build their own information bases. A professor to Norway found that his lectures were best comprehended when he organized them around a Norwegian context:

> *In my field of national parks and wildernesses, at first, I used examples from the U.S., Canada, Australia, and New Zealand. But I soon found I needed to put them in the context of the Norwegian situation. I tried to learn as much as I could about how Norway manages its wilderness so that I could compare sys-*

tems. . . . It is not necessary to be a Norwegian expert prior to arrival, but a real
effort must be made to learn the Norwegian situation as soon as possible.

Soon after his arrival in Malaysia, CUNY law professor Sid Harring "set out on a
crash course on Malaysian history and politics . . . thirty or forty books, . . .
everything I could find on anthropology, sociology, economics, history,
politics . . . so I could become competent to teach law in an Islamic Society."
Lectures tailored to situations encountered by the students and audiences in
the cross-cultural setting were rated high on measures of effectiveness by the
hosts. This cultural relevancy in lecture content, though difficult at first, was
reported as "appreciated by the students" and "worth the effort." One Fulbright
professor in Malaysia used the local English language newspaper extensively
which, because of its editorial nature, she deemed excellent to promote discussion. Another professor reported that when she changed all the names in her
illustrations about children and schools to local Thai names and place names, the
interest in the material dramatically increased. A Fulbrighter in China interviewed
his students extensively for details about their backgrounds, skills, interests and
families, which he then incorporated into his lectures. Another found that,
perusing government documents and international agency reports with summaries of issues or projects in Asian countries was useful for formulating culturally
sensitive and relevant examples.

PLANNING FOR GOOD DELIVERY OF LECTURES

During my research on and participation in cross-cultural teaching, I have filmed
many and attended hundreds of lectures by American professors in various disciplines. Sometimes these lectures were in English, sometimes in native languages,
and sometimes used translators. They have been delivered in grand lecture halls
with multi-media screens and in tiny classrooms with no electricity. Many of
these lectures across cultures (including some of my own) were so ineffective in
terms of fostering comprehension and motivating attention that I decided to find
out what "delivery strategies" would be the most effective. Guidelines for Effective Classroom Lectures across Cultures in Figure 5-3 summarize some of these
strategies for lecturing to students in regular classes.
    A recent study provided some information about how foreign professors'
lectures are evaluated in Japan (Iizawa, 1991). Lectures given by Western professors to Japan were characterized as effective when the lecturer 1) adjusted to the
students' language levels; 2) spoke very slowly; 3) repeated and repeated again;
4) wrote down all difficult words; 5) handed out summaries and outlines of the
lectures; and 6) used visual aids. It is my hope that further discussion and research will provide additional observations and furnish a basis for sound, workable models for planning and delivery of good lectures to students and other
audiences across cultures.

1. **Plan the lecture using a structure.**

   • Make the thesis, main point, or problem extra clear.
   • For note-taking, follow a similar structure routinely.

2. **Use an advance organizer.**

   • Outlines, models, concept maps, etc. support conceptualization of problems and memory for the main points.

3. **Adjust your language.**

   • Slow your pace of delivery.
   • Use simple English constructions and declarative sentences.
   • Preview key vocabulary with definitions and glossaries.
   • Control your vocabulary. Keep to familiar, defined terms.
   • Remember to repeat, sum up, and repeat again.
   • Consider amplification if ambient noise levels are high.

4. **Use some culturally or geographically relevant examples in every lecture.**

   • Search for regional data and illustrations, gather local testimonies, and think of U.S./host country analogies which will inspire interest and promote relevancy.

5. **Keep straight lecturing to fifteen minutes segments.**

   • Break up lecturing with demonstrations, audio-visual interludes, and break-out activities.
   • Demonstrate alternatives to lecturing for students who will likely become college teachers.

6. **Engage students with participatory activities embedded in the lecture.**

   • Try intermittent discussion dyads, questioning methods, whole-class discussions between lecture segments.
   • Use cooperative methods, e.g., collaborative note-taking and learning partners to promote learning of the lecture material.

FIGURE 5-3   Guidelines: Effective Lecturing in Cross-Cultural Classrooms

Timing Lectures

In classroom situations where English is a second language and the learning culture is unfamiliar, one key to effective lecturing is careful timing. Straight lectures (without demonstrations, audio-visual segments, or break-out activities) should be short. Research on student note-taking during lectures has found that those listening to a fifteen-minute lecture recorded about forty percent of the main points presented, those listening to a thirty-minute lecture recorded about twenty-five percent of the significant material; and those listening for forty-five minutes recorded only twenty percent (McLeish, 1976). The research supports a fifteen minute maximum length for good attention and retention. The Thai proverb that the "professor talks until even the monkey goes to sleep" should serve as a constant reminder to be brief. Another point about the timing of lectures is when to continue or discontinue a topic. One professor to Japan, who was evaluated as being an exceptionally effective senior Fulbright lecturer, suggested that "each lecture should be a 'stand-alone unit' of learning instead of expressing continuity between lectures." Students have difficulty following the complex content material in one lecture, and even less if that lecture refers to material presented last week or last session. He added, "I just develop each of my lectures as if the themes were being heard for the first time."

Fostering Comprehension and Attention while Lecturing

The good news about students' poor facility in English is it requires me to formulate my ideas as succinctly as I possibly can—a useful teaching practice anywhere! (A California Tech professor, Nepal)

Remembering Advance Organizers. Many American professors abroad say their most useful technique for fostering comprehension while lecturing is the *simplified outline* prepared for their own and the students' use. Some professors find the overhead projection of these outlines necessary to focus students' attention. Others suggest that the photocopied outlines with "lots of white space so students can take their own notes and make translations right on the sheets" work best. Outlines work well, in part, because they serve as the "advance organizer," or the mechanism to establish the conceptual framework, that is particularly necessary for students in cross-cultural situations.

Using Verbal Supports for Comprehension. You probably have never monitored your *pace of delivery* as much as you will be called upon to do during this new assignment. A slower pace of delivery is, of course, critical when speaking in English to audiences for whom English is a second language. A Fulbrighter to China said he got so accustomed to talking slowly that when he saw a video of his class, he wanted to play it on fast-forward so he "could actually get something said." The feedback from almost every student of every American professor teaching abroad is "go slower, go slower." The admonition sounds like an easy one with which to comply, but the practice is difficult. Whether you do what others have reported—"get excited about the content," "have so much to cover," or "forget myself"—most lectures cover too much material at too fast a pace for most cross-cultural settings. As attested by a professor to Pakistan who "tried to speak slowly and distinctly, but I'm sure I didn't get through to most of them," speaking slowly is necessary, but not sufficient.

Additionally, *amplification* serves as an important support for comprehension. Students cannot understand what they do not hear. The level of volume needed may have more to do with ambient noise in the classroom environment than poor projection. Actor and professor Bernie Dunlop described his experience in Thailand:

> *I didn't realize the extent to which I would have to adopt their conventions. . . .*
> *I did not want to use a microphone in a small class and dictate. I am a trained*
> *performer, so I was confident I could project my voice to the back of the auditorium full of students. But even after I assured myself I was clearly audible,*
> *many students complained they couldn't hear me. . . . I was eventually obliged*
> *to use a microphone [which further distorted the voice] and confined me to the*
> *podium.*

You may not want to use or may not have available the tools for amplification You then will probably need to consider other strategies to minimize competing noise. A professor from Pakistan complained, "Due to the noise of street traffic, students talking, and birds screeching, the university was not a conducive place to learn." Another from Indonesia recalled, "My students complained that they could not hear me when I used an overhead projector [with its fan]. So I had to turn it on and let them copy the material, then turn it off to talk—it was a hassle!" While the environmental noise in some of the bustling cities of Asia and Latin America, for example, makes lecturing at urban universities almost impossible without amplification, the noise level in Irish classrooms, caused by the din of off-task talking, was described as "deafening" by one professor and "completely unacceptable" by another. "Irish instructors told me that I would get used to it, but I did not," reported one Fulbrighter.

Another verbal support for comprehension is the use of *controlled vocabulary*. A professor to Turkey "struggled to find the vocabulary that was simple enough to be understood in my lectures, but still sophisticated enough to say something meaningful." Most professors lecturing in English to non-native English speaking audiences complained of the same problem. A controlled vocabulary is one in which you use the most common and widely comprehended usage of a word and maintain that usage. For example, instead of saying, "The boy sustained a leg injury," you might say "The boy suffered a leg injury," or more simply "the boy injured his leg" and always say that term the same way.

Verbal cues are other verbal supports for comprehension in lectures. Cues such as, "This is important," "Now, note this," "This is the author's main point," etc., highlight key ideas for students. Connectors such as "because," "in order to," "if . . . then," "therefore" note essential relationships and are easily missed in translation. They should be emphasized for students who understand them and reviewed for those who do not.

More language supports for comprehension are needed in the cross-cultural situation than might be expected. Many professors recommended identifying and defining *key vocabulary* before the lecture (and perhaps directly on the outline). One professor warned that in Japan a lecturer cannot assume student comprehension of even common vocabulary in a field. He argued, "Professors cannot expect that students have been exposed to the literature or working vocabulary of their particular discipline before his or her class. Even if students have taken a previous basic course, professors cannot assume that they know the meaning of a given concept." However, despite efforts to use this form of verbal support to promote comprehension, one Fulbright professor in Nepal contended, "Still, major and complex concepts required translation, even when English competence of an audience is high."

Using Nonverbal Supports.   Typically, professors in many countries stand in front of the class lecturing, more authoritatively but far less animatedly, than typical American professors. Some American instructors used the novelty of posture, movement, and gesture to their advantage, but one professor warned, "Be subtle rather than grandiose!" Because a commonly reported problem of visiting lecturers (coupled with lack of language comprehension and limited student participation) is coping with students' inattention, boredom, and drowsiness, you can increase attentiveness with *emphasizing gestures*. Boldly pointing to main points on your overhead projections or blackboard material, using hand motions to emphasize points, or giving a cue when students should definitely get a point in their notes serves both to punctuate sections of material and to promote attention.

Teacher proximity has been shown in American educational settings to affect student attention. For example, students closest to the teacher are more attentive than students who are not and, as a teacher moves around a classroom, students' attention increases as the roving teacher nears. You may wish to arrange seating in circles, concentric circles, or horseshoes so that you can stand closer to more students than in typical row and column format. Because of differences in patterns of proximity in cultures and classroom subcultures, as discussed in Chapter l, you will need to be alert to possible discomfort among students as you approach or stand near them.

Student feedback regarding the effectiveness of such verbal and nonverbal methods, cannot be assured. Asking for reactions from host colleagues may be necessary for you to discriminate between the methods that serve you well and those that call excessive attention to themselves. Because understanding of lecture material was limited, one Fulbrighter lecturing in Thailand became discouraged:

> *I knew I was not being understood. If the faculty could have admitted that in the audiences many students and even faculty do not have good English skills, I could have concentrated on supporting the language ability of the slower group. . . . But trying to address the full spectrum was almost impossible.*

Because comprehension includes many other issues related to vocabulary, language clarity, and techniques for using translators, read Chapter 9 on Structuring Language Supports for Teaching for more details. Even with verbal and nonverbal supports for comprehension, understanding of lecture material is problematic.

ENHANCING LECTURES WITH MATERIALS AND METHODS

Because even the best lectures delivered in the cross-cultural setting are often not well comprehended, supplementary materials and methods are needed to promote attention and comprehension. Three areas of enhancement are Handout Materials, Audio-Visual Materials (with a broader discussion in Chapter 10, Enhancing Learning with Technologies) and Participatory Activities.

Providing Handout Materials

Preparing Outlines. Supplementary handouts and written material to guide students during lectures is one of the most common ways to promote comprehension of lectures. For example, a well-planned outline of the lecture will provide both a framework for conceptualizing the main points and an outline for note-taking and language supports. A biology professor to Indonesia received the following note one day from a student who benefitted from outlines:

> *I am glad to be a student in your Palynology [sic.] lectures although I don't understand most of what you are talking about. I suggest you to give us an outline for the next lecture a week before, so that we have time to read over and over again and will grasp the ideas in it.*

Effective outlines we observed included simple linear outlines, skeletal linear outlines and "webbed" outlines. The *simple linear outline* using standard outline form and listing main points in chronological (as delivered) form is often used. One professor to Thailand resorted to very detailed outlines for his students because they "took such impossible and unworkable notes on the lecture." Providing the outline works differently than providing the full paper, as one lecturer described, "When first to Japan I made every effort to have copies of paper I would be presenting in the hands of the audience prior to my lecture, but I found they would then not pay attention. Once I started giving the outline only, they paid attention and expanded on my outline notes." Sometimes these outlines included translations of key materials and other language supports. A Fulbright professor to Hungary found his lectures increased in effectiveness when he "gave out a three-page outline of my lecture in English and a short summary of main points in Hungarian." In Japan, where there is a tradition of "closest colleague" and counterpart participation, professors sometimes were helped to prepare summaries or outlines in Japanese to hand out before the lecture.

The *skeletal linear outline*, following the structure of the lecture, shows only main points or key words and provides cued spaces for students to fill in the rest of the lecture information. The advantage is that students must pay attention to fill in the blanks, yet a supporting structure is there for them. Figure 5-4 is an example of a skeletal linear outline.

TOPIC: AMERICAN UNIVERSITY LIFE

Subtopic: Social Groups in American Universities

I. INTRODUCTION – Identification of Main Groups:

    A. Ethnic groups:

    B. Age groups:

    C. Gender groups:

II. Background Readings:

    A. Social stratification (Bell, 1993):

    B. Socioeconomic trends (Smith, 1992):

III. Social Groups Overview:

    A. Stereotypes:

    B. Discrimination:

    C. Laws and policies:

IV. Chinese-American Experience:

    A. Data:

    B. Court cases:

FIGURE 5-4   Skeletel Linear Outline

The *webbed outline* is gaining popularity with instructors, who find that students do not share their fondness for linear thinking. Often, in a "linear type of lecture," the third point (rather than the first) may be the most important, or a point may be closely related to or even a corollary to another point. Webbing allows students to see the full array of points and their connectedness. Figure 5-5 illustrates an example of a webbed outline.

Preparing Written Materials.   In many countries it is likely that you will not have clerical and support personnel to help prepare course and lecture materials.

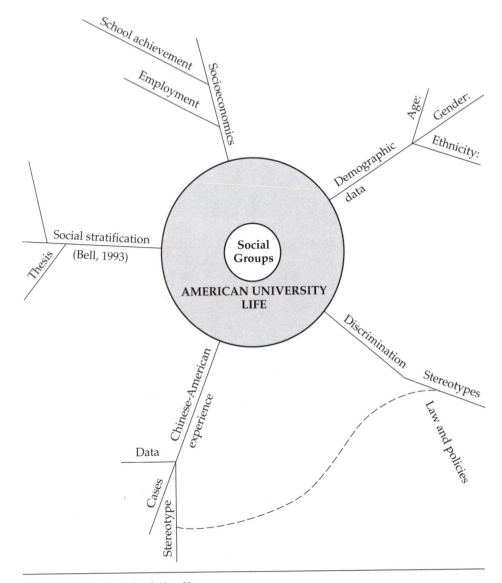

FIGURE 5-5   Webbed Outline

Typewriters and word processors may be scarce. Typists may not type well in English and your directions to clerical staff, which often will be given in the native language, may not be well understood. Managing your own copying was recommended by some professors, because "you have more quality control over your work." One colleague reported that her clerical staff "will run-off illegible copies because legibility is not obvious to the nonEnglish reader."

In preparing materials, a concise and well-spaced format is useful to allow space for student translation and restatement on the page. Native scripts—Thai and Arabic scripts, for example—require more space than English script. Proof-reading materials carefully also is recommended, because students will not be able to easily decode errors or abbreviations. Writing translations of key words on the materials before their reproduction has proved useful. A religion and philosophy instructor suggested a *class glossary* of key and often-used English terms was a time-saving device.

Participatory Activities

Effective lecturing involves supplementing well-planned and engaging presentations with other, more participatory techniques to help keep students attentive and involved with the material. A few are mentioned here—Intermittent Discussion Groups, Question and Answer Pairs, and Collaborative Note-taking.

Intermittent Discussion Groups. By interspersing mini-discussions between pairs or small groups seated near each other, long periods of uninterrupted listening and information processing can be broken up. Recall the research finding that even among native English speakers, fifteen minutes is the maximum for good attention and retention. With discussion groups, the audience or class is assigned into dyads, or triads (or some other small group depending on the room arrangement). These assignments are usually made prior to the beginning of the lecture and based on the best way participants can move in to and out of the groups with a minimum of lag time and noise. After each segment of lecture material is delivered, groups are asked to react to the material in several ways:

1. To formulate personally or culturally relevant examples which illustrate, expand upon or counter a point delivered in the lecture material.
2. To summarize in their own language the main point previously delivered in the lecture.
3. To relate an assigned reading to a lecture point (Here you assume that someone in the group will have done the assignment and will be rewarded by the chance to relate this information).

Question and Answer Pairs. Johnson, Johnson and Smith (1991), well-known advocates of cooperative learning methods, use another method to supplement lecturing. Each audience or class member takes as partner the person sitting next to him. Having just heard the lecture segment, one partner asks the other a question on the material. The lecturer should have some questions available to "prime the pump," if necessary, for the initial rounds. Next time, the other partner asks the questions.

Collaborative Note-taking. The notes students take during a lecture in a cross-cultural situation are often incorrect and incomplete. Students may be unskilled in note taking. A University of South Carolina professor of American Literature posited, "Taking lecture notes means discerning what is significant and deciding what to write down. Many Thai students did not know how to take notes, not because it was beyond their ability, but outside their training." White and Tisher (1986) suggest that students with little prior knowledge of the content take poor notes due to "information processing overload." With oral delivery (often in a foreign language), verbal material (handouts), and visual material (overheads, maps, graphs, models, charts, etc.), a student is pressured to take notes from too many sources. In cross-cultural situations you add the elements of culturally different teaching styles, and overload is likely.

With collaborative note-taking, participants work together to assure that each has the lecture material covered in the notes. After each segment of lecture, each member of preassigned dyads (usually seat mates) reviews, checks, and expands her own notes with the help of the other note-taker.

LECTURE TOURING

Have Fulbright; will Lecture. (Business card of a lecturer to New Zealand)

The opportunities for lecturing to faculties and professional organizations abroad outside your assigned university are plentiful for American professors abroad who are interested and energetic enough to seek them. An American Studies professor to New Zealand was surprised by the scope of her lecturing opportunities, "Having no idea, before I arrived, what was expected or what the standard visiting professor does, I gave more lectures on diverse topics to diverse audiences than I ever thought possible." A professor to Eastern Europe whose specialty was mental retardation was asked to lecture on everything from early childhood education to educational policy in America, to speech therapy and applied behavior analysis. "Because of tremendous interest in all things Western right now," he explained, "requests often extend far beyond one's area of expertise."

American professors abroad report they lectured in such diverse settings as provincial colleges and universities, government training institutes, national and international professional conferences, American studies associations, American university alumni associations, teacher training programs, learned societies, U.S. military posts, news conferences for national papers and syndicates, national and international radio broadcasts, U.S. Embassy and other diplomatic programs, host country ex-patriot gatherings, American Chambers of Commerce and civic clubs abroad, U.S. study abroad programs and many others. "Sometimes I lectured to groups of four to six, other times two-hundred to four-hundred with everything in between!" exclaimed one Fulbright lecturer.

Arranging Extramural Lectures

Lecture tours are usually arranged directly between the lecturer and the inviting institution or group, but sometimes sponsoring organizations facilitate these connections. An economist arranged his lecture tours in the common way, "I arranged two lecture tours, both to universities—one to the western part of Malaysia and another one to Thailand. I arranged them by writing that I am a Fulbright professor assigned to Malaysia and would like to speak on the following topics at their institution. The reply was prompt—they were very interested in having someone lecture on those topics of interest to them." Typically, you would send:

1. a *one-page introductory letter* listing three or four topics about which you are prepared to lecture (usually these topics are more generic than you would lecture on in the United States.)
2. a *short vita* (no more than one page)

As a Fulbright Lecturer to Thailand, I participated in eleven lecture tours in a year and was invited to do even more. While the opportunity to visit so many areas was enjoyable, eleven tours were difficult to manage while also teaching. In my case, both my university and the sponsoring agencies were busy "making good use of their visiting scholar" and arranging more of these invitations than I could accept. Others reported similar experiences. "I was told to try to take as many lecture tours as possible. The interest is not only in the professional experience, but also in the opportunity of going around the country and seeing different environments. By lecture touring, I was able to travel to four major islands in Indonesia," offered a history professor from the Arizona State University. A management professor from American University took three commerce workshops on tour around New Zealand. A Fulbright professor to Norway lectured on national parks in America at national parks around Scandinavia.

Other professors arranged lecture tours en route home from their assignments, garnering the added benefits of seeing other cultures and breaking up long journeys. For example, a professor in Hong Kong, through contacts with the United States Information Service, arranged to lecture in both Nepal and India on his return to the United States.

Additionally, it is not uncommon for two or more American professors in a country or region to arrange "exchange lectures" between themselves—each visiting the other's university. Sometimes the university provides lodging and meals. Occasionally, host organizations have small travel budgets set aside for in-country or regional lecture tours such as these, and provide small stipends for transportation, room, or board. A typical tour was explained by San Diego State professor Hari Singh. "Basically a lecture tour involved traveling to one, two or three distant universities for about a day each. I would lecture on a specific topic for about three or four hours with a question and answer session at the end of each talk for ten or fifteen minutes. Then I would go out for lunch with the host and talk about professional activities. Then come back for another session or some kind of group discussion."

Not all lecture-touring goes without a hitch. Problems with unreasonable expectations, with little or no direction from the host, or with the lecturer's dislike of the lecture-touring process were reported. "Exchange lectures in Brazil were frequently requested, but arrangements were poorly carried out," maintained one lecturer. "On one series of lectures, I was not informed until twenty-four hours in advance that I would be presenting four days of eight-hour lectures (as if that were possible!) and providing a concert every evening," complained another. As part of their staff development efforts, universities may invite you for as much time and as many lectures as they can squeeze into one visit. For example, the expectation that you give four, three-hour lectures in two days can be gruelling, especially if the honorifics of "courtesy visits, faculty lunches, teas and administrative consultations" are added to the expectations.

A professor to Norway who was invited to lecture in many classes campus-wide lamented, "I found it difficult for my hosts to narrow down what topics they sought and to identify how my lectures might fit into their teaching objectives and program." Another lecturer to Eastern Europe complained, "I never knew ahead of time what I would be expected to talk on. I always had to have a cache of overheads that I prepared before I came and I carried them with me from place to place."

Those with negative reactions to lecture touring include a veteran American professor who expressed the following:

> For me every lecture day feels like my first day of school with all the appropriate anxieties. I hate facing lecture halls full of strangers. I've had to devise whole new pedagogic approaches appropriate for this work in New Zealand.

A professor to Japan disliked lecture touring because he disliked dependence on a translator, "I don't lecture. I *talk* to my students and colleagues and try to *communicate* with them using anything I can think of, rather than being totally dependent on the translator. Of course, the 'anything you can think of' is the hard part."

Preparing Lecture Tour Topics

Preparing topics for lecture tours in advance may be the best idea. One instructor to Pakistan advised, "For extramural talks, the idea is to bring a couple in the bag with all appropriate research and visual aids." Obtaining key references, preparing overhead transparencies, making master copies of outlines and handouts, and preparing back-up materials (in case there are no overhead or copy facilities) could be done before departure. Additionally, developing your lecture-tour proposal and short bio (duplicated on high-quality paper often unavailable overseas) would be an asset. You also might consider creating some "marketing" materials for your tour, such as a flyer or program announcement describing your topic and including, perhaps, a picture. This later suggestion is not without a cautionary note. Once on a lecture tour in Southeast Asia, I was driven to the front gate of the university past a billboard that looked like the giant movie posters one sees in Bombay or Jakarta. With a double-take, I realized the "blond movie star" on the billboard announcing my lecture that day was supposed to be me. Students had painted the picture from the photo on my flyer. I was so embarrassed I promptly forgot every word of my greeting speech.

Topic choices for lecture tours are often very general. For example, two American geographers talked on "National Parks in the U.S." and "Walking the World's Cities"; two historians lectured on "Agrarian Life in the U.S." and "American Small Towns"; an educator spoke on "Educational Reform in the U.S."; two sociologists lectured on "People's Movements in U.S. History" and "New Trends in Evaluation Research in America"; a psychologist talked on "Raising Children in a Multi-cultural World"; and a biologist on "Americans View Rain Forests." These topics have wide appeal, do not require audiences' specific knowledge in a field, and serve another of the lecturer's functions—that of representing or being a "cultural ambassador" from the United States. One Fulbright lecturer to Mexico said that the lecture topic most enjoyed, most responded to and most often requested for repeat performances was his "A comparison of U.S.–Mexican University Life." Caroline Alexander (1991) told of her first public lecture in Malawi:

> *There being a dearth of visual entertainment [no television at all and, in my city, no cinema to speak of], I decided to give a talk on "classical Western art" and thus make use of my modest collection of color art slides, which I sensed would do more to draw a crowd than anything I might choose to discuss. [With slides of a few nude and partially clothed statues from ancient Greece and Rome] my strategy was successful to a degree that I did not anticipate.*

BUILDING AN ETHIC OF GENUINE COMMUNICATION

Western academics are generally deserving of the criticism that they use a rather "heavy textbook style" of lecturing in cross-cultural contexts—a style described as "pedantic, formal, or boring." Recently, I spent a sabbatical as a visiting scholar at the University of Hong Kong, one of the true multi-cultural universities in the world. In my research capacity I observed professors and scholars from Australia, the United Kingdom, New Zealand, Canada, the United States and several European countries lecture to Asian students and their culturally diverse colleagues. I am more convinced than ever that the extraordinary expense and energy expended to bring together academic scholars and university professors from around the globe argue for a better sense of academic discourse and genuine communication across cultures.

As a visiting professor in a cross-cultural situation, it is likely that you will address, not only classes of student with whom you often interact, but also faculty and professional groups with whom you rarely interact. On such occasions, you will likely do much more than give a scholarly paper like those you have given so often in your careers. In this role of "guest lecturer," you will "represent" your sponsoring U.S. or international agency, the cooperating national commission or organization, your home university, your host university, and your disciplines. For many Americans, this role of "cultural ambassador" is unfamiliar and even undesirable. Even the concept of a worker being a "life-long member of his work-place family" (such as the case with the *donwei* in China or the "corporation family" in Japan) is fundamentally foreign to many Americans. So how can American professors be expected to "represent" anything other than himself?

Effectiveness, as you consider this "ambassadorial" task, comes with first asking some essential questions: "How can I work toward a goal of genuine comprehension in my lecturing and teaching?" and "What can I do to avoid the mistakes of the guest professors whose lectures are sometimes criticized as pedantic or irrelevant. An overview of some guidelines for addressing the cross-cultural audience might serve as gentle reminders.

Define What the Audience Wants. The questions you need to ask are: What do the people here in this room today *want* to know? Along some continuum of experience or understanding, where do these people generally fit? Those who start with what the listeners want to know seem to lay a background for telling them what they need to know. Unlike the guest lecturer who passes through town on a "lecture tour," or is "just in town for a conference," you are in a position by working in country to talk with program coordinators and colleagues about what your listeners want from your presentations. Finding out what listeners want to know takes some research, for hosts will often be politely sweeping and say something like "anything you want" or "whatever is going on in physics in the States." One professor to Turkey whose specialty was research methods learned, prior to a lecture tour, that "a debate raged in his field about the use of qualitative methods (driven by European-trained professors) vs. quantitative methods (championed by U.S.-trained professors)," and it was hoped he would "settle the score." He shrewdly chose to revisit the strengths of different methods for different research questions, because he had been forewarned.

Introduce an Advance Organizer. With listeners for whom English is a second or foreign language, an introduction or overview which makes clear what is to be covered and what issues, questions or main points will be addressed is essential. (Advance Organizers are discussed in Advancing Concept Attainment in Chapter 2.) The accompanying advice is that brevity is the essence of a good introduction. As the Louisiana adage goes, "If you don't strike oil in the first three minutes, stop boring." The purpose of the introduction is to propose a framework on which to hang your lecture's main point. Details and examples follow the framework.

A professor on a lecture tour to the University of Singapore remarked on the utility of providing an outline or overview of the lecture. He had prepared two separate lectures for two situations (one a small round table graduate seminar and the other a formal lecture for the large general university audience). So important was the advance organizer to his host that they passed out his notes for the "formal lecture" to accompany the roundtable, even though they were an entirely different topics (Bailey, 1993).

Tell a Good Story to Promote Attention. Many audiences in cultures where oral traditions are still valued are spellbound by a good story. Whether it is because of the tradition of using fables and parables to illustrate important and complex ideas or because of the love of illusion, stories seem to be an invocation. I remember opening a lecture I was giving to Chinese colleagues with a story of my grandmother's first flight with the barnstormers who visited her East Texas farm. The image of the poor country girl's confrontation with the dangerous world of urban excitement was remembered long after the lecture topic was forgotten. With stories, attention follows and, hopefully, memory and learning too.

Build an Ordered, Logical Case. You need to examine your main points to make sure they are ordered and logical for the listener who is new to the content. You can order them chronologically, by importance, by cause-and-effect, or topically. Your choice of organization may differ for more experienced listeners (faculty and colleagues) and for inexperienced listeners (students). The principle-centered and problem-centered models of lecture progressions discussed earlier in this chapter serve as two possible ways to organize information.

Make Main Points Visible. You will want to verbally and visually punctuate your main points. Listeners operating in a second language need to hear you say, "The second main characteristic is . . " or "The most important finding of the research was . . .". In overhead projections and printed material, these points need bold highlighting and enumeration. Repetition and exaggeration, sometimes thought of as redundant or inappropriate in our home settings, may be necessary in the cross-cultural situation. (See Chapter 11, Enhancing Learning with Technologies, for information on uses and availability of audio-visual materials and equipment.)

Be Clear and Culturally Alert. The old COIK (Clear Only If Known) principle is forgotten in some American professors' lectures. Like the direction-giver who says, "You can't miss it," some lecturers assume "general knowledge," but such knowledge is often very culture-specific. One Fulbright professor was surprised when his sophisticated students at the Foreign Affairs Institute in Beijing were baffled by his reference to a "hamburger."

Make Lecture Information Personal. Reading newspapers can give you a quick lesson in useful styles of communication. For example, in the Philippines, letters, editorials, and conversation are often printed as news items. By using real people, names, dialogue, personal stories, and testimony in your presentations, you can make data and key points more personal, simple, and powerful in this cross-cultural setting.

Invite Listener Questions. The best lecturers explicitly or implicitly answer the questions of the audience. One visiting lecturer I observed had an interesting technique: He gave a lecture as if it were an interview. He planted questions among the audience beforehand. Since mass communication research shows that interviews are easier to read and more widely read than articles on the same subjects, interview-style lectures make sense. Obviously when listeners identify with our message, they attend to it better. One professor of philosophy reported that to invite listener participation in her lectures she had students write down their questions about the readings and materials before class and pass them in. She then tailored her presentation for that class based on these questions in students' own words—and emphasized the points she wanted embedded in them. She used their questions as the springboard for the ideas she wanted to teach.

Use Illustrative Examples. As with other standard practices of lecturing, using specific examples is more necessary in this new setting than in the United States where your and your audiences' sets of general knowledge are roughly equivalent. Use anecdotes, examples, and cases to illustrate your main points. The professor's standby, "*You* can think of examples," is not sufficient in this case. A well-known American lecturer in Thailand lectured to an audience on "Strategies for Optimal School Achievement in the American Experience." As part of her lecture she described research findings on the efficacy of "early intervention programs" (day care, Headstart, etc.). Because institutionalized day care was a rare practice there, one good example of a typical day-care program in America would have illustrated what forty-five minutes of lecture did not.

Simplify the Vocabulary. In years of teaching your own language peers, you may have forgotten how to use short, simple, vivid, easily understood words. Instead of "confronting" problems, you can "face" them. A "multifaceted" issue is really "many-sided." Do not "proceed on the assumption," but just "assume." Your objective here is to illuminate—not to dazzle! Professional and technical words are sometimes necessary, of course, and university professors and students in the cross-cultural university setting may want to learn or practice complicated English terms. Explaining them in ways that do not insult the sophisticated listener is sometimes difficult. Some professors use students as their target and say, for example, "For any student who might not know the meaning of this term, it is . . . ," and the full audience benefits.

Repeat and Summarize Carefully. As you approach the end of your lecture, you need to restate the questions you were to answer. If you have covered more than three main points, you may need to carry them along as you go (with restatement). Then you need to repeat the main points in the summary, although recasting these points in a fresh way may be more interesting to the sophisticated listener. Some effective lecturers use the United Nations' custom of the "rappateur" whereby a bilingual listener reviews and summarizes the highlights of the lecture for the audience. This method is discussed in the section on Employing Translators and Translations in Chapter 9.

The Final Dash.   And when all these guidelines are reflected upon and incorporated into this otherwise good presentation, the final dash of artistry, creativity, and personal style can be added. Many American professors have a bit of "saw dust" in their blood, so when they get before audiences, their capacity for theatrical provocation and humorous interludes is abundant. I remember one very formal and distinguished American professor in Thailand who wore a blinking bowtie to a lecture that fell on Christmas Day. However, for a cross-cultural audience, for whom communication comes harder, a mammoth supply of creativity will be useless if good principles of instruction and a sound ethic of universal communication are not heeded.

Concept Map

6

BUILDING SUPPORTIVE
WORK SETTINGS

*Cooperation and generosity are plentiful here. I am
reminded by contrast, what a 'fighting field' academic
work life in America has become.*
—A PENN STATE PROFESSOR, MALAYSIA

For most Americans teaching in a host country, colleagues and students become
the best "guides" to the workplace and the most useful "informants" on the culture. Indeed, these relationships become the small keyholes through which American professors witness other ways of working, thinking, and being. To examine
these and other essential relationships and the issue and roles of work relationships in successful academic sojourns, information concerning the following questions was gathered in interviews:

1. Which work relationships strengthened over time?
2. What behaviors seemed to facilitate or to inhibit these relationships?
3. How did professors make friends?
4. How did teachers cultivate relationships with students?
5. When and where were there relational conflicts in the workplace?

Just as in Chapter 1, Examining the Culture of the Classroom, the danger of
painting with too broad a brush and identifying narrow observations as general-
izable experiences is real. But it is hoped that through observation, mutual discussion, exploration, and research on behaviors and attitudes in the cross-cultural workplace we can build a better understanding of work relationships and
their roles in professional integration across cultures.

FOSTERING CONNECTIONS WITH
FACULTY AND COLLEAGUES

Fostering effective relationships with colleagues in the university workplace requires American professors to reconsider the cultural context of their customary professional and personal behaviors. For example, Americans challenge authority, status, and protocol almost by instinct (where other nationalities may treat them with reverence). American academics engage in professional debate and criticism and assert positions readily (where academics from other cultures may find such directness out of place). Additionally, fostering workplace relationships in new cultural situations often necessitates the use of modified or less familiar professional and social strategies. Examined here are experiences of professors who have used such strategies to build supportive collegium and make good friends in university workplaces across cultures. Figure 6-1 provides a set of guidelines for Fostering Connections with Faculty and Colleagues.

Recognizing Cultural, Political, and Structural Hurdles

Cultural Hurdles to Effective Relationships. There were many cultural differences involved in relationships in university workplaces around the world. However, among those differences there were a few hurdles that persistently affected American professors' efforts to build supportive work settings. The first of these hurdles is *compartmentalization*. In contrast to our practice of compartmentalizing worklife and work relationships apart from our social or family life, many other cultures see work as the place of primary social, as well as professional, relationships. In such a setting, workplace lunches may become big social occasions lasting for hours, while the American instructor keeps looking at his watch wondering when colleagues will ever let him "get back to work." In such a setting, there may be few boundaries around roles. For example there may be the expectation that a professor's spouse will serve the university or department in some capacity (as teacher, English instructor, tutor, "first-lady" hostess, etc.), perhaps without remuneration.

Another area of difference acting as a hurdle is *directness*. American academics pride themselves on "telling it like it is," and eschew meandering methods of interpersonal interactions hosts sometimes use and prefer. In the intercultural setting, bold assertions, criticisms, debate points, opinions, and boasts stated directly were sometimes viewed by hosts as inappropriate. The particular type of self-promotional directness common among American academics was often identified as a hurdle. Thais criticize the Western professors' practice of *yok tua* (lifting oneself up). A Norwegian colleague advised American Fulbright professors there "not to engage in those forms of self-aggrandizement that so punctuate academic discourse and behavior in the United States." Another professor to Turkey warned, "It seems important to be down-to-earth and to avoid the subtle kinds of self-promotion which are all too common in American universities."

1. **Anticipate common hurdles**

   a) Cultural hurdles (e.g., compartmentalization, directness),
   b) Political hurdles (e.g., departmental camps, prejudice toward Americans, salary disparities),
   c) Structural hurdles (e.g., space, language and schedules).

2. **Cultivate collective work arrangements**

   a) Team-teach with a colleague or junior faculty,
   b) Hire or trade for translators, tutors, or research associates,
   c) Seek a "closest colleague."

3. **Network early and often with professional groups**

   a) Discipline groups (e.g., local, national, or regional)
   b) American studies or alumni groups (e.g., American Studies Association, American University Alumni, Fulbright groups),
   c) University-based faculty development groups.

4. **Seek advice, counsel, and help from faculty colleagues**

   a) View colleagues as "key informants,"
   b) Consider collaborative research projects where colleagues' expertise is valuable.

5. **Use social systems of the local hosts**

   a) View "socializing" as part of your work experience,
   b) Participate in dining events (e.g., tea breaks, business lunches, "compa" time),
   c) Play departmental sports,
   d) Do annual rituals (e.g., festivals, pilgrimages, graduations).

6. **Be guided by the Chinese "3 P's"—Patience, Politeness and Persistence**

FIGURE 6-1   Guidelines: Fostering Connections with Faculty Colleagues across Cultures

Views of authority is a third area of difference that affects work relationships, as identified by John Paul Fieg in his insightful texts, *Common Core* (1989) and *Thais and North Americans* (1980). American academics are notoriously distrustful of authority and view it as something to be challenged. They often encourage such challenges to their authority from students. In some of the other cultures examined, host professors and students revered authority which they perceived as derived from age, position, family background or moral excellence. Similarly, *attention to status*, was a major difference. "I found that as an exchange professor with roots in a big American university, I automatically had status that set me apart from others," observed one professor to New Zealand. Some American instructors were slow to recognize vertical social status hierarchies as a workplace framework. Their attitudes of friendship toward support staff, drivers, custodians, language instructors, translators, and even their students were viewed as peculiar. Their egalitarian gestures of seeking everyone's participation or contribution were sometimes only tolerated.

Political Hurdles to Effective Relationships.   Political as well as cultural barriers serve as hurdles to building supportive relationships in the workplace. University politics is not a new phenomenon to veteran American scholars, but the inscrutable nature of politics in cross-cultural situations makes the situation more perilous. A visiting professor to Mexico told a common story of some bitter *political divisions* among her faculty,

> *As a consequence, each group tried to pull me to its side in order to increase its numbers and influence. It took considerable effort on my part to avoid taking sides and not getting entangled in these power struggles, but it paid off.*

Professors who were cognizant of such political divisions and able to avoid them more likely maintained cordial, professional relationships with their faculties. Another instructor described a negative outcome after affiliation with one faction:

> *Some faculty were displeased with the department head. I was associated with him and, hence, some faculty members who didn't even know me went out of their way to ostracize me. This resulted in months in which I was assigned to do relatively little. This mutiny was unfortunate since it contributed to department disharmony and resulted in a failure to use an important resource—me!*

Other political hurdles affected relationships. One professor to Eastern Europe reported *prejudice toward American academics*, "Despite being forewarned of the attitude toward Americans as 'not being professional, not prepared to teach, not having information regarding teaching methods, not able to handle students and lazy,' I was still quite shocked by it." Another reported *resentment over salary disparity*, "The best explanation for the Polish faculty's resentment of American faculty is salary. Americans receive considerable more salary than they do. The amount of my Fulbright grant was told to someone in the university and the gossip spread like wild fire." Yet another described *innovation as a barrier*. Tone Carlen, a business professor to Czechoslovakia, found, "Cordial relations with faculty easily turned hostile when I adopted a nontraditional teaching style and became popular."

Structural Hurdles to Effective Relationships.   Cultural and political hurdles are not the only barriers to the development of effective workplace relations. Structural hurdles such as *no office space, rigid disciplines, language barriers and disconnected schedules* present real challenges as well. An American instructor to Hungary described such a structural barrier:

My interaction with my faculty is limited because they come to the department mostly to give lectures. Other than that, they work at home or at other institutes and jobs all over the city. They earn so little that even with a working wife this mode of work is necessity.

Another professor to Mexico agreed, "There is almost no collegial interaction, as professors come on different days and stay only the time it takes to teach their class. Curriculum is often organized around professors' schedules, who can teach on a part-time basis and what these profs can teach." University of North Carolina sociologist Tony Oberschall found that "establishing professional contacts among Chinese sociologists was difficult from my university, because of sharp disciplinary boundaries among organizations and professions in China" (1986). A University of Utah professor to Indonesia summed up his and many others' situation: "The main difficulty I have in establishing relationships with colleagues revolves around the fact that I don't have an office. I work at home, therefore I don't run into my colleagues much."

Fostering Connections Using Professional Strategies

In a cross-cultural setting, American professors give much attention and energy to building collegial relations and report frustration when they do not make personal connections with colleagues. Disappointment was sometimes registered, as heard in this example from Nepal: "Relations among my faculty are cordial, but distant"; or from Japan, "My interaction with colleagues was disappointingly minimal." Yet some professors' energy and attention to relationships met with success, because they were more skilled at fostering connections through collective work and professional networking.

Fostering Connections through Collective Work

Some professors build strong relationships through cultivating collective work arrangements. Often co-teachers, translators, language tutors, or fellow researchers became the "guide" or "key informant" or friend many American professors had wished for. A professor in China related,

I developed a close personal friendship with my translator whose home village I have visited often. I have even arranged for him to come to America as my doctoral student.

A professor to Czechoslovakia reported:

For my lecturing outside of the university, I hire [for a small honoraria] another faculty member to accompany me for needed translation and logistics work. It actually gives him much needed exposure in academic circles and serves me well. Additionally, we have become good friends.

As another way to foster relationships with colleagues, an American professor in Mexico suggested, "Collaborative research is extremely valuable for building collegial relations. Mexican faculty often have little experience in research and have few opportunities to engage in it. On the other side, without collaboration, the foreign professor is less likely to do relevant work or get to know colleagues very well."

Fostering Connections Using Professional Assemblies. Another common way professors build effective work relationships is through professional gatherings. An American history professor offered an example, "In Hong Kong, my department sponsors weekly seminars which allow the members the opportunity to share their research with colleagues. Doing this again, I would sign up as early in my stay as possible." Joseph Mestenhauser, well-known researcher in the area of cross-cultural communication and a Fulbright professor to Czechoslovakia, remarked:

> *I utilized the time they required to 'figure me out' by attending every faculty meeting they had. Attending these meeting gave me not only needed exposure, but the topics they discussed gave me valuable insight on the level and quality of thinking people expressed about their educational programs.*

A professor of Women's Studies to New Zealand suggested, "A conference presentation early on in country seemed to be the most effective way to get the word out that I was doing work of interest to others and wanted to make personal and professional connections." Explained a professor to Egypt, "I arranged to give a departmental seminar fairly early during my assignment in order to get information to colleagues regarding my work. Later, when I did have some problems with computer access on campus, it helped, because a colleague who had been at this seminar remembered me and helped me find a computer for my work."

And still others created their own assemblies, like this visiting professor to Malaysia:

> *My hosts provided me with a lovely office. It was embarrassingly better than the offices of all of my colleagues. It even had air conditioning. I suspect some administrator was moved out of it so its value could be used to create 'matching' funds for the grant I came on. Nevertheless, I decided to use it as the 'Faculty Development Lab' and hold faculty seminars, courses, brown bag lunches, etc. in that nice space. It was a hit!*

Another to Malaysia also created his own gathering. "I have an office, but I don't really work in my office. . . . I do all my research and writing in the departmental library, because it is accessible. Colleagues can see me and talk with me there."

Fostering Connections by Seeking Counsel and Advice.   Like the adage "the best way to make a friend is to ask to borrow a quarter," some visiting professors find the best way to make a friend is to seek help from a colleague. CUNY Law professor Sid Harring recounted his experience in Malaysia:

> *I try to ask people about their work, what they teach...I professed an interest in Islamic law. I felt totally ignorant about this great legal order. One faculty member brought me her books on the subject. Now I'm a student of Islamic law and she's the teacher. It's a good connection . . . good exchange.*

Another professor in China sought advice from the senior staff. "My colleagues are tremendous teachers. I enjoy long conversations with them. One of my closest colleagues is 80, another is 66, and they tell me things about the legal system that my age peers can't—the historical perspective." Many professors find, among the junior faculty at their universities, professors who are open to an active exchange of ideas and view the relationship with the visitor as a chance for professional development. CUNY law professor Sharon Hom, who held weekly gatherings of junior faculty at her apartment, described her connections:

> *Young teachers who have graduated from colleges in the last 5 to 6 years come here from all over the country. They tell me about training and developments in various areas of law and a great deal about what's going on beneath all of these laws. They even share with me their concerns about the new legal system, questions about the lack of clarity in the new laws, and what it would take to implement them. They talk about their dreams for China and for their own professional lives—We talk a lot about that.*

Fostering Connections Using Social Strategies

> *Faculty gossip tastes sweeter over food. (Thai proverb)*

Using Food to Nourish Relationships. A Wayne State professor to New Zealand offered his favorite way of developing esprit de corp with his colleagues: "Tea time at 10:30 and 3:30! The conviviality and conversation of tea time has been delightful and helped me foster professional and informal relationships." Professors in the present or former British Commonwealth countries often report they build collegium by "joining the faculty commons" and "taking tea." Several visiting professors to Japan reported spending "much 'compa' time talking over drinks and snacks at a bar or cafe with colleagues after work as a means of creating bonds and exchanging useful information." They recounted that Japanese colleagues suggest that those who do not attend "compa" are "peculiar and left out of the in-group network." A Fulbrighter to Malaysia expressed, "I always try to go for lunch with people. I hang out around the office around noon and ask people to go out. I've been to lunch with almost everybody and we've talked about people's work, Malaysian life . . everything."

Because Thailand is a place where food and relationships in the workplace are so intertwined, it serves as a good example of this phenomenon described by many professors—with varying degrees of delight and dissatisfaction. One lecturer to Thailand who observed this culinary expression suggested, "Thais speak two languages—Thai and food—and I don't speak either one very well!" Visiting professors to Thailand observed that most university events involve eating, and much business is done over one of many "snacks" during the day. It was recommended by one visiting professor that any serious scholar to Thailand should "recognize that Thais love their food and regard it as a national treasure. So learn about it, name it, and praise it!" A professor to Indonesia agreed. "Departmental business and in-service training happens over food. It is the place that a visiting professor's expertise is sought and much mutual learning happens."

Using Sports and Extracurricular Involvements. For many visiting professors, sports is the vehicle. An American literature professor to Korea remarked, "The best way to make friends here is to express your affection with food or teach them your slam-dunk." Another American professor mentioned that his relations with faculty "turned around" when he made an important realizations: "Prestige among students and faculty came from involvement in extracurricular not academic activities." With this information, he was able to reshape the way he chose to foster connections with his peers and he "played with them more often." Syracuse University professor Peter Bell recounted his basketball season in China:

> *In the beginning of the year, the faculty fielded a basketball team. So I asked if I could play. They said, 'Sure,' looking up [this professor was 6'6"]. So I wander over to this game. I hadn't played in nine years. I get there—uniforms, referees, and this great court that seemed a hundred yards long. I am 43 and they are younger, but they were very nice to me. Fortunately, my memory of my basketball skills was good, though my body's ability to connect to that memory was limited. But their skills were very rudimentary and lacking some fundamental things guys here get growing up. Plus I had six inches above anybody else. . . . And they loved it. It was a trip! Every time I did something great, like block a shot, there'd be a murmur. People flocked to see the foreigner play. My faculty won the finals and got in a tournament for the first time. It was great!*

On Saturday mornings at a Malaysian university, American professors sometimes do calisthenics with their colleagues on the playfield. "The whole of Saturday morning is a working day used for a kind of group physical fitness. There are no other classes or instructional activities. Faculty exercises, a phenomenon which has been borrowed from the Japanese, are supposed to build physical health and teamwork," explained a participating American instructor. My own experience of this team-building phenomena was in Thailand where a university aerobics dance class capitalized on my singular ability to dance to the beat of American jazz and rock music.

The amount and intensity of socializing in some university workplaces across cultures aggravate some of the more task-oriented American professors, as conveyed by one economics professor:

> *One thing that bothers me about teaching in Malaysia is the leisurely pace of activity here. A lot of time is spent talking to each other. If you don't do that you are classified as a loner, so you have to socialize. This kind of socialization takes away a lot of your time. On an average day, I would spend three hours talking with colleagues and that really cuts into productive activity. As useful as it might be, the* extent *of it is what I don't like!*

A professor of comparative politics in Turkey described a similar aggravation. "After arriving at 8:30, by the time student consultations, class, and the inevitable departmental tea were over, it was 1:00. Then a professor would invite me to one of those lengthy faculty lunches. It meant I had less than an hour of afternoon left for preparation and library research." Another professor to Pakistan regretted that he was not able to find enough time for his own personal academic work. "I suppose I could have safeguarded my time better, but the faculty was always so solicitous and the food was so delicious, it was hard to take leave."

Fostering Relations Using Patience, Sensitivity, Flexibility, and Conviviality

> *Tea first, business later. (Chinese Proverb)*

A University of California at Berkeley professor to Nepal expressed the often discovered truth in intercultural relations: "It took a long time to be accepted and trusted." *Patience*, a virtue that many visiting professors found elusive, seemed the key. Connections with colleagues in the cross-cultural setting, it is often said, require "3-P's—patience, politeness, and perseverance." The patient effort to build trust is especially necessary. Another professor to Nepal concurred, "Patience is essential when working in any type of educational or rehabilitation work involving the introduction of new ideas." Another offered:

> *Patience and flexibility go a lot further in maintaining good relationships with my Turkish hosts than my brilliant theories or my irate comparisons of our educational systems.*

One instructor commented on the need for patience at the beginning of a work effort. The Chinese proverb above suggests that you should make efforts toward building friendship first, before business can be accomplished. One Fulbright professor explained, "I found that Turkish teachers would not listen to me unless they knew and liked me personally, which meant a lot of informal conversation and joking at tea parties. Hard work is not praised here—friendship is more important and connections are essential."

One demography professor to China recounted a story illustrating what happened when he temporarily forgot this "tea first" lesson. He had earlier been a major consultant on the first computer-based empirical census effort in China in 1985. Three years later, he returned as a distinguished visiting professor with many international credentials and honors. As part of his exchange year there, he planned to examine and reanalyze some of the population data he and his colleagues had worked on. Following customary protocol, he asked his university officials to request permission for him to talk with the officials in the Census office. They did, but the demography professor was rebuffed. Frustrated, he went to the Census office himself and was again put off. He asked the young demographers there if they knew of his data set. One retorted, "We know of the data set, but we don't know you!"

Another behavior identified as essential for developing effective workplace relations was *sensitivity*. Blatchford (1983) described intercultural relations with his Chinese host as "a game of cat-and-mouse, each party trying to divine what the other really wanted or felt, with exchanges being covered with an aura of politeness." In that game, it is difficult to ascertain right actions. The best that you can expect to do is be sensitive, aware, and empathic. Recent research and practice in multicultural education in America has put forth the position that in cross-cultural situations, a group or subgroup identifies its *own* values, norms or sensibilities (Cushner, et.al, 1992). If a group perceives an action as insensitive—then it *is*, despite what tradition posits or what the dominant or majority group dictates. Some host professors we interviewed in this research offered American professors their advice on ways to show sensitivity in their university settings:

- *Know our religion, if you teach anything about the way people think or behave. (Malaysia)*
- *Understand our respect for seniority. (Thailand)*
- *When you talk to students and faculty, use clear English, thoughtfully and simply. (China)*
- *Have a sense of humor every day. (Sri Lanka)*
- *Know our system, if you want to organize anything. (China)*
- *Be patient and make us feel at ease. (Thailand)*
- *Take the time to establish relationships (Hong Kong)*
- *When you lead a discussion, we may keep quiet. Know it does not mean that we are not smart. (Thailand)*

Another attribute associated with building effective work relationships is *flexibility*. American professors advised similarly when they encouraged future academics in cross-cultural settings to be "adaptable," "changeable," and "compliant." Law professor Sharon Hom articulated this need in China:

Flexibility—that is the key. And it is more important in a multicultural worksetting. Not everyone is sharing your assumptions or your work style. Even in the States, not all your colleagues or your students will share your vision of life, your workstyle, your way of learning, or your way of teaching. But it is more obvious here, where people come from very different backgrounds and values. There is a real need to be flexible here to be effective.

A professor to Thailand described his flexible, compliant method: "I always say yes!" Another adapted the Thai way of accepting assignments or invitations. "Rather than giving an abrupt negative response when asked to do something I don't have time to complete, I shake my head yes and postpone doing it."

To illustrate the value of being adaptable, one professor in the Philippines shared the story of a research trip around Luzon he arranged with his department chairperson to document the work of Filipino village faith healers. Since he was funding the research trip, he had a tight deadline, strict interview protocols, and a limited budget. Three other professors (whom he had not invited) accompanied them on the excursion, and he was angry about their coming. The American conveyed he had learned some important lesson about "being adaptable":

These 'interlopers' kept introducing time-consuming 'detours' into my itinerary, such as stopping at cathedrals along the way for prayers and confessions. After a long day of travels and interviews, at midnight on a dark mountainous dirt road, hours from the nearest town or mechanic or electricity, the van broke down. My anger by now was barely containable. Then one of these colleagues went to gather young men from a nearby house to push the van to level ground; another pulled a flashlight out of his bag; another rebuilt the distributor there on the mountainside, and my department chair shared food from a cache of 'loaves and fishes.' Before dawn, the caravan was safely heading back to Manila."

Conviviality was one of the most functional behaviors American professors used to overcome hurdles to relationships. In contrast to professors from other Western countries, who are sometimes reported to be "mirthless and aloof," American instructors were often viewed as "friendly, likable, and energetic" and "responsive to overtures of friendship." One such amiable professor expressed,

The first thing I learned was that I needed to spend as much time listening and learning as I did trying to tell and teach . . . adjusting to people and their styles of relating . . . trying to be of help, being warm, and friendly.

Finding a "Closest Colleague"

It is commonly observed in work relations among American professors abroad that personal relationships are not numerous. As one professor described it: "My relationship with the faculty has been limited to one close colleague." This relationship should not be minimized, for instructors who develop or luck into close, personal, and satisfying work relationships report the smoothest and most favorable academic sojourns. Japanese universities have a tradition of assigning "closest colleague" status to a professor who works closely with the visiting professor. An Arizona State history professor found similar support in Indonesia:

> *The situation prevails with foreign teachers that you are unofficially assigned an Indonesian who speaks English and any problems can be explained to him and it gets worked out. But he is more than someone to complain to and work things out with. We have become very good friends— we go on trips together and to dinner frequently.*

I too had a fellow faculty member (who had studied in the United Kingdom and spoke reliable English) assigned to help me "settle in." She became my "closest colleague" when our time together was greatly increased by my suggestion that we "team-teach" a class.

The language instructors of some professors often become closest colleagues and friends. A professor in China told of her experience. "Though I've made efforts to make some friends, my concerns about not having relationships with colleagues still dominates. My closest friend is my language teacher. I really like my relationship with her. She shares much with me about her life and about China. With this relationship, I don't feel totally isolated."

CONNECTING WITH STUDENTS

> *The thing I miss the most is real involvement with students . . . with a two-hour course that meets once a week, there isn't much connection. I need some new ideas to try or I'll be disappointed and ready to get back to the U.S. classroom!*
> *(A University of Oregon professor, Norway)*

Initiating Interactions with Students

For some professors in the cross-cultural setting *greeting and addressing students* provokes initial anxiety. One teacher to China found he could "never get used to the use of surnames alone for addressing students and especially awkward when addressing women." Another reported:

> *It is really important to me to learn my students' names. I didn't know whether to try to learn their Chinese names, knowing that I would mispronounce them most of the time . . . or to assign them American names. At the suggestion of the monitor in my class, I tried to learn their names in Chinese, but it took me all semester.* Oo-ii *sounds like a song, not a name to me.*

Because of the awkwardness surrounding greetings, one professor commented, "Many students are unable to greet or take leave of me in a casual manner." One

American professor in Thailand told of her students' coming to class. "They came in staggered or late but always going through their formal bowing and *waiing* interminably." Another found the Thai greeting convention of literally "Where are you going?" particularly troublesome.

Some professors found that initial interactions were facilitated with the use of some formal structure like an *interview or personal survey*. A Fulbright professor to Ireland described such a survey. "In the beginning, in order to learn more about the general outlook of my students, I constructed and administered a short questionnaire. In addition to finding out a lot about their personal lives, I sampled their perceptions of the role of women in Irish society, which is a research interest of mine." Another to China related,

> *One of the things I did to break down barriers was to spend some time early on with my students. My first activity was to get them over to the apartment in groups of two . . . talk to them, interview them, find out about their background. My aim was to try to find things in them I could relate to in teaching the course and to find examples for teaching. I wanted to get them to be a little bit more comfortable talking to me. Force them to talk a little in English and have them realize that it was OK if they didn't speak perfectly.*

Another professor to Hong Kong planned *field trips* early in the year to "break the ice." He recalled one. "I organized a trip with one of my classes and got the department here to pay for the transportation. We danced at the hostel where we stayed the night. I danced with some of the women and taught some men to dance who had never danced before. It really broke down some barriers. All of a sudden they saw me as an individual, throwing them the Frisbee, joking—not as the distant professor asking them questions in literature but asking a lot of questions of a personal nature. It took extra time but the reward was there."

Meeting Students on Their Territory

Because of social distances between professor and student in some cultures, discussed more broadly in Chapter 1, American professors sometimes find the need to interact with students in ways not customary in American universities—e.g. meeting students on their own territory. "It is hard to get them comfortable. It always has to be on their terms," said one professor to Turkey. From Norway, a visiting professor remarked on his students' relative comfort. "Although very shy about speaking English, they miraculously overcome this reluctance when they invite me to *their* homes, or include me in *their* social gathering—it's amazing!"

Most professors reported it was much easier to develop personal relationships with students outside of class. A visiting professor to Korea advised, "The best way to get to meet and know students is to be available in the campus cafeteria." Another to Japan said she often goes to the cafeteria with students after class "because students say they want to continue the class discussion in a 'relaxed atmosphere.' " A University of Kentucky professor to Beijing similarly reported:

> *Students asked, 'Why don't you come and eat lunch?' I did and it was fun.*
> *Then they asked, 'Why don't you come one day a week?' Then they asked me*
> *twice a week . . . then every day of the week. It's fun for me, because it gives*
> *them a chance to ask me question they would feel uncomfortable asking in class*
> *or even on the break. One student asked me, 'What is a hamburger?" I was*
> *amazed. And they ask me about boy-girl relations in America . . . everything*
> *you can think of! I really wanted to give them an opportunity to have a comfort-*
> *able, talking relationship with me.*

Another instructor remarked about the atmosphere of lunch dates with his students. "At first, it was very formal, but after a week or two, I was just another person eating lunch with them. Now, if they want to ask me something or suggest I come do something, I'm there." A Syracuse University professor related a way he met students on their terms in China:

> *Students suggested that we meet where they could ask more questions. They*
> *wanted to meet in one of the dorm rooms which are very small [with four bunks*
> *to a room]. So half the class met one afternoon and the other half the next day.*
> *My teaching assistant would come to do any translation that might be neces-*
> *sary. They'd ask questions and have discussions in Chinese. I'd just sit there*
> *sipping my tea and answering questions. In winter, with wind coming off the*
> *lake, it was absolutely freezing [there was no heat in China south of the Yellow*
> *River]. I would just layer-up (four layers and my down coat) and I would sit for*
> *an hour. I would be cold, but not freezing. They like the fact that I come to see*
> *them.*

CONSIDERING GENDER AND ETHNICITY ISSUES

> *Women here wear tudung to obey Koranic command to cover their attractive*
> *hair. Male and female students are not allowed to hold hands in public. They*
> *enjoy telling vulgar stories in mixed company, but not dancing. No sex either—*
> *it might lead to dancing? (A Catholic University professor, Malaysia)*

An American literature professor upon his first encounter with fundamental Islamic students captures, in the above quandary, many professors' puzzlement about the roles of gender and ethnicity in the cross-cultural workplace.

Considering Gender Issues

Gender disparities in rank, status, and work-loads have significant influences on interactions with colleagues in cross-cultural settings. The issues of cultural views of women and differential classroom interactions have important impacts on relationships with students.

In a 1992 symposium of the Comparative and International Education Society, faculty life and work at universities in Turkey, China, Indonesia, Thailand, and Korea were examined and compared. Information on faculty women's roles in Thailand can serve as one example for illustrating the role of gender issues in relationships with colleagues. Within the Thai university setting, 49.2 percent of the professors are male and 50.8 percent are female. This near parity does not, however, statistically reflect Thai faculty women's leadership at the universities. Men hold 80 percent of the full professorships in Thai universities and women hold 20 percent. While male professors in Thailand do hold twice as many Ph.D's as women, the 400 percent rank differential is not be explained entirely by this 200 percent Ph.D. degree differential (George, 1992).

In an effort to understand the role gender plays in the university workplace in Thailand, researchers with the Women Studies Project at ChiangMai University examined achievement and career aspirations of Thai university female faculty members at three major Thai universities (Purisinsit and Pitackwong, 1986). Some of their findings reflect cultural differences between American and Thai faculty women and address issues raised by researchers from Korea, Indonesia, Japan, and China at the CIES meeting mentioned earlier. First, this team found that Thai faculty women resolutely accepted the lack of career advancement and identified personal deficiencies (e.g. lack of Ph.D, lack of enough time for work due to family duties, and personal inefficiencies) as the reason for this inequality with male faculty members. Women did not use the concept of "discrimination" to describe reasons for career lags. Secondly, the researchers found that Thai faculty women accepted the traditional social roles of Thai women in society (i.e., women as primary caretakers of family and children) as their primary responsibilities and saw their careers as important but secondary.

A third finding of the Women Studies Project was that Thai faculty women worked longer hours than their male counterparts. This theme of women as the "harder worker" or "putting in the longer hours" was often reported among both male and female American faculty abroad. For example, professors to Pakistan reported "women students worked harder and more professionally than men students."

Finally, it was reported by Purisinsit and Pitackwong that, while 48 percent of the nonPh.D faculty women indicated that holding a doctorate was important in their work, only 21 percent indicated that they plan to pursue further studies. Family obligations were seen as their major commitment by those not planning to pursue their Ph.D.. One interesting and unnoted paradox in this research is that 77.4 percent of the women interviewed who "resolutely accepted their lack of career advancement" had recently applied for rank promotion.

In my interviews with Thai faculty women, they consistently remarked in uncomplaining tones that they carried more of the faculty clerical, teaching, and extracurricular workload than their male counterparts and usually did not have responsibility for faculty leadership. Most Thai faculty women reported that they tend to nominate and select male faculty members as faculty leaders. When asked why this occurs, one Thai female professor reported, "It was expected."

One American professor remarked that he was bothered that in his department women professors "peeled the fruit and made the tea."

Gender issues, similar to those in Thailand, are felt as well in China. CUNY law professor Sharon Hom described her experience as a female law professor:

> In China, contact with the American legal world has been primarily through the individuals who have come here—for the most part male, white and older. When someone came who was not that, they were taken quite by surprise. Being a woman law professor, in the Chinese context, I'm in the minority here. . . . The female teachers say, if they go to a Chinese law firm, they are not wanted. They are told there are things they couldn't do, like attend conferences, stay outside the home overnight, or hold late business meetings. The employers say, 'We couldn't let you do that. If we hired you, we'd have to send a male lawyer to accompany you. That is why it would be inconvenient to hire you.' The women students accept this even though they are very, very competent and qualified.

A classics professor to Malawi observed some discomfort with women in authority. She related, "A student sitting dead center in the front row was clearly the self-appointed spokesman. [He] already read Latin . . . and was a good deal older than the other students...He also had an unfortunate contempt for women, which he believed he concealed beneath an unctuous politeness" (Alexander, 1991).

Richard Burg, a Fulbright professor to Pakistan and Indonesia, defined another gender issue—that of communication between faculty and students of the opposite sex. He explained, "The trouble I have had is in dealing with female students. They are very hesitant about speaking to me inside or outside of class. The male students are very friendly and you can chat on virtually any topic. I don't know of any easy way to overcome that problem. The way I've dealt with it is that my wife is very friendly with these female students and I ask her and she asks them and gives the information back to me." Additionally, professors in Indonesia, Korea and Japan commented that female students rarely speak English as fluently as male students.

American professors register some befuddlement in their relationships on faculties with unfamiliar patterns of gender relations. Women professors were not certain when and if they should travel with their male counterparts. Single professors questioned if and whom they should "date." Fulbright parents puzzled whether their American sons should court the Dean's daughters. Some professors reported that patterns of flirting, teasing, friendly touching, or other gestures of familiarity, which characterize much of the social interactions between the sexes in American universities, are often perplexing in the cross-cultural setting. One American male said that it took him a year "to recognize that students did not openly display affection [like hand-holding], but did slight, subtle touching."

American women faculty sometimes wanted the perceived situations of women in the subordinate position within universities worldwide to reform and tried to be instruments of this reformation. A female professor to New Zealand declared:

I am very aware of the gender dynamics in the classroom and among those that will become teachers themselves. I hear how they talk to each other and how I talk to them. My presence has the impact of opening [the] perceptions they've held of teachers. I want to help them see that definitions of who they are were socially constructed, which means they can be changed, if they are not happy with them! They can stop being an object, a goose that is being stuffed with education and everything else, and become persons who take some charge of their own lives.

Whether or not you share this visiting professor's sense of mission, research and observation across cultures indicate that males and females still have significantly different university experiences which emerge from differential teacher-student interactions, expectations, and curricula and from unexamined gender bias in the university workplace. Some guidelines for Avoiding Gender Bias in the Classroom are provided in Figure 6-2.

CONSIDERING ISSUES OF ETHNICITY

Ethnic diversity in an already foreign cross-cultural context adds another layer of complexity. While many classrooms in cross-cultural settings are less diverse than the American classrooms you leave behind, some are more diverse. One American Studies professor based in Jerusalem expected students to be "older than American students," but did not expect the " huge variety of different ethnic and linguistic backgrounds [e.g., Greek, Rumanian, British, South African, Argentinean, Australian, as well as Israeli] all in one classroom."

One of the major considerations in this discussion of ethnicity is the *debate on the language of instruction.* One professor to the Philippines observed the difficulties the large minority populations were experiencing with the nationalizing trend toward teaching all university classes in tagalog, the language of the capital and the major island of Luzon. "Students from the Vasaias [central Philippines] fared better at university when English, the *lingua franca,* was the mode of instruction," he asserted. Similarly, another professor in Turkey worried that "the reintroduction of Turkish as the instructional language limited access to the nonethnic Turks and minority students" he had in his classes. Of course, with the disassembling of the former Soviet Union, the reversion of Hong Kong to the PRC, and vast independence movements world-wide, this discussion of national and instructional languages and access of education to majority and minority groups will be an increasingly interesting and relevant one.

Another consideration of ethnicity in the cross-cultural setting is the observation of *discrimination on the part of the hosts toward minorities*—ethnic Tibetan students in Beijing, ethnic Chinese and Indian students in Malaysia, Cebuano students on Luzon in the Philippines, any nonJavanese in Indonesia, hilltribe students in Buddhist Thailand . . . the list goes on and on. Beyond the social and economic justice issues of this discrimination, which are major themes of academic

1. **Check that teaching materials and texts present an honest view of options open to both males and females.**

   - See if both males and females are portrayed in traditional and nontraditional roles at work, leisure, and home.
   - Discuss with students traditional/nontraditional roles in the host country and have them report sex-role biases in the teaching material.

2. **Watch for unintended biases in your own classroom practice.**

   - Do you group student by gender for certain activities? Is this grouping appropriate?
   - Do you call on one gender more often or for certain answers?
   - Do you meet with students of one gender more often outside of class?

3. **Use gender-free language.**

   - Have you updated your English vocabulary to gender-free terms (e.g., "law-enforcement officer" for "policeman," "chairperson" for "chairman," etc.)?
   - Do you balance class illustrations, examples, and test questions with male and female referents?

FIGURE 6-2   Guidelines: Monitoring Gender Issues and Sexism in Teaching Across Cultures

Source: Adapted from Anita E. Woolfolk, *Educational Psychology,* 5th edition. Copyright © 1993 by Alln and Bacon. Used with permission.

discourse in our own culture and country, this issue of ethnicity has an impact on alliances and relationship in the university workplace. Some professors reported that minority students sought *their* support and alliance in the "chilly climates toward them at the majority universities." One instructor sympathized, "We are, after all, also alien, outsider, other!"

Yet another element of diversity, unplanned for by the professors who encountered it, was the *presence of foreign exchange students* in their classroom—students from still other cultures. A visiting professor in Israel reported he "did not anticipate the large number of American students taking their junior year abroad here who threatened to dominate class discussions." A director for a consortium of Midwestern university students studying in Thailand recalled a "persistent problem in class was these American exchange students, their separatism, and the resentment toward them." Another visiting professor to Portugal lamented the "relative immaturity of the American [exchange] students, who had a more casual attitude toward their educational goals [than their Portuguese counterparts]." "Classroom Culture Shock" was coined by a professor to Israel trying to explain his "extreme embarrassment at the disruptive behaviors of American exchange students" in his Israeli classroom.

Revisiting Historical Relationships

A brief discussion should be made here about the experiences of exchange professors who visit or return to ancestral homelands. For example, a second-generation Chinese-American professor returned to the homeland of her parents in China; Indo-Americans returned to India, Malaysia, and South African birthplaces; Jewish Americans fulfilled dreams of parents and grandparents to work in Israel; and African-Americans traced their family roots back to Ghana and Liberia.

On these academic sojourns, a mixture of embrace and discomfort was often reported. One Fulbright professor returning to Hungary puzzled, "This has been a difficult assignment, even though I have a decent knowledge of Hungarian, was born in Prague, and spent my youth here. Why is this the case?" One Chinese-American instructor to China reported a disturbing incident where she was refused, without cause or explanation, admission to a store that sold Western food in Beijing. Another Chinese-American Fulbrighter to Taiwan explained, with discouragement, that his contributions were not as highly valued as other Western experts' and rationalized that "prophets are never honored in their homeland." An Indo-American economist reported Malaysian officials' suspicion of his legitimate research interests in the economic progress under the National Economic Plan (a program aimed at redistributing and equalizing wealth between Chinese, Indian, and ethnic Malays). An African-American colleague reported her work in West Africa as "triumphant" and "unfortunate"—the first time she had ever felt in the majority and the first time she realized that "culture was more influential than race."

Another African-American professor told of his "long-awaited-and-dreamed-of year" on an academic exchange to Africa:

> *Upon my arrival at my Nigerian host university, all my preconceived notions of what I would be doing at this fledgling institution had to be carefully re-evaluated. There were a so many questions regarding the operation of the program (e.g. faculty, courses, and materials—just to mention a few) and so many disagreements that needed resolution (e.g. policies and resource allocations—just to mention a few) . . I found in myself prejudices and biases toward Africans I never imagined I had.*

ANTICIPATING POTENTIAL CONFLICTS

Don't sweat the small stuff! (*A University of Tennessee professor, Thailand*)

Every scholar involved in an academic exchange experiences some conflict with the host institution, the students, government officials (customs, postal, research, housing, etc.) or colleagues. Each country and culture presents its own peculiar reasons for these conflicts and particular resolutions of them. It is beyond the scope of this text to present the myriad discomforts, altercations, resentments, confabs, and irritations reported by all the professors whose work we examined. There are, however, some consistent and common sources of conflicts in almost all the exchanges which we did uncover and report here: inscrutable schedules, erratic attendance, cryptic feedback, unpredictable notice, and perplexing procedures.

Inscrutable Schedules

Among the consistently reported exasperations: deciphering enigmatic university calendars and baffling course, exam or curricula schedules with unfixed starting dates; invisible holidays; flexible ending dates; and last-minute alterations.

Spontaneous or unscheduled holidays were cited as a major cause of lost class time. Visiting professors to Brazil lost Thursdays and Fridays to holidays "it seemed every other week." A professor in Chile maintained she "lost nearly one-fourth of all my teaching time due to spontaneous holidays." "Some were even last minute events, unscheduled, nontransferable days," complained another professor. "In Mexico," said another, "there is a student custom of stretching holidays by taking extras days off before and after the official holiday." Another added, "These *puentes* [extra days] can add up and have a limiting effect on what can be covered in a semester." A professor to Pakistan said, "I lost five lectures because of a holiday which appeared at the last moment." "The academic calendar, if there is one, is a mess! There were 165 holidays last year in Nepal," a disgruntled academic observed. Chinese New Year celebrated throughout East and Southeast Asia is an "impenetrable calendar of events aimed to keep my students away from campus for as long as possible!" argued a professor to Asia.

Undeclared semester beginnings and endings were identified as major schedule conflicts. One Mexican professor commented that, unknown to him, "Classes started one month before I arrived." "The academic calendar is not very fixed. Heck, it's not fixed at all!" described a visiting professor to Pakistan. "Spring vacation wasn't set until a few days before; the end of school was extended an extra week; and the beginning of the term in October didn't start until November," offered another. "No one knows in Hungary in mid-December exactly when the next semester will begin.... Planning seems to be done as they go along," griped a Fulbrighter. Another to Portugal described a similar irritation. "It's an irrational system of not requiring all classes for a semester to commence on a common date!"

Professors on exchanges to Southeast Asian countries often cut their own semesters short, then rush furiously to begin semesters in Thailand, Indonesia, the Philippines, and Malaysia which "amble lumberingly" and often do not begin until weeks later than the posted starting dates. One instructor complained, "I nearly killed me and my family trying to get in my grades, to ready my house, to prepare my teaching materials, to handle the 4,000 things that have to be done to be away for a year .. all to begin my classes in Thailand ... and we didn't gear up for weeks."

Professors to Eastern Europe during this time of great transition reported *unfathomable class schedules*. One professor of linguistics to Czechoslovakia said, "There does not appear to be an actual schedule of classes, only a temporary one at the beginning of the term. This means each instructor has to meet students and then negotiate the actual schedule—days, times, and then find a classroom. Due to conflicts, faculty signing up for more than one room, students refusing to attend classes late in the day or on Mondays or Fridays, classes got started a month late."

Schedules are often affected by *political events and disruptions*. A University of Idaho law professor was dismayed that the law program at his university in Nepal was ". . . closed much of the time due to upcoming elections." Another English professor reported, "Political unrest sometimes prevented my students from traveling to class." A chemistry professor to Pakistan said "Over two months of instruction time was lost due to suspension of classes during elections."

Complaints about the irregularity of the university calendar and schedules ranged from mild frustration to militant anger. An Iowa State professor in Nepal expressed, "At times I felt frustrated, even furious, because of enforced inactivity—holiday breaks, political strikes, etc." Another professor to Czechoslovakia, whose classes ended abruptly on April 1 (though the university calendar published June 15 as the closing day), felt so strongly about these irregularities that he tried to rewrite his contract requiring his classes to meet the full term or he would resign. An epidemiology professor to Nepal offered his solution for schedule conflicts:

> *I learned a great deal of tolerance. I learned to have my time schedule flexible enough to accept delay as part of my original plan. I learned to start each class with a simple approach that could lead to an accomplishment within that class-time . . . with no holdover or continued assignments.*

Erratic Attendance

Students' lack of attendance was a constant complaint from professors all over Eastern Europe. Business instructor Tone Carlen said, "Czech students' not attending classes [with no punitive consequences] was a real problem. They sign up, then not show, then sign up for exams, then beg to pass [because a low mark is a coffin nail]." A Fulbrighter to Hungary asserted, "Nowhere do students and teachers attend class as regularly as they do in the U.S. . . . they definitely don't here!"

Attendance is "highly fluid" in a Nepalese university, one professor stated. "We held classes on Mondays and Fridays for whomever wanted and was able to come." An academic in Pakistan criticized his class. "Of the fifty students on the role, only ten were regulars, and then only two or three students did the assigned work outside of class." A University of California at Santa Barbara professor to Israel was vexed by how few classes she actually was able to hold ". . . because of once-a-week meetings of grad classes and the many holidays, students were seldom present. On top of that, attendance was not required." From Norway, another instructor resented that he had "to repeat constantly for the benefit of students who had not attended previous lectures." Another from Ireland added, "I was shocked by 150 students signed up in each class. Students showed up in small numbers at the beginning [about one-third], but after a few weeks the attendance rose. However, cutting was common." A Fulbrighter to Poland concurred, "About 30 students are listed in my official role book, but about half attend regularly."

Many reasons were offered for erratic student attendance. "With no clear admission or placement requirements, no real control of the numbers of students enrolled in a program, and huge classes of students with a wide range of proficiency in English—how could I have expected it to be otherwise?" rationalized a professor to Yugoslavia. Another reason for erratic attendance in Japan, American professors complained, is that "students take up to eighteen courses—a ridiculous overload and extremely conducive to shallowness and absenteeism." Annoyed by the disruption absenteeism caused his course plans, an archeology professor griped, "Attendance is very irregular in Israel—first, male students invariably get called back into the army for a few weeks during the semester; second, the rules here permit students to take two courses in same time block [of course ensuring they will miss classes in each]."

As is said, sometimes the problem is its own solution. One Fulbrighter to Japan contended, "In the beginning classes are large, but nonserious students drop out like flies. Some courses taught in English have one or two students left per class after mid-year! . . . The workload becomes easier and easier!" Offering another solution, one teacher argued, "Pakistani profs will often repeat lectures when one half of the students appear one day and the other half the next . . . I was pleased to discover by not doing so, my classes had better attendance."

Cryptic Feedback

> *My dean arrived at my apartment around noon. I asked him if he would eat lunch with me and my family. He said, 'Thank you.' Because he was the Dean, I cooked this and opened that and put on a spread. But when I served the lunch, he did not eat. So I asked him again. And he said, 'Thank you.' (A contract professor of TEFL, China)*

From colleagues, students and authorities in cross-cultural situations, *feedback is sometimes given in unfamiliar ways* to American professors. "I was determined to give a high quality class the fall semester on 'The U.S. Confronts Revolution in Latin America,' " a professor in Mexico explained. "I think I did give a good class, but the students were not all that happy with me. But I never found this out or how to deal with it until the end of my time there." Another professor from Old Dominion University related:

> *Students in Pakistan are extremely skilled at talking faculty into reducing course requirements. If they are not successful, they drop the course, replace it with one which is less demanding, or wage some 'go-between business' behind the professor's back. I stuck to my guns and kept my standard high. But as such, my initial enrollment of fifteen students became six by the end of the semester.*

A lecturer in women studies to New Zealand recounted an example of *conflicting feedback.* She had been encouraged by the interest of New Zealand faculty and students in her areas of research interest: women and aging, women and madness, bisexuality, African-American drama, lesbian women in U.S. history and culture—all topics of cultural conflicts. However, one day at her university-wide lecture on "Women of Color in American Society," she encountered a small but vocal demonstration and disruption. The demonstrators took offense that a white lecturer was talking on women of color. They argued (yelled) that it was politically incorrect. She said, "My rather innocent and inconsequential lecture on Audre Lorde's autobiography, *Zami*, fell into this bubbling cauldron and left me a bit battered, but also reflective."

In some cross-cultural situations, *feedback may be surreptitious.* Professors sometimes report that there was (or they suspect there was) a class "monitor," "reporter," "plant," or "spy" in their classes whose responsibility (by official or informal assignment) was to report to the university administration or political entities the content and processes of the classroom. Caroline Alexander, a visiting professor to Malawi (1991) said:

> *Somewhere among this engaging group and their classmates was almost certainly a government spy. It was generally accepted by the university community that a least one 'plant' was present in every class, and that anything remotely suspicious on the part of the lecturer or the students would be reported. About halfway through my stay at the university, I returned to my office early one day to discover a strange man, implausibly dressed in a raincoat, leafing nonchalantly through my papers. When I asked him what he was doing, he smiled, turned up the collar of his coat, and calmly let himself out the door.*

Sometimes cryptic feedback came in the form of *anti-U.S. sentiment.* One political science professor to New Zealand warned, "Visiting scholars from the U.S. should not be surprised to encounter anti-U.S. attitudes. Ironically and inevitably the radical left-wing political fringe groups, with whom I have always sought to associate, were the ones most likely to be hostile to American experts."

Another source of confusing feedback from students comes in a more positive package—*gifts.* In many cross-cultural situations, especially in the Asian countries we observed, giving gifts to professors is common. The gifts mentioned included everything from food items and small crafts made in hometowns and family kitchens to expensive watches, clothing, and electronic equipment. Some American professors reported the troublesome situations of gift-giving around the time of assignment of grades and other student evaluations. But one

Fulbright professor to Malaysia defended this custom and explained his experience:

> *One way students here say thank-you or reciprocate is to bring gifts for the professor. In some instances this would be considered as bribes or a form of corruption, but not so here. The gifts are rather small but symbolic and show their appreciation and praise for your teaching.*

Unpredictable Notice

Another complaint that sometimes precipitates conflict for American professors abroad is the unpredictability or lack of any advance notice of important events, meetings, holidays, visitors, schedule changes, examinations, or conferences. One TESL professor to Turkey conveyed, "There is no attempt to post important messages for the faculty. Rather, people seem to rely on verbal communication. Because I don't speak Turkish very well, this has resulted in my frequently missing meetings or other important events." Another remarked from Poland, "I have problems with no one bothering to communicate important information to me, mostly, I think, because they forget that I do not know the system here. For example, my schedule was changed twice without telling me. The result was that I missed two weeks of classes for one course."

International relations professor Al Bailey agreed. "It is not one of the strong points of the Chinese university of giving advance notice for events or sufficient notice to plan things either academic or social. That practice causes a great deal of difficulty for many Westerners here. Putting up notices, perhaps a day or an hour in advance of an event, causes quite a hassle."

Perplexing Procedures

A final source of job and interpersonal conflict for American professor abroad was "puzzling," "confusing," "bewildering," and "perplexing" procedures for managing daily university life. "I needed a coach to help me figure out how to get things done at my Irish university!" declared one Fulbrighter to Galway.

CUNY law professor Sidney Harring, trying to do some legal research in Malaysia, explained how he butted up against perplexing procedures:

> *I went to the National Archives, they wouldn't let me in because I'm classified as a 'lecturer' not a 'researcher.' Then, I went to the Prime Minister's office for Economic and Political Research and was told I needed a permit for which I should have applied for before I came. I said, 'I didn't know that; no one ever told me that.' Now, I've applied for a research permit, but it could take months.*

Another academic wanting to pursue her research interests while teaching in Mexico was also frustrated. "I was unprepared for the extreme centralization of everything in Mexico and the belief that nothing important happens outside of Mexico City—and *my* university is, of course, outside the city. Misunderstanding this was the contributing factor in my failure to gain access to the officials and data I needed," she complained.

A Fulbright professor hoping to do research in Turkey encountered all manner of perplexing procedures . . . "being informed that documents were unavailable due to rebinding [when the same documents were made available to Turkish scholars] . . . being informed that documents I had ordered to see were not germane to my research topic . . . finding out documents we consider historical [e.g., prior to 1918], they don't consider historical and are not classified as such." Obviously, a researcher needs, as one said, "a third eye and a great deal of patience."

To ameliorate the sense of utter frustration in the face of perplexing procedures in the academic environment, Lehigh professor Peter Beidler advised reframing the question:

> *There are lots of difficulties in getting along in China. Somehow everything I do here has to involve my Waiban [foreign affairs office]—even totally academic things! There is lots of bureaucracy I had to learn to deal with and, in doing so, I learned a lot about China and a lot about myself. When something that seemed stupid, strange or difficult happens, instead of saying it is really stupid, strange or difficult, I try to ask* why—*Why did it happen? Once I started asking why and finding out the* real *reasons, things here began to make sense.*

Another teacher concurred with Beidler and told of a class trip where two (uninvited) people from her department came along. Because one of them was a secretary, the teacher thought surely this person was "a plant to check if we do anything unpleasant or anything that smacks of unusual freedom." But, upon investigation, the reason this secretary had been invited was, as she told it, "to take care of the Fulbright professor, the older foreign guest. If she was hurt while hiking up the mountain I would need to find her a hospital." Another professor, familiar with bewildering bureaucracy, kept this sense of perspective in Malaysia:

> *They tell you there is a government bureaucracy, but I work in New York. I can't call the New York Office of the EPA and get anybody to do anything for me! You get layers and layers of people who are overworked. . . . Malaysia, like any other country, has this bureaucracy. It means you have to keep calling and finding the right person. By and large things open up to you!*

Not knowing where to start was the common complaint. For example, as one professor stated, "At my university, my major problem is finding out who is in charge of what and where they are." A professor from Mexico said, "It took me a long time to really understand how the program and the university work— which affected my teaching." Another woman declared, "I'd like to have been able to 'get in' more easily. To say that this assignment requires self-sufficiency and assertiveness is an understatement."

American professors interviewed suggested two ways to learn the procedures for managing university worklife smoothly when you first get in country:

1. A *Campus Tour*. It was suggested that you "request it as part of your first week on the job."
2. A *"Routine Jobs" Tour*. Some professors advised, "Have your hosts take you around to all the service areas for you to record the steps for making phone calls, getting copies, borrowing audio-visual equipment, requesting library materials, applying for permits, etc."

Concept Map

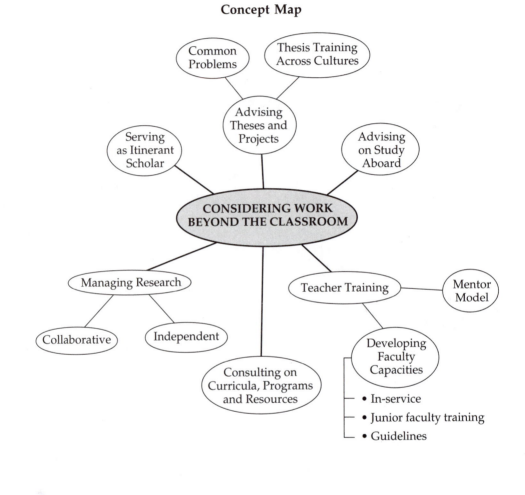

7

CONSIDERING WORK
BEYOND THE CLASSROOM

My work here is much bigger than my job.
—A UNIVERSITY OF HAWAII PROFESSOR, MALAYSIA

Just as an American professorship includes work assignments beyond teaching regular classes, teaching in the cross-cultural setting may include work beyond teaching and even work beyond the university job itself. Figure 7-l provides an overview of the expansiveness of the roles of many American scholars abroad. A few of the most common roles beyond classroom teaching will be examined here.

ADVISING STUDENT THESES AND PROJECTS

Often, visiting professors are requested to serve as theses, dissertation, or project directors for graduate students. Theses supervision is by far the most common request. This supervision task may be a much larger work assignment than when working with U.S. students. Theses in countries where the masters degree is the usual terminal degree (often leading to the profession of college or university teaching) may be given more emphasis than in the United States. In these instances, a year or more of a graduate program may be given solely to thesis preparation. A Fulbright professor to Ireland, who found the extra work rewarding, stated, "While directing student research was extremely time consuming, that was the very best and most rewarding form of teaching, and was what I came over for. The interaction with the graduate students enriched the year."

Identifying Common Problems with Advisement

It is often reported by teachers in an intercultural setting that there is considerably *more student anxiety surrounding thesis proposals, research and projects* than is

University Teaching	Work Beyond Teaching
• Teaching regular classes • Teaching graduate seminars • Instructing in English • Supervising student projects and theses • Modeling instructional strategies • Serving as an itinerant scholar or instructor	• Training faculty • Developing resources, programs & curricula • Advising on study abroad • Managing research • Lecturing on tour • Building institutional linkages • Serving as "cultural ambassador"

FIGURE 7-1   Work Roles Beyond the Classroom of American Professors Abroad

typical in the United States. Writing in English or under the scrutiny of a foreign professor may provoke this anxiety. One professor explained his experience:

> *Ours is the onerous task of encouraging students to do what is particularly difficult and unfamiliar to them, at the same time we are evaluating the product. Students are very sensitive to any criticism—so the work goes very slowly.*

A professor to Pakistan warned, "One consideration for thesis advisement is whether I will be here long enough to supervise the entire project. Students worry they will not finish within my year. If they can, I work with them; otherwise I avoid working with them."

The thesis period is a time when students, who may prefer to work together, must work alone, autonomously, and under duress. Students who do not like to impose on professors must now request meetings and assistance. Students who have been lectured to for years must now answer the questions and even initiate them. In this situation of heightened anxiety, students need more initial support and direction, but they may be more reluctant to ask than American students (who may feel that they have rights to them). In Poland a Fulbright professor found, "Polish students lack experience in writing literary and research papers. Their theses must be at least sixty pages long, exclusive of bibliographies, and they have many difficulties in organizing large amounts of material." Anxiety is understandable.

The second problem area with thesis advisement is that *research expectations differ dramatically across cultures.* Research questions are often unworkable. The topics that students submit are often those that would "take five years and five million dollars to investigate," observed a professor of research methods. Another Western professor in Thailand reported, "Students' topics are rarely hewed down to small, workable theses questions." Two of his examples of student proposals illustrating this broadness were: "An Evaluation of Educational Radio in

Asian Countries" and "Attitudes, Community Values, and Aspirations of Hill-Tribe Communities in Thailand" (where he added, "There are thousands of tribal communities and presumably no small number of attitudes"). Because faculty research in many locations consists primarily of "consultancy reports" for hire by government agencies, students may model their large, sweeping, policy-oriented, uncontrolled form. The enormity of the proposed research questions were often way beyond the scope of the students' resources.

A converse problem of expectations existed for some professors who reported that *many student projects were replications of previous studies.* One complained, "They are often done the semester before by another student or by their advisor with only slight variations in the variables. University of Minnesota ecologist Edward Cushing reflected on these differences in research expectations between his and his Indonesian colleagues':

> *The important thing about science is not what you know about nature, but how you use what you know about nature to find out more; research is finding new things. The students and their advisors typically take a technique published in a book by other scientists and apply it to a new setting or organism—which is applied science. But they do not think in terms of finding new techniques that are not in the textbook. That's what's foreign about science . . something most difficult to teach.*

Additionally, proposed studies were sometimes entirely descriptive in nature with little empirical substance. A sociologist to China had difficulties expanding research explanations beyond rhetoric:

> *The hardest concepts for me to get across were experimental and quasi-experimental designs incorporating random sampling and comparison groups, without which nothing beyond description can be done. As for modes of explanation, it took me some time to banish the phrase 'it is because of our feudal past' as the typical social science explanation.*

A final problem area for thesis advisement, which makes it more difficult in the cross-cultural settings than at home universities, is the *limitations of library resources.* The problems mentioned in terms of student anxiety and inappropriate questions are sometimes directly related to the availability of research materials. For example, a Brigham Young professor to Mexico remarked, "Library facilities were minimal in comparison with most universities in the U.S. and were inadequate for much of the research students needed to conduct for their theses. [Therefore], I encouraged students to choose thesis research topics involving observational or survey research in a Mexican context." Another instructor to the Philippines concurred. "Library acquisitions are very limited so my plans to require more literature review had to be limited." The section in Chapter 4 on Working in Environments Where Resources are Limited expands on the issue.

Providing Thesis Training in the Cross-Cultural Context

Some professors found it necessary to train students (and even receptive faculties) in research methodologies before they could pursue thesis advisement. In New Zealand, an American studies professor argued that limited experience with research methods and practice inhibited thesis preparation and claimed, "Students had little or no instruction in research methods and techniques of documentation—I concluded they most would benefit from some formal instruction in research methods." An American history professor to Indonesia was another who found sufficient deficits among his advisees that he had to formulate a robust seminar in methodologies. But he still was unprepared for how far back he had to start:

> *In a seminar on writing theses, I explained what we might be doing in the class and I gave a handout of an exercise to begin with. One student clearly understood what I was going after; the other six just wanted to ask what they would be writing their thesis on. I realized I was way too far ahead when I thought we would be going over the elements of developing a thesis and hypothesis testing...I wasn't prepared for that.*

Another professor in biological sciences to Norway found that, instead of working with individual doctoral students, spending time helping faculty understand various research methodologies they might use with their graduate students was more useful. He observed a formulaic version of research going on which describes the experience of many other American professors abroad:

> *Research to many of the faculty is something you do by formula: Pick a topic titled 'The effect of _____ on _____,' collect some data, apply some cookbook statistics, and there you are! Don't bother too much about whether others have done similar work already, and don't worry about trying to understand underlying processes or to generalize the results to other organisms or situation.*

Similarly, an American botanist in Indonesia bemoaned the student research he described. "The students wrote research proposals for the course that were to be their own thesis research. Despite my pleading and exhortations, nine of the ten proposals indeed had a formula title, such as 'The Effect of Soil Moisture on Bean Yield' [with anticipated result of 'too little or too much moisture is bad']." Another professor to Indonesia reported that one of his graduate students was writing his thesis on the environmental effects of PCB and was pursuing some creative avenues of work. "But," relayed this professor, "this student confided that he was writing two versions of his proposal: one for me and another for his faculty advisor, who wouldn't understand the deviations from the formula." The title of the other advisor's version was "The Effect of PCBs on Trout Reproduction in Farm Ponds" and it followed the typical formula.

ADVISING STUDENTS ON STUDY ABROAD

One of the common "informal" advisement tasks of visiting professors from the West is helping students seeking educational opportunities at American, Canadian and European universities. A list of resources for this advisement activity is found in appendix C—Resources for Advising Foreign Students Informally on Study Abroad in the U.S.A.

On his informal advisement role, a University of Montana professor, assigned to Hungary, reported:

> *As things in Eastern Europe thaw daily, there is considerable interest in professional and graduate study in the U.S. . . . Students need to be advised about what universities might be best for them, what their endorsers ought to say in their letters of recommendation, what exams they will have to take (e.g. GRE, TOEFL, etc.), where to look for financial aid and the imminence of deadlines.*

Tone Carlen, a professor to Czechoslovakia, held, "Students' expectations about study in the West are very unrealistic. They are especially naïve about competition and costs."

Vincent Linares, a two-time Fulbrighter to Srî Lanka and Malaysia, said of his advisement abroad, "On this campus, I initially assisted about twenty students who approached me seeking help with applications to American universities. I acted as an advisor to help them out. The thing I have done the most is connecting them with the U.S. Embassy and United States Information Service (USIS) for resources on study in America. I had so many requests that I offered a two-day workshop and set up sort of an 'advisory service' for any students who wanted to come in. I found it most helpful to gear my advising to what American professors expect of students." Richard Burg, an American History professor, remarked of his study-abroad advisement work in Indonesia:

> *I spend a good deal of time doing things that most Americans think very basic like teaching them how to write a letter of application to a university explaining what they are interested in studying . . . how to address a letter . . . what a Zip Code is . . . how to find out the address of a university in America . . . how you find out what programs a given university has . . . how much travel costs and how to figure the costs of going to a university where it snows [they'll need warm clothes].*

TRAINING STUDENTS FOR TEACHING

Many of my students will themselves be teachers in the not-too-distant future. I hope when they reflect on the different experiences they've had with teachers in the classroom they'll remember this American Fulbright professor who talked about teaching in a different way. (A Lehigh professor of literature)

In many countries, especially in the Third World, graduate student training is often teacher-training for post-secondary institutions. For most American professors in the United States who prepare, for example, biologist or lawyers, the training of teachers is "not in the bargain." In the cross-cultural setting, the situation is quite different. Professor Peter Beidler described his revelation about teacher training in China:

When I first came here I was thinking of my job as a teacher of American literature—to tell my students about Hawthorne, Faulkner, Hemingway, little bit of Melville. It gradually became clear to me that I had a wider responsibility to them than that. They were to become teachers, *but they were not at all convinced that they wanted to be the teacher they were almost destined to become. Suddenly it came to me that I had to do work in pedagogy, in the experience of teaching. In a sense, I turned my courses into a scientific laboratory in the technique of teaching.*

Another Fulbright professor to Thailand realized that his graduate classes in American Literature were made up entirely of instructors from the teacher-training colleges. While he had never had any pedagogical training himself, he found he was training teachers and even teachers of teachers. A public health professor to Brazil concurred. "Because my graduate students were all prospective teachers, I also used the class methods and processes as a way to do teacher training. I think they will undoubtedly implement some of the innovative things I taught them."

Some of the professors who realized this extra responsibility of teacher preparation examined more carefully the ways teachers were trained in their host countries. Often to the minds of these American professors, the training contained minimal uses of progressive pedagogy. A University of North Florida professor described the Chinese matriculation process which trained China's new professors and teachers in higher education:

I have sat on five different M.A. oral examining committees here in China. It has occurred to me that these students have had six years of university education. They have spent these six years mostly in silence. Now to get their Masters' degrees they are being asked to talk. These young adults 23–25 years old are coming into the examination room quaking. They are terrified, because now they have to speak to win the right to write their thesis to get their M.A.

degree to become a teacher. If they are successful, they get to lapse back into silence for one more year. Then suddenly they are the teacher who goes into that classroom full of silence that they have to fill up with their own words. Suddenly they are the 'paid talker.' What I want to know is how do you get from absolute   silence   to   total   speech?

A Fulbright professor to Nepal, mindful of supporting the future teaching roles of the students he was preparing, suggested bringing "a few handbooks on teaching techniques for teacher training." But he warned the techniques will have to be "low-tech and transferrable to large classrooms of between 60–120 students." Another visiting professor to Turkey advised a "utilitarian view of your own teaching methods." For students who would be teachers, he protested, "They were already overburdened with twenty-five or more class hours a week, had little interest in modeling my new ideas, or in learning them, if I didn't make them practical and applicable to their less-than-optimal teaching situations."

Using the Mentor Model

The reward of being a good teacher is that once or twice a year, if you're lucky, you get to turn a life around. (A Lehigh University professor, China)

One of the ways some of the American professors abroad serve in the unexpected role of teacher-trainer is to serve as a mentor for a few graduate students who will become teachers. Two exceptional Fulbright professors, whose cross-cultural work my colleagues and I have had the opportunity to film during the last few years, chose the mentor model for training young teachers. One of these was Peter Beidler, a literature professor from Lehigh University who has received national awards for distinguished college teaching. Beidler described his training of a group of English majors at Szechuan University in western China to become university teachers:

Almost all my students are post-graduates and here it means they will get their master's degree and go on to become teachers. For at least two women and three men I have become a mentor for them in their teaching. They have told me they will never teach again in the same way as in the past. They may not teach the way I teach, but now they have alternatives to the way they teach here in China.

He described his teacher-training approach, "I would use a method to teach a story or a passage and then I would ask, 'Why did I just do that?' Or I would use the discussion method or Socratic questioning technique, so they could have a sense of being on the receiving end. Then I would ask, 'How does it feel having a teacher force you to speak? What happens when a teacher waits until he gets a response from you?'" With his approach Beidler wanted his future teachers to focus on the teaching/learning process. And "I wanted them to know how much fun teaching really is!" he added.

The second professor who took on teacher training as a primary role was CUNY law professor Sharon Hom, who spent one year in China teaching law and then a second year training young law teachers. She remembered how she became aware of the need for teacher training among her Chinese law faculty. "I talked a lot to my colleagues and my students—not how would you train, but how were you trained? They said, `Not at all!' So I asked, `You graduated, then you started teaching?' They said, 'Yes!' " She was aware of the limited repertoire of teaching strategies her colleagues had to use to make their legal teaching memorable and meaningful and she sought a way to expand their teaching options. She explained:

> *I really wanted an opportunity to develop ways which we could train young teachers in explicitly developed teaching methods. I wanted to do teacher training—training young law teachers. It was a concept that I think the Chinese didn't understand. So they said, 'Oh, great, you can give lectures to the young teachers.' In their head, substitute "young teachers" for "graduate students." But my assignment is shaping up to be what I really wanted to do, i.e., develop a program with young teachers and somehow leave something behind of that approach, so other people can build on it.*

She created a resource manual from the training experiences with Chinese teachers "so other people can see that's what we tried and that's what happened." In doing so she developed China's first text for the teaching of law (Hom, 1991).

Hom developed her training methods by experimenting with training five young law teachers per semester. She selected teachers who had her content course the semester before and used them as the "teachers" in the same course the second semester. She met with them each week to cover the processes of legal teaching and general pedagogical practices where they covered everything from discussion techniques to objective test preparation. From my observations and filming of Hom's classes, featured in the documentary, "Teaching the Chinese Student" (George and Ward, 1989), I observed that the method produced inordinately well-prepared teachers skilled in a variety of teaching strategies. But the preparation was not without challenge:

> *Initially, the students perceived the young teachers not as the experts or voice of authority. If a young teacher asked a question, students kept looking at me hoping that I would answer the question. And the young teachers were quite uncomfortable at first with the structure of the room. We had set up five small work groups where students suddenly were face-to-face with a classmate! For young teachers who had little experience with group processes, it was a stretch!*

Hom reported she knew she had been successful when she heard young teachers saying to students, "What do you think?" and "Do you agree with that?" She added, "They were trying to be inclusive of everyone in the group. . . . We talked about that and I consciously tried to model it."

A Fulbright professor to Mexico also followed the mentor model to train young teachers. He explained, "I taught six graduate students in a seminar in international economics and they, in turn, taught undergrads the same subject matter under my supervision. It served to fulfill both of my personal goals—to do good undergraduate teaching and to train graduate students who would become teachers." A professor in Ireland described his mentoring of future teachers: "I worked with a group of graduate student 'demonstrators' who would eventually become university or college instructors. My goal was to help them develop materials and pedagogical strategies for their own teaching."

American literature professor Bill Slaughter held similar goals, but was discouraged by students' limited exposure to alternative or more participatory teaching strategies. "So students know what you're talking about when you try to explain American teaching styles, strategies, and techniques to them," he advised, "show them models." He suggested:

> *If I had known and fully accepted that I was going to be training teachers, what I would have done is videotaped myself in my own classes in the States and shown Chinese students what an American class is like. Chinese students don't get to see their American counterparts. They get to see me—an American professor conducting himself much as he would in a classroom in America. But it is not at all the same experience, because they don't get to see or understand the student role, e.g., in the discussion method.*

Developing Faculty Capacities

> *I became a one-man demonstration project of American academic procedures.*
> *(A Villanova professor, Poland)*

Another way American professors abroad participate in the training of teachers is through developing the capacities of host faculty and staff. In the situations studied, this training was accomplished through in-service training workshops or seminars and "shoulder-to-shoulder teaching" with junior faculty members. Some visiting professors expected or were requested before they arrived at their host country to do staff development work , but some gravitated to it when language barriers or circumstances prohibited them from the direct classroom teaching they had originally planned for.

In-Service Workshops and Seminars.   Coe College English professor Robert Drexler expected to do faculty development activities as part of his Fulbright assignment in Thailand. "I run two seminars for the faculty. One has been on using techniques they haven't used before. When I show them how to use videotapes in class, or how better to teach poems, they are very responsive and take it right away," he explained. But his original plans for this training were not so successful. He recalled:

When I first came, I thought the best way to do staff development was to observe the Thai staff teach, to talk to them afterwards and to make suggestions—that was not the right thing to propose! Nobody was interested in it. Then I decided to demonstrate teaching methods and talk about them afterwards. That worked out wonderfully!

Drexler described the challenge to develop faculty capacities: "Thai teachers told me students were not interested in the literature classes here. They wanted me to give them some sort of magic. There is still a lot of straight lecture, translation of works, and a lot of reading that students find far too difficult. I felt my role was to give the teachers methods to get students to participate in class and to give them some sense of what material is too hard."

Linguist Vincent Linares on a TEFL faculty in Malaysia said, "I duplicated and condensed a sixty-hour workshop I do in Hawaii for my faculty here. Fifteen colleagues have participated in approximately twenty hours of in-service instruction for them to promote critical thinking skills through writing. There was some reluctance on their parts to participate . . . they were skeptical at first. So it has been fun showing them that these methods can work." Sharon Hom, whose innovative mentoring model for teacher training in China was mentioned earlier, also organized a national meeting on legal teaching which she reported:

Seven foreign professors and I structured a two day conference for Chinese law faculties aimed at demonstrating actual teaching exercises where each of us was responsible for demonstrating a particular approach (e.g., case method, lecturing, role-playing, problem-solving, questioning and giving instructional feedback). We structured the conference so there was a little introduction to the method and then one of the professors demonstrated it with the rest of us as students. Then we did a double level of feedback: first, the American professors gave feedback on the exercise, and then everyone gave feedback. That was quite innovative in China.

A professor to Malaysia remarked on the dedication of faculty and staff to their own development. "I'll have a workshop on a weekend or at night and everyone will show up. No school I have ever taught at did I find that experience. That is what makes it so worthwhile here." But a professor to China reported another experience (Blatchford, 1983). He offered:

My specialty being language teaching methodology, I was asked to train faculty in linguistics and methods. Upon arrival, I conferred with the department leaders and at their request submitted a list of eight methodologies I could teach. The department members then discussed these and selected their choices. After three sessions, it became clear that some were uncomfortable with my approach. I realized the introduction of new instructional techniques can be upsetting for at least two reasons. First, many new techniques require departure from the text and a degree of English fluency that the teachers do not have. Second, the potential that students might rebel against new methods is a great threat.

Individual Training of Junior Faculty.   The opportunity to improve the capacities of one or a few junior faculty members was reported by American professors abroad as "special" and "rare in American academia." A professor to Indonesia said:

I work with two young faculty members who are interested in improving their research skills and helping students get research projects started. They never exactly asked me [for to do so would admit that they lacked these skills], but rather expressed an interest in a very diffident kind of way. They come in and we talk about possible research in more detail and I show them many examples, so it has to be a one-on-one tutoring situation. They are excited about it and eager to come.

A professor from Brigham Young relayed a similar experience in Mexico. "Many of the things I did in my courses [such as socratic questioning, group work or designing objective exams] were innovative to my colleagues. I involved two junior faculty [my team-teaching partners] with those activities and used the occasion to teach the process. They often took careful and copious notes on what I did in class." Ecologist Edward Cushing found that training some of his colleagues in Indonesia in research skills developed faculty capacities in important ways. He described a collaborative research effort where he incorporated skills training while remaining respectful of the contributions of his hosts:

I have four faculty members who have three different kinds of skills and they want to work together. We created a research team and have gotten a small grant to do some work here in Java. . . . I teach about the vegetation of the world. Everybody is interested in what is going on in the tropical rain forest. But how do the people here feel about that. I need that information to be a teacher and to be an ecologist.

Additional guidelines for Planning for Training Students as Future Teachers is available in Figure 7-2.

CONSULTING ON CURRICULA, RESOURCES, AND PROGRAMS

Another way that American professors abroad serve in ways beyond classroom teaching is consulting and developing curricula, resources, and programs in universities abroad. A few visiting professors arrived at their new assignments, following grueling U.S. teaching loads or exhausting administrative duties and hoped to have a "more leisurely year to reflect and write," only to find that they

1. **Recognize your possible role as a teacher trainer.**

    • Much tertiary education, especially in developing countries, is the preparation of future college teachers.

2. **Plan ahead for teacher training.**

    • Take materials on pedagogy, teaching strategies, curriculum development, and teacher training in your discipline.
    • An education text on generic teaching strategies will help fortify your teaching repertoire.
    • Bring video-tapes of your classes in the United States to illustrate how students perform using teaching methods other than lectures.

3. **View your own teaching strategies as "models."**

    • Demonstrate a *variety* of teaching methods for students.
    • Discuss your methods with students as you use them and have them evaluate the methods.

4. **Consider a "mentor" model of teacher training.**

    • Train a small group of graduate students or junior faculty to teach an undergraduate course under your supervision.

5. **Propose short workshops on pedagogical methods.**

    • Include some examples of large group discussion, small group problem-solving, role-play, use of audio-visual equipment, case studies, debate, or cooperative methods.

6. **Video your teaching and your students working.**

    • Video can facilitate discussion of methods. It allows both repetitions and psychological distance.
    • Students will likely evaluate taped segments more candidly than live ones.

FIGURE 7-2   Guidelines: Training Students for Future Teaching

had been assigned to "develop the Classics Department" or "serve as Acting Dean of Humanities while the former Dean is on a foreign fellowship" or to "set up the Masters' program in Communications—and, by the way, there are fifteen new students." However, more typically, American professors who serve as consultants are requested to share their experiences and contacts with their university administrators and committees. One such professor of American literature to Thailand remarked:

> *One thing that my university wanted a foreign 'expert' to do was to advise on changes in the curriculum. It meant sitting in on endless committee meetings. The second thing they wanted to do was put in a new master's program. [They had three years of meetings that never got anywhere]. Just last week we presented*

the proposal for this new program to the university. You could hardly ask for a better situation than to come in where they are making important changes and be on the ground floor."

Sometimes this consulting requires representing the university or faculty to external bodies. For example, a professor in Hong Kong assisted his faculty in planning a world congress held by a U.S.-based professional organization. In the case of other professors, consultations included service on government commissions. Several American teachers served on national testing commissions (representing both their universities and their disciplines) that dealt with designing and setting policy for national examination programs. One professor with experience at the Berkeley Center for Studies in Higher Education served on a commission whose task it was to evaluate "five major five-year plans for higher education submitted by the Czechoslovakian Ministry of Education." Another American Fulbright professor of law to Israel consulted on the introduction of conflict resolution programs into the Israeli judicial system. He reported that his efforts were met with enthusiasm and suspicion and said, "In the beginning, one group of lawyers said, 'That is all well and good in the U.S. for the goyim, but it will never work here for the Jews.' Clearly, it is a long-term education project."

MANAGING RESEARCH ACTIVITIES

A university-based visiting faculty member on an international exchange may have ample research opportunities, but they often may be different than he or she is accustomed to in the American university setting and different from what was expected. Some of the typical research activities identified by American professors abroad included:

- Translating (or polishing the English of) articles for journals, law reviews and bilingual publications;
- Serving as the research methodologist on hosts' research projects;
- Completing or polishing articles based on research work from home;
- Building collaborative research teams and proposals;
- Developing research proposals for whole departments or faculties;
- Supervising and/or participating in graduate theses and dissertations;
- Analyzing/interpreting data bases for university, government or agency policy reports;

Self-Directed Research Activities

Many professors who participate in international exchanges do so during a sabbatical year or its equivalent. Most expect, or dream of, "a more manageable schedule" and "time to write." Some hope to finish a text or polish articles for publication. As discussed in the Chapter 2 section on Safeguarding Research

Time, it was routinely reported that protecting research time in academic exchanges is difficult. The complication seems related to *views of a professor's role* in the culture as a "scholar" and *norms which exist for teaching loads* including levels and class sizes. The Fulbright professor to Mexico who reported that "Course preparations and consultations with students have taken much more time than I had anticipated and have left me with little time for my own research and writing" seems to articulate the prevailing sentiment. Other professors to Sri Lanka and Nepal advised, "It is important for any professor planning to do any research to guard the research aspect. The tendency is for research time to be eaten up by increasing requests for lectures, thesis advising, etc."

But some visiting professors do manage successful self-directed research activities abroad despite the odds. One strategy is to *craft a research agenda not dependent on library resources.* This strategy was described by a University of San Diego economist to Malaysia:

> *I realized before I came here that I couldn't do the same research I was doing in California—so my home research was shelved temporarily. The library here is very limited in terms of journals, publications and books. So research requiring literature reviews can't be done here. I can still do research, but my agenda had to change tremendously.*

A second strategy for managing self-directed research abroad was to *focus a research agenda on the issues of concern in the host country.* A law professor from New York City subscribed to this strategy:

> *The hottest case history in Malaysia is the mandatory death penalty for drugs, but no one has studied it systematically. So I copied the hundred or so cases and read them all and am trying to make sense of them. It has allowed me to be a researcher in my infancy here where I don't know much about Malaysian law . . . It gives me a vehicle to talk about the issues and research with colleagues.*

Other professors following this strategy surveyed and interviewed their host faculty, students, and officials. They studied public records and government documents in their host countries. They wrote journal articles, newspaper accounts, conference paper proposals, and memoirs about their investigations and experiences.

The third strategy some professors used to manage research activities abroad was to *bring self-contained research projects from home.* Some researchers carry computers, software, databases, unfinished manuscripts, and even small libraries on their exchanges. Some professors gain access to university and government computer centers. A University of Tennessee professor, who was analyzing data from a large survey done in the United States before he left, reported, "I brought my data and my own software (to Thailand), and the university made their computer center available to me two to four times per week." This professor was lucky, as well as resourceful. As the section on Planning for Computer Use in Chapter 10 describes, computation resources vary much in availability and quality.

Collaborative Research Activities

In some cultures and academic environments, the research tradition is a more collaborative one than in the United States. Americans are accustomed to setting their own research agenda, to being rewarded with tenure and promotion for sole-authored articles, and to managing research processes from conception to publication "as horses for single harnesses." To illustrate the difference in a culture with a more collaborative tradition, a Fulbright professor of educational research reported the following conversation:

> *I lunched today with two Deans—both distinguished, intelligent, and ambitious men. We discussed research and how it impacts on policy decisions in Thailand. The inspiration for the discussion was my preparation for a lecture tour on 'Policy Research Methodologies.' Both of these administrators seemed compelled to state their positions on research which were: First, individual research projects done by single researchers to study isolated effects are of the lowest priority and not to be supported. And secondly, research projects by collections of colleagues addressing problems defined by people directly involved with or affected by a program or policy are worthy and should be supported.*

University of Minnesota professor Ed Cushing, whose collaborative research efforts on Indonesian rain forests with local ecologists was funded by the National Geographic Society, found his cooperative research "the most exciting thing I'm doing!" He explained why he chose this collaboration:

> *I have always felt really strongly that I didn't want to come here to do my research and go back. I want faculty here, if they are interested, to do this research. They are the ones who have the most reason to know about their environment. If it is of value to them, then I can help them. . . . The success of what I do depends on meeting people here, not on my terms, but on their terms.*

A major advantage of collaborative research activities is the help it offers in dealing with the many bureaucratic hurdles that burden a research project in an unfamiliar culture. It was often reported by visiting professors managing research activities that the best way to deal with institutional and government permissions, authorizing documentation, library cards, etc., is to work with host colleagues and deans to try to handle them. Visiting researchers are advised, however, to be aware that colleagues also may have many bureaucratic constraints and "social costs" related to seeking excessive permission and authority beyond the ordinary.

Not every visiting professor agrees with the advantages of collaboration. Research done collaboratively, like other cooperative efforts, is subject to human idiosyncrasies and cultural foibles. A California State University at Fresno psychology professor who attempted to do research during his teaching assignment in Brazil stated (Levine, 1985):

. . . The Handbook of Research Methods in Social Sciences *never warned me about the difficulties which occurred while I was a visiting professor in Brazil...Every instructor I asked to help me was quick to offer whatever resource he had available. Nao tem problema? went the replay...[But] On every occasion, when the appointed hour arrived, no instructor did . . . I later learned that my colleagues felt they'd be insulting me if they said no. It was politer to offer assistance and then not give it.*

He later added, "I learned from my Brazilian experiences that the less I relied on assistance, the more smoothly my research proceeded. Happily, I was able to design a series of measures that would allow me to gather data without depending on local helpers."

Suggestions and guidelines for working with colleagues on cooperative research endeavors are provided in Figure 7-3, Managing Collaborative Research Activities.

SERVING AS AN ITINERANT SCHOLAR

Roving Scholar of American Studies. (Business card of a Fulbrighter in Norway)

A final way American professors work in cross-cultural university settings but outside the traditional classroom is serving as an itinerant scholar. Sometimes visiting faculty members are shared by two or more institutions and the visiting faculty member rotates between them daily, weekly or monthly. In other situations, the visiting professor circulates among faculties in a university system, providing faculty and staff training, giving special seminars or doing in-service workshops.

While the itinerant faculty positions were given mixed reviews by visiting faculty, they do serve to enhance the objectives of some countries' programs. Norway's "Roving Scholar" concept is a good example of a program that is particularly well-suited to the country's aim to provide in-service faculty development to its provincial institutions. In this setting, roving professors provide workshops and short courses for faculties across the country. The Fulbright professor whose business card read "Roving Scholar of American Studies" in nine months provided twenty-three short courses throughout Norway. Similarly, a management professor from American University provided business seminars on tour around New Zealand.

One professor who rotated between two universities in Hungary described some of the difficulties of itinerancy:

On days when I had assignments in both places I would really have to hustle to get back and forth between location. . . . More importantly, each institution [or at least my supervisors there] wanted my efforts directed toward the task at that

1. **Describe collaborative research activities as "joint ventures."**

    - Think of, refer to and address collaborators as bona fide colleagues, not as research assistants or translators.
    - Describe your work as collaborations to officials, funders, and collaborators from the beginning.

2. **Expect to compromise on design, methodology, and interpretation issues.**

    - Avoid "pulling rank" when differences arise.

3. **Recognize different incentives for research participation.**

    - Publishing may be less of an incentive than intellectual stimulation, advanced training in research methods, interest in the issue, or professional advancement.

4. **Value and recognize the role of "official go-between."**

    - Institutional and government permissions, authorizing documentation, library cards, and other bureaucratic obstacles may be numerous.
    - If you use your host collaborator(s) to manage these difficult tasks, recognize this important role.
    - Be aware that colleagues may encounter bureaucratic constraints and "social costs" related to seeking excessive permission and authority beyond the ordinary.

5. **Praise colleagues amply but honestly for their work on the project.**

6. **Try to avoid power or status imbalance in the collaboration.**

    - Expect that colleagues might defer to you or place you in a leadership role (e.g., in design, procurement of resources, credit, etc.) out of respect or custom.
    - Avoid imbalance by being facilitative but not directive.

FIGURE 7-3   Guidelines: Managing Collaborative Research Activities

particular organization . . . often wondering why I could not give as much as they had hoped.

Another professor to Thailand concurred. "It is understandable that a sponsoring program wants to cover as many bases as possible with my services, but by touring all around giving lectures, I miss out on developing close relationships with a small group of faculty and students which is the best part of a cultural exchange." Two "rovers" in Norway suggested that the experience, however, could be a rich one if you "are an opportunist" or "really want to see the world." But they advised, "Don't expect lots of guidance and be prepared to set your own goals."

PLANNING THE RETURN HOME

A plan for re-entering American academic life and "taking the exchange experience home" is something too many American professors abroad give insufficient consideration. The re-entry process completes the academic sojourner's cycle, and involves both *readjustment* and *integration*.

Readjusting to American University Life

Marcia Miller, an English professor who spent a year in China, described her anticipation of re-entry into a rich academic and personal life in New York City (1990):

> *I was certain that people would be as interested in hearing my story as I would be in telling it. My personal relationships, I assumed, would be easily resumed because I had been a diligent, attentive correspondent. I had prepared for going to China by reading widely, speaking to returned teachers, and trying to learn as much as I could about the country. I did not prepare for re-entry . . . Why should it be necessary to prepare to go home? After all, I knew exactly what I was coming back to. . . . I was wrong!*

Personal Readjustment. Stories of "reverse culture shock" abound from professors who return to the United States and feel "strange," "awkward," or "diffident" in their homes and departments. Fulbrighters to Indonesia Jim and Jill Aton dubbed it *"back* pain." Some college teachers abroad return "supersensitive" to American cultural norms, which often are in sharp contrast to norms in their host countries. Some find their students' casual behavior repulsive. Others note oddities of "green- and pink-dyed hair standing up four inches," tee shirts and shorts that reveal breasts or genitals, or barefeet in the classroom (which they never attended to before) are now bothersome. Some professors are appalled by the waste, excess, obesity, and opulence in their homes and neighborhoods. When she and her husband, upon return, paid the equivalent of a Chinese faculty's salary for six weeks for one modest restaurant meal, Marcia Miller felt "consumption of the meal was reprehensible, that I had committed an immoral act."

Some professors upon re-entry report that they feel "isolated," "like strangers," "disinterested," or "psychologically distant" from students, colleagues, and former work routines. This "distance" seems to be the case even among those with positive home and work environments and relations and among those who "yearned to return." One professor describing this distance and disjuncture recalled, "My father used to say that we lose 100,000 brain cells a day. I think they disappear faster when you go on sabbatical" (Gold, 1993). Feeling like a stranger in his own department, he mistook a long-time colleague in the copy room for a graduate student, introduced himself, and asked what was his specialty. He related, "That question particularly confounded the colleague looking inside the photocopying machine . . . 'My specialty? Lack of toner,' " he responded after a pause. " 'That and jamming, I guess.' " For some professors, this sense of "distance" last longer than one semester.

Those professors who had enjoyed some release from home-based routines of committee work, advisement, heavy teaching, and supervision loads, etc., reported that when faced again with those routines upon return felt *excessively* burdened. Those (especially women) who had had support staffs and household help with child care, cooking, transportation, and housekeeping found it hard to give up "all the time freed up for professional work when others take charge of domesticity."

Professional Readjustment. Some professors report they return to a disinterested or hostile university environment and experience a difficult period of professional, as well as personal, readjustment. Miller, who was eager to share with colleagues her experiences teaching in China, reported:

> *For the first month after my return, there was only one reason for a conversation and that was to talk about China. But after the first few times, I saw a glazed look pass over my colleagues' eyes; I could hear them thinking: Oh here she goes again! . . . But to me it was the only vital topic.*

Similarly, an art professor who wanted to share her particularly satisfying exchange experience to Mexico, where she surmounted the tribulations of the cross-cultural classroom, greatly improved her Spanish, and enjoyed an unfamiliar prestige as a faculty member, found that "American colleagues would ask, 'How was it?' and allow me about a twenty-five word answer before changing the subject!"

Others complained that they were "punished" by chairs, deans, and colleagues who were envious or angry about their leave. Upon return, some found their teaching schedules or loads had been altered or extra courses assigned them. Others reported finding some aspect of their leave governed by new rules. Professor of English at the University of Kansas, Joel Gold, returned to find new rules his sabbatical leaves had provoked on his campus were referred to as "the Gold Rules" (1993). An example of such an "after-the-fact" rule occurred when another successful Fulbright professor to China was requested by the Chinese to stay a second year and his university responded to the request with a new rule— "A sabbatical year can not be extended by a year's leave of absence."

Some professors respond to the perceived hostile and disinterested university environments with feelings of "impotence" rather than accustomed vigor and self-righteous indignation. "Returning Fulbrighters often don't feel as if people are aware of their experience or are interested in what they have done," reports Jan Anderson, executive director of the U.S. Fulbright Alumni Association. "They come back full of the experience with great propensity for international exchange, and they feel no one cares" (Watkins, 1993).

Suggestions of ways to manage your re-entry into daily and academic life, which can personally empower you and professionally connect you, are provided both in the guidelines on Planning the Return Home in Figure 7-4 and in the following discussion.

1. **View readjusting to American university life and integrating the exchange experience as part of your work.**

    *   Prepare for your return by reflecting on ways your overseas experience and newly acquired cross-cultural skills and learning might be useful in your home environment.
    *   Plan for one or two simple ways to share the experience with colleagues, students and friends, e.g., a slide or video presentation, short articles in the popular or professional press, a feature story for the university or local newspaper, etc.

2. **Acknowledge the likelihood of some re-entry "trauma" and plan for it.**

    *   Organize a schedule that will allow for the blocks of time necessary for sustained work.
    *   Honor continuing needs for intellectual stimulation, disequilibrium, social excitement, and adventure.

3. **Find ways to integrate the exchange experience into your ongoing professional life.**

    *   Advise others who are interested in studying or teaching abroad.
    *   Maintain a correspondence with host colleagues.
    *   Network with professional organizations involved in international education and area studies (See appendix D).
    *   Consider the establishment of institutional linkages.

FIGURE 7-4   Guidelines: Planning for the Return Home

Integrating the International Teaching Experience

Building Networks. Some professors returning from international teaching have found that joining and participating in groups and organizations which study and promote international education and academic exchanges, e.g., the Comparative and International Education Society and the National Association for Foreign Student Affairs, have helped integrate their experiences abroad with their present professional lives. Active national alumni groups, e.g. Fulbright Alumni Association and the Returned Peace Corps Volunteers, provide ongoing support for some college teachers. Additionally, participation in professional and advocacy organizations focused on area studies (even for the nonspecialist) maintains networks for resources and information about the host country and region. Appendix D—Resources for Affiliations and Linkages upon Re-entry to the U.S.A. is a list of some of these organizations specializing in international education and area studies.

Advising Others on Teaching and Studying Abroad. Some professors find it helpful to advise others who are considering teaching abroad. One way is to share experiences with faculty at programs planned by international program offices of their colleges. Miller identified the utility of this kind of advisement:

A few months after my return, I was asked to speak to a group of teachers who were considering work in China. In order to prepare for that presentation, I was forced to organize my thoughts in a logical manner. That was a steadying and extremely beneficial exercise.

Others write about their experiences in professional journals, campus newspapers, and union newsletters. Writing about the triumphs and tribulations of cross-cultural work may help with your personal and professional readjustment and with integration of the experience by codifying and synthesizing what you have learned.

Another level of involvement in promoting academic exchanges upon return is advising students who are considering study abroad. Working with your college study abroad office and affiliating with organizations such as the Institute of International Education, the National Association of Foreign Affairs, and the Council on International Educational Exchange (listed in appendix A and D) are good ways to begin.

Putting your Host Country into Your Curriculum.   One of the "lessons" many participants in academic exchanges report is that "the host culture and American culture take from and give to each other." Cultures cross-fertilize and do not exist independently. John Buescher at the National Endowment for the Humanities advocates that teachers with Asian experiences "put Asia into the core curriculum" because if a core curriculum is an assembly of main ideas then Asia should be allowed to "negotiate and parley on equal terms with the West in sending representatives to the assembly" (Buescher, 1991). When curriculum is flexible enough that professors, upon return, can introduce contemporary poets from China, national parks management strategies from Malawi, or industrial management techniques from Japan, the exchange is made more meaningful. Beuscher describes this integration as recognition of ". . . the cultural gene pool, a vital buffer against stress and unforeseen circumstances, a range of possibilities toward which our own culture might evolve . . . conceptual germ plasm that we might use to make exotic medicine to cure our cultural diseases."

Jody Olsen, executive director of the Council for the International Exchange of Scholars (CIES) and her staff produced "The Fulbright Scholar Program: Expanding the International Involvement of Higher Education," a guide booklet which discusses policies and practices to promote greater faculty involvement in universities' internationalization efforts. Increasingly administrators are acknowledging that their universities can never send as many students abroad as they would hope. But they can internationalize the curriculum and the experiences of the faculty who teach those students. According to a recent survey of returned Fulbright lecturers 1985–1992, almost 60 percent have developed new courses based on their experiences abroad and 80 percent added more international perspective to their course content (CIES, 1993).

Establishing Institutional Linkages. A final way American professors integrate their academic exchange experience into their professional lives is through linkages with host-country institutions. These relationships range from government and foundation supported programs to direct institution-to-institution affiliations. These connections may include many permutations of exchange agreements, e.g., short-term, nondegree-oriented coursework or research, credited study-abroad exchanges, professor exchanges, and field-based placements for pre-service teachers. An example of this kind of linkage is the exchange program in theater and dance at Indiana University, Bloomington. This program is an outcome of Beverly Stoeltje's Fulbright exchange to Ghana. "Ever since my Fulbright, the university has had scholars coming and going to Ghana," said Stoeltje, an IU professor of folklore and African studies (Watkins, 1993).

Two sources of support for institutional linkages are the United States Information Agency's Academic Exchange Programs, USIA, Washington, DC, 20547, which provide direct support for institutional linkages, and the Council for the International Exchange of Scholars (see address in appendix A), which offers support for visiting foreign professors to American universities that provide some matching resources.

According to Swierczek (1987), who has studied university linkages in Southeast Asia, a professor who helps facilitate these linkages often develops strong, on-going relationships with host faculty that lasts for years. Some of the suggestions for facilitating successful institutional linkages include:

1. Build support for institutional linkages while at the host institution.
2. Recognize that the linkages which work best are primarily professor-to-professor based and identifying "key faculty participants" early.
3. Solicit additional support for linkages from officials (e.g., administrators from departments, schools, area studies, study-abroad programs, and research centers).
4. Budget parsimoniously because resources for linkages are usually small and spread thin; and.
6. Negotiate an "exchange agreement" with the host institution which articulates realistic expectations.

Concept Map

8

IMPLEMENTING EFFECTIVE INSTRUCTIONAL STRATEGIES

If one could learn by observation then all dogs would be butchers. —TURKISH PROVERB

As an effective and dedicated instructor in America, you have undoubtedly developed some excellent and time-honored instructional methods that work well to promote learning. But teaching across cultures often taxes the most dedicated and creative teachers. In this chapter, methods of instruction to encourage student participation and progression to higher thinking processes are discussed in an effort to reinforce your repertoire of instructional strategies and to suggest modifications of those strategies where language and culture are different.

Before you read about these strategies, it might be useful to examine the approaches you typically use in your current teaching. Figure 8-1 provides a Self Assessment Guide developed by law professor Sharon Hom in her faculty development work in China and the United States (1989).

ENCOURAGING STUDENT PARTICIPATION

By far the most common frustration for most American professors teaching across cultures is the limited amount of student participation in class. Syracuse University law professor Peter Bell described this frustration with his classes in China:

The most difficult thing is getting the students to participate. I think of participation as one of the strengths of my classes in the States where they are mainly discussion classes.

Thinking about when and why this pattern of participation or "wall of silence" occurs is to contemplate, as we did in Chapter 1, Examining the Culture of the

---

I. **YOUR TEACHING METHODS**

   A. **Which of the following methods do you now use? Next to each one, approximate the percentage of use.**

   1. *Lecture*
   2. *Discussion*
   3. *Case analysis*
   4. *Problems method*
   5. *Role-plays or simulated exercises*
   6. *Individual or small group feedback*
   7. *Other (specify)*

   B. **Which of the following factors have affected your choice of methodology?**

   1. *Context*
   2. **Students**
      • Number of students
      • Your perception of the abilities of the students
      • The interests of your students
      • Previous experience of students
   3. *Yourself*
      a. Your perception of your own abilities, knowledge, and interests
      b. Do the methods you use contribute to developing and expanding your abilities, knowledge, or interests?
   4. *Method*
      a. What demands are placed on you and your students?
      b. How much preparation time and energy do your methods require? How much class time is required?
      c. What materials were required?
   5. *Other factors*

FIGURE 8-1   Self-Assessment Guide

Source: Sharon K. Hom (1989), *American Legal Education Methodology in China,* p. 105. New York: City University of New York Law School. Used with permission of the author.

Classroom, important interactions of classroom behaviors and general culture attributes of the host country. Figure 8-2 provides general guidelines for Encouraging Participation in Cross-Cultural Classrooms.

Recognizing the Nature of the Silence

American visiting professors to foreign classrooms perhaps talk more about the silence of these classrooms than any other characteristic. Reports on students'

1. **View participatory teaching strategies as innovations.**

    - Most university teaching traditions use lecturing as the sole instructional method.
    - Ask students to try discussion methods, breakout activities, collaborative problem-solving, etc., as an "experiment."

2. **"Prime the pump" to initiate student participation.**

    - Solicit easy responses initially until students respond freely, then increase the complexity.
    - Start with the "facts" then move to the inferences.

3. **Demonstrate participatory practice.**

    - Have a small group of graduate students, colleagues, or former students demonstrate Q/A, role-playing, group discussion, etc., for the class.
    - Bring and show a videotape of your class in the United States where students are involved in participatory learning activities.

4. **Solicit student responses randomly.**

    - To distribute solicitations equally and maximize attention to questions, draw a student's name or group number randomly from a deck of cards.

5. **Allow "Think-Pair-Share."**

    - Students formulate their own answer to your question, pair with a partner to exchange ideas, and share their best idea when called on.

6. **Invite participation of reluctant students.**

    - Allow extra time for reflection or formulation of answers into English when mecessary.
    - Encourage a reluctant student to check with another student first and then respond.
    - "Scaffold" or construct a partial response for the student to complete.

7. **Activate participation with small groups.**

    - Small group discussion and problem-solving will bring some students "to life."
    - Anticipate setting work rules and group processes.

8. **Avoid grading participation.**

    - Where students are reluctant to participate and/or have limited English facility, evaluating "class participation" may be a disincentive.

9. **Reinforcement participation.**

    - For correct responses, uses of praise should be specific and descriptive (example: "Correct! That *is* the author's main point" rather than "Good answer").
    - For incorrect responses, encourage students to "Try again" or direct the response to another student, "Do you agree with her?

10. **Persevere with participatory practice.**

    - Most professors who use participatory methods do not meet with immediate success. With skill, persistence, and demonstration, students come around slowly to the practice.

FIGURE 8-2   Guidelines: Encouraging Student Participation in Cross-Cultural Classrooms

silence described it as "unwillingness to participate," "inability to openly discuss," "bred-in passivity," "shyness," "timidity," "reticence," "reserve," "diffidence," "bashfulness," "reluctance," "disinclination to take part" and "aversion to talking in class." The plethora of these observations (usually in tones ranging from dismay to exasperation) probably attests both to the ubiquity of the phenomena as well as to the uniqueness of the American education experience wherein student-teacher interaction and inquiry is an expectation. Some of these observations included:

- *The only question I was ever asked in any course by a Japanese student raising his hand during class was to confirm the pronunciation of the word 'multilateral,' since my pronunciation did not match that in the dictionary.*
- *Israeli students generally won't play along!*
- *For someone used to American students, the passivity of Irish students is frustrating, for they simply do not ask questions in class.*
- *Chinese students are quiet—they do not talk much or at all. I did not come uninformed about this, but I have enough of the reformer in me, having come of age in the 1960s academically and intellectually, that I thought in my own small way, in my own small classroom, I could do something about it, I could change that. I have not been successful.*
- *Because Irish students are so quiet, it is difficult to determine how well the subject is understood.*
- *New Zealand students, if they talk at all, tend to let their neighbors do the talking for them. . . . Those who talked a lot were viewed critically by their peers.*
- *The natural habits of Australian students lead them to sit back and take notes . . . It is difficult for me to draw them into a genuine case discussion.*
- *Japanese students do not participate in class discussion spontaneously . . . Professors have to struggle to break students' reticence.*
- *Korean students are accustomed to teacher-dominated classes and expect me to deliver knowledge to them.*
- *For Japanese students, it is a role—the role of recipient. . . . I guess my role is dispenser!*
- *Czech students never interrupt with a question and rarely question me. They told me it is because it is deemed rude to the teacher or presenter.*
- *Malaysian students expect that professors' lectures must be learned almost verbatim, so they quietly take copious notes in class.*
- *While I personally enjoy the teaching in Norway, I have major education difficulties adapting to the difference in student involvement in the learning process.*
- *It is uncommon to receive from Thai students obvious facial or body cues that register agreement, comprehension or quandary familiar to us.*
- *You find yourself teaching your heart out trying to seduce your Hungarian students into the process and find them most resistent to your attempts to make them speak. I feel like I'm forcing my children to play piano for Grandma! . . . It doesn't make for a very dynamic classroom.*

- *Malaysian students want the answer without talking about it . . . they want the teachers to provide the answer which they write down. They want to think about it and memorize it and reproduce it.*
- *In China, I don't lecture, I talk with my students, but often times I find that in class I am talking to myself.*

Predicting Levels of Student Participation

American professors, who are clearly both annoyed and challenged by this lack of student participation in the classroom, often spend much time reflecting on the traditions and cultural practices that foster this difference between American and other students. Some report that their students "have the expectation that university classes will be taught in a lecture format and their expected response is to sit quietly and listen." These professors often blame the educational traditions perpetuated by their host faculty. A Fulbrighter to Thailand observed:

> *Thai professors stand almost still as they lecture from the front of the class. If they use overhead projections, they are usually from the text or typewritten notes which students copy. Body motions are restrained. They rarely move to different quarters of the room. They emphasize points with quiet restatement.*

In Japanese tradition, "teachers give lectures and students listen to them passively. It is strictly a one-way system," another professor added. "Only when teachers ask students if they have any questions are they allowed to speak in class," another said.

A journalism professor criticized his colleagues. "In the Pakistani method of teaching the *practice* of good journalism, the practice part is minimal—which is unfortunate because good journalism education must have a healthy dose of practical training." Practice and participation are discouraged, several argue, when students are not free to err. "Hungarians teachers train students to speak only when they are absolutely right!" a Fulbright professor to Hungary explained.

A University of North Florida professor observed that the typical Chinese method of teaching a class is to "sit at a table with the text or notes and to *lecture*." Another added, "I've told colleagues that in a two-hour class in America I would probably speak for twenty minutes and my students would talk for the rest of the time . . . I am more like a choir director, a facilitator, keeping the discussion going and steering the conversation . . . but not lecturing ever. They don't believe me!"

Other observations reflected similar American conviction on the value of student participation. A professor to Egypt said, "When I see a faculty member lecture unceasingly for over two hours, it violates the conceptions I have of how *good* professors function." Another concurred. "Teaching in Malaysia is not student centered—the professor lectures and the students listen quietly, very passively. There is no interaction." Criticized another to Thailand, "For me, teaching undergraduates may be communicating a body of knowledge, but when teaching at the graduate level, there should be much more emphasis on developing an understanding, learning to solve problems, and establishing relationships between different variables. This cannot be achieved by one way communication."

Oren Moffett's summary of teaching methodology in Chinese universities (1983) describes many of the situations American professors will face:

> . . . *a predominance of teacher-talk over student-talk, the complete absence of visual aids, and the proclivity to use the tradition-bound lecture technique. This latter practice will be hard to change since administrators, instructors, and students alike seem to be enamored of it.*

Facilitating Classroom Discussion

> *If I tell you something, you will write it down and forget it. If you tell me something, you will not write it down, but you will not forget it. (An American Literature Conference Theme, China)*

Breaking with Tradition. Some teachers were able to break with tradition and facilitate enough student participation to feel some sense of satisfaction. From New Zealand a professor offered, "Students were far more diffident and passive at the outset, but after much encouragement and adjustment to my more informal teaching mode, they began to respond and to contribute to the discussion." Another professor from Malaysia reported, "Using a fair amount of humor, I was able to get most of them to participate fairly actively in class. In general, I found the students more flexible and accepting of innovation than my academic colleagues suggested they might be." While Thai students admit that they do not like to be singled out when called on, Western professors using the Socratic method suggested that students "initially had trepidations, but got used to the technique— and eventually do well using the method." John Roger, a law professor in Beijing, also broke with tradition:

> *We were repeatedly warned in orientations that the Chinese students do not want to talk in class, they don't want to put themselves above their fellow students, and they do not want to say something wrong. The reason I took that with a grain of salt is that at my University in Kentucky, you hear the same thing. I think that it is used as an excuse to lecture to students.*

Being "Theatrical." The image of "teacher as performer" often came up in discussions with college teachers abroad who struggled with the challenge of facilitating class discussions. One teacher in China supported this idea, "Like a stage performer, I kept looking for tricks that would work. I think, 'They didn't like this, so I'll try that.' I've got my bag of teaching tricks, but when I'd go through the bag, some things work and some don't." Another from Thailand:

> *I must appear like Phil Donahue brandishing his probing mic. They must think I prance around and wave my arms with exaggerating gesticulation. I'm sure*

students feel I intrude into their space as I circulate observing their notes and that I violate their privacy as I call on them for responses.

An American literature professor in Pakistan "often felt like a guinea pig—a type of experiment—the purpose of which was to prove the worth of American pedagogical methods!" A professor in Korea reported that after one class where he had attempted to ask questions, a student said to him, "Going to class is like watching television. But the television started asking me questions. How can this be?"

Being Controversial. Some professors reported that their participatory methods were controversial and provoked discussions among colleagues and students. A professor to Japan was lamenting the inability to foster any discussion in class when her closest Japanese colleague articulately and perceptively advised her:

> *It is only through gradual and sensitive introduction of learner-centered methods that they will come to accept a* radical *shift in their classroom role. Mutual dissatisfaction may arise between teacher and students, if the foreign teacher is not prepared for the painstaking work that is called for to introduce the change."*

A graduate student in China reacted to a Fulbright professors' "pressure" in class to participate by commenting, "At first his discussion method annoyed me, because I am a lazy student, but he has proved that this method is really a good one. It puts us to think about the story." Another commented, "In the very beginning the foreign teacher made us to suffer a lot . . . we were not used to her discussion method. Before going to class we had to read the material very carefully and we had to struggle to think up a good question. Gradually we get used to it and we have grown to like this method after half a semester."

University of Connecticut professor Bruce Stave related an example of being controversial (1986):

> *I had been warned that Chinese students would be passive in comparison to those I teach in the States. I was delighted to find, especially in the graduate seminar, that this was not the case, at least not to the extent I anticipated. I will always remember one of our early discussions in which I tried to stimulate conversation by asking for a comparison of the American and Chinese revolution. One student asked me if I knew the three mountains of China. I shook my head in ignorance. 'Professor, they are feudalism, capitalism, and imperialism!'*

Stave further described how using controversial topics such as the "three mountains" (and how they apply to America as well) often led to good discussions. However, he warned, "Discussants were usually limited to those who could express themselves well in English."

An opposing view to this "go ahead and be controversial" attitude came from a Chinese faculty member who warned, "Some foreign teacher starts a class with a topic or a question which in his own culture would arouse the interest of the students and start a lively discussion (e.g., sexual promiscuity, or what to do with sudden wealth). But because the topic or question is inappropriate in the students' culture or outside their experience, students fail to respond or feel uneasy about the teacher's intention. Teachers who expect the students to participate in such class discussions will be disappointed in the outcome." Further discussion concerning the use of controversy in the classroom can be found in a later section on Teaching for Critical Thinking Across-Cultures.

Priming the Pump. American teachers abroad who had noticeable levels of class participation practiced a kind of successive approximation toward full group discussion. They started with the simple material that was obvious and that any student who was even a little prepared, or had been present at previous classes, or had just heard the short lecture presentation, could answer. Examples included naming the title or characters in a story or the location of a work or other easy points. One law professor explained how he got students talking:

> *You ask them the facts of the case...you ask them who the plaintiff and defendant were [right on the title page] . . . and you've got them talking! Now, if they say something wrong they have at least part of it right . . . then they'll keep going.*

Being Patient. "Silence...for most teachers that is the nightmare," declared CUNY professor Sharon Hom. "Now I am working on not filling too fast. I've found if you let it go for a bit, they'll look for it. And if I let the empty space be there, I'll pick up on a student nodding or whispering to herself or thinking out loud, but without the courage to raise her hand in the silence. Since I saw her, I can call on her then." Another declared, "I have gotten a little comfortable with that silence, obviously not as comfortable as they are, but as stubborn as they are!"

Inviting Student Participation in Whole Class Discussions. It takes skill and finesse to facilitate a class discussion which encourages reluctant, shy, or low achieving students to participate. According to Woolfolk (1993), you need to "invite" the diffident student to participate with solicitation, directing other students' questions to them, probing for more information and pausing after the questions. Figure 8-3 offers some practical suggestions for engaging such students in whole class discussions.

Letting Go. Some teachers never find a way to facilitate the kind of student participation with which they are familiar or comfortable. A professor in China shared, "In terms of my teaching experience here, lack of student participation has been the most trying part of it. I am learning to live with it—to relax. I am learning that I am not going to change the Chinese students in one year."

An American studies professor reframed his expectations. "I don't care anymore if they talk in class—what I want is for them talk about the ideas I share with them *after* class, in the dorms, in the cafeteria!" Another shrugged his

1.   **Recognize when the whole group discussion method is foreign.**

     • Students will avoid eye contact, "outwait" you, and fidgit in noncompliance.
     • Only students facile in English will venture comments.
     • Dead silence will characterize attempts to solicit views.

2.   **Move from simple to complex, from familiar to unfamiliar.**

     • "prime-the pump" by first soliciting the facts of the case, the "who, what, when, where" of the story, or the bold headings.
     • Allow students in dyads to formulate their ideas and get/give feedback before dealing with the whole group.

3.   **Invite participation in the discussion.**

     • Ask "Tomas, what is *your* view?"
     • Ask "Can we hear from another?"
     • Invite equal participation by drawing names at random.

4.   **Keep students talking and thinking.**

     • Get students to expand on cursory comments with:
       "Can you tell us how you developed that idea?"
       "That is a good/strong/controversial/novel idea, what is the rational/evidence for it?"

5.   **Use students comments and questions to facilitate more discussion.**

     • Ask "Kea, do you agree with Semi's comment?" "Ran, what are your thoughts about Jan's idea?"
     • Ask "Erik, how do you think Heidrun got to that idea?"
     • Ask a student to restate or summarize another's point.

6.   **Keep students "on course."**

     • Reframe students' comments which seem tangential.
     • Summarize the discussion periodically.

FIGURE 8-3   Engaging Students in Whole Class Discussions in Cross-Cultural Classrooms

shoulders. "It is one of the things that I find lamentable in my experiences in China that I am not able to break down that conditioned or bred-in passivity."

Some professors who held a student's questioning of them to be a mark of the student's competence, intelligence, preparation of the material, or respect for them as teachers were disappointed. But some were able to overcome students' reticence to speak in class by finding other contexts to share conversation. American literature professor Bill Slaughter contended, "I'd love to be challenged by my students. I'd love for a student to disagree with me powerfully and articulately. I know they are capable of that, but what is interesting to me is that they don't do that in the classroom." Then he noted the contextual shift. "However, they cluster around me after class, follow me home, knock at my door and speak very articulately, about their concerns, about a text, about questions they have. They just don't do it in class!"

Another professor described his Israeli students in another context. "They rarely ask a question in class, although they may well challenge a statement of mine after class in the hall. It seems they will speak only from positions of assumed or real strength." Yet another professor reported that "in the Korean class, students typically ask questions after the period is over . . . and then only very modestly." Suggested one undaunted Fulbright professor to Eastern Europe who especially appreciated the value of student participation, "Trying to create situations where students would interact with me became one of the most challenging and enjoyable aspects of my job."

Questioning Students to Further Participation

Questioning strategies are useful tools in university teaching across cultures. Both the professors' asking of questions and the students' reactions (despite traditions of classroom silence) can be mastered with practice. Whether you choose to use questioning methods referred to as "Socratic questioning" or "guided inquiry" or just to use questions as a preview to a discussion, questioning methods further student participation and help the professor gauge comprehension of the material presented.

Professors who used questioning strategies reported that students responded with discomfort and noncompliance at first. Law professor Peter Bell related his experience with this noncompliance in China:

> *I would say, 'What about this?' And then I would wait. And I would sit there. Nothing. Then I would call on somebody, 'Chung, what do you think?' He would look down at his book . . . (silence) . . . (silence). I have no experience with this—that of calling on a student and the ability of that student to outwait me.*

Thai university students reported that they were unfamiliar with the practice of professors' asking students questions or of being called on to answer questions in class and felt "uncomfortable with the request." A Fulbright professor reported similar attitudes among Malaysian students, but found, after sticking with the practice for some time, these students performed as well as his students in the United States.

Asking Clear, Brief Questions. Questions are best prepared ahead of time so that careful language and definite concepts can be clarified in their construction. Questions should be as short as possible and avoid ambiguity, confusing constructions and extra phrases. Two examples of the same question illustrate differences in clarity and brevity:

Q1: In your opinion, from the assigned Jones and Renard reading, do the authors agree that the trend is toward many operating languages with the new hardware or only a select few?

Q2: What does the Jones and Renard article say—there will be many or few operating languages in the future?

Socratic questioning can be modified to work in cross-cultural classrooms when questions are comprehensible and the session is slowly paced. Pausing ten seconds before designating a respondent and 10–15 seconds after designating a respondent allows for translations and reflections.

Distributing the 'Risk' of Responding. Effective questioning strategies distribute questions and avoid mechanical response systems (e.g., calling on students in alphabetical or seating order) or selective response systems (e.g., calling on students who are cognitively and linguistically competent). One example of an effective strategy was the "luck of the draw" solicitation used in China by University of Tennessee law professor John Rogers. Every student had an equal chance to be called on and "air-time" was shared by all. Rogers described the simple method:

> *There are some things you can't do, whether you are in Beijing or Kentucky. If you get up in front of a class and say, 'The facts of the case are as follows . . . The court said this...Does it make sense?' Nobody is going to answer when you ask a question out to the whole group! So I just write one person's name on each playing card and shuffle the deck. I draw a card and that is the person that I call on.*

A Fulbright professor to Nepal agreed, "I distribute questions equally by calling on students randomly. If left to volunteers, few students [and only those very comfortable in English] will answer." In Turkey, one professor warned, "If I ask, 'Does anyone know?' or 'Who can tell me?', the class will always look to the student most proficient in English to answer." Randomizing the solicitation of responses assures that equal "time" is offered male, female, bright, average, quick, reflective, fluent, and nascent students.

Using Native Language Cues and Constructs. Attention to native-language patterns of questions may help formulate more easily comprehensible questions in English. For example, in Thai, the question tag usually comes at the end of a sentence, such as *prysanii yuu thi nay?* (post office is where?). If a professor poses a classroom question similarly constructed, it registers more quickly with the Thai students, e.g., "Bartlett's Five Year Plan was chosen by the Ministry. Why?"

Choosing Levels of Difficulty of Questions. If you consider questions in some kind of taxonomy, you might ask simpler ones first to "prime the pump" when students are not used to teacher questioning, and move toward more difficult ones to probe students' understanding and prompt their critical thinking. For example, the professor might open a questioning session on a piece of literature just read with "What were the names of the main characters in the piece?", "Where did the opening action take place?", and "What did we see the old man do during the first chapter?". These are all easily answered questions on elementary material. Then she can ask, "What did that action (e.g., a prophetic act of the old man's) mean for the other characters?" and can hope for some response. Common questioning terms (e.g., "enumerate" or "contrast") should be defined (using English and the native language) in some kind of working glossary, if you plan to use questioning as a major instructional strategy.

Many sophisticated question taxonomies exist which move students from simple cognitive levels of recall to higher levels of application, but effective questioning (like other favorite teaching methodologies) does not transport across cultures accidentally or incidentally. Much attention has been given in recent years to the American educational values of "critical thinking" or "higher order processing" and professors admonish students for not using them. Research in U.S. classrooms suggests, however, that American teachers themselves seldom question students in ways that would move them beyond simple recall and recognition. With this perspective, a Fulbright professor to Thailand described his situation, "In essence, we have had a rote learning system here . . . which causes students not to approach their real level of intellectual potential. They are rarely asked to stretch their minds beyond passive note-taking in class." But a competent professor with an effective questioning strategy can stretch students in an American or cross-cultural classroom. The taxonomy in Figure 8-4 suggests ways to recognize and develop those questioning strategies.

Increasing Student Responses Through Reinforcement. In a cross-cultural classroom, students' responding to professors' questions may be new behavior, and as such should be rewarded continuously if you want the behavior to increase. Encouraging participation may require more effort, initially, than you are accustomed to with your most reluctant American students. In the case of a student providing a clear, correct answer, your best reaction is to reinforce the response by saying "correct" or repeating the correct answer for all to hear the repetition. However, what should you do when the student's response is slow, reluctant, only partially correct or wrong? One way suggested was to "cue the reluctant student by giving a hint or beginning a response and allowing the student to finish it." Another way is to listen for a student's response that is "near, but not on the mark" and restate the answer in a clearer, more correct way formed on the student's idea and/or in his words. In both cases you have rewarded approximately desired behavior.

A questioning technique used with students who give incorrect responses is to react, not by saying "Wrong!" or "Incorrect!" but rather by "Try again!" or "Can you give another answer?" Additionally, you can minimize the risks of incorrect responses by the use of the paired response technique called Think-

Recall Questions bring forth data from students which can be used at the next level of questioning:

Enumerate	Describe	Match
List	Complete	Recite
Observe	Define	Identify
Recall	Count	Select

Process Questions draw from students information about relationships and causes by asking them to:

Infer	Sequence	Classify
Explain	Organize	Contrast
Analyze	Group	Experiment
Compare	Distinguish	Make analogies

Application Questions asks students to go beyond the data of concept which they have developed and to generalize, or use a new hypothetical situation, by asking:

Apply the rule	Extrapolate	Speculate
Build a model	Imagine	Evaluate
Forecast	Modify	Invent
Generalize	Theorize	Find examples
Predict	Judge	Hypothesize

FIGURE 8-4   Taxonomy of Questioning Strategies

Pair-Share, discussed in the Chapter 4 section, Setting-up Cooperative Learning Systems. With this technique, you call on students paired with learning partners who collaborate, choose a best answer, and share it with the class.   In some cultures "face saving" is so strong that few students will risk incorrect answers unless extraordinary means are employed to support their efforts. Your respectful attitude toward approximately correct answers "headed in the right direction" and your sensitivity to "face-saving" will provide the needed support.

Scaffolding.   One of the teaching approaches that I have observed to be the most effective in stimulating participation is "scaffolding," i.e., building supports (cues, prompts, structures, etc.) to help students initially. In this case, "scaffolds" are the prompts or structures to help students produce the correct responses.   As they are practiced, the scaffolds become less necessary. Some examples include:

   1.   *Provide students with partial answers and ask them to complete them.* This can be expanded to half-done examples of problems, briefs, or reviews which they complete.
   2.   *Progress from least difficult to most difficult.* Using the "prime-the-pump" idea, start with simple questions or tasks and move to the more complex.
   3.   *Provide prompt or cue cards in English.* To help students formulate the correct linguistic structures in English, provide a glossary of "cues words" (e.g.,

"who, what, where, when, how, why, because, etc.) and "answer openers" (e.g., It is my [his, the author's] opinion [belief, finding] that_____.)

4. *Get students to "Think out loud."* When a student gives a thoughtful answer or asks a good question from the readings in class, ask them to "think out loud." By doing so, they will model their thought process, choices, and reading strategy for other students.

ARRANGING FOR GROUP AND INDIVIDUALIZED WORK

Sometimes I start off in the big group and it's dead. I say, 'Let's break into small groups.' Those I thought had fallen asleep or died come back to life and start talking. (A CUNY professor, China)

One common sight in Asian universities is students gathering before class comparing assignments and after class comparing notes. In the university and cultural context of Southeast Asia, students usually work in groups and report they prefer to work collaboratively in and out of class. A professor to Thailand reported that students' anxiety surrounding his assignments was markedly reduced when he allowed students to work with partners or groups to do the assignments. Variations in English language proficiency among a class of university students might encourage students to seek out more language proficient peers to help them with assignments. Or additional expectations created by the "foreign professor's odd ways" might provoke a need for more affiliation. Whether it is to deal with a "homework cartel," as one American professor called it, to encourage ad hoc groups to work on assignments, or to create cooperative learning teams, good management of small-group work is a necessary instructional strategy.

Organizing Small Group Work

UNY professor Sharon Hom used small discussion groups to increase participation in her classes in China—a practice her students had never done before. She explained the rationale for using these groups:

The reason I like to structure small group work is that students who are uncomfortable speaking in a large groups will speak in a small group. I use them to get the juices going. To start cold on a discussion in a big group setting, there tends to be a kind of chill. But in small groups they talk the problem . . . they get their mouth going, their brains going. Then when you go into the big group discussion, the participation is much better.

A visiting professor to Prague used small groups similarly. "I opted for beginning with the Czech method of lecturing to the large group. But before they fall asleep, I break the large group into small groups for discussion, Q&A, and exercises." University of Tennessee professor Fran Trusty described his use of groups in Thailand to solve simulated problems:

> *At the first class [the 'lecture session'], I give the students a problem which is an application of the concepts covered in the lecture. At the next session [which is the 'problem-solving session'] I present a restatement of the problem. Then I divide the class into groups of eight to work on the problem. At the end of the session, each group makes a short report. A translator makes sure they understand the directions and concepts. The technique works well.*

Typically, the professors who used the small group discussions rotated among the groups, served as a resource to participants, and checked on comprehension of the concepts and compliance on the task procedures.

Role-playing has been one group simulation activity American professors have introduced in many cross-cultural settings. A Fulbright professor to Prague, with the help of two Czech colleagues, translated a simulation game requiring students to role play. Each member of the class received a specific role assignment regarding a proposed educational reform. They researched this role and presented its arguments in class. The professor remarked:

> *It worked amazingly well. Students showed an amount of originality, creative thinking, and seriousness that had escaped me before. When they had to act out a situation that related to something tangible in their experience, they went out of their way to search independently for material not prescribed. They uncovered works we did not know existed in Czechoslovakia.*

Debates are another form of group work organized by some professors in cross-cultural settings. Earlier discussions on both classroom culture and conflict address the need among students in some cultures to avoid confrontation. A professor to Thailand reported being surprised that his students "seem to enjoy debating tremendously—as if the medium gives them a reason and license for mental and verbal jousting." But it was remarked that "disparities in status between debaters provokes some discomfort." It was reported that in debate activities, students often "document poorly, talk too much from personal testimony, and often veer from the main points"—not unlike American students, just harder to correct.

Managing Group Assignments. To manage group work effectively across cultures, you will need to establish an expected set of procedures for group assignments. Because routine can communicate often when language fails, routine can be used to your advantage. Do not assume students know the common rules for group work. Some of the procedural considerations include:

1. *Work Materials.* Do students bring books, writing materials, English dictionaries, etc., with them to the groups? Do you provide the work materials, worksheets, models, etc.?

  2. *Work Rules.* How do the groups get formed? Where can they work? Where do they get help, and how do they signal for help? What do they do when they are done? How do they have work checked? When are they "done"?

  3. *Work Product.* What is the expected product (quality, quantity, complexity)? How do you check it for completion or correctness?

Troubleshooting Problems with Group Work. Learning activities, such as using a class model, discussing a theory in one's own words, or solving a simulated problem, lend themselves readily to group work. Students' inherent interest in working in groups may motivate them to participate in the routines and expectations of the class. But there are three major problem areas in the use of group work: language barriers, difficulty of evaluation, and limited individual practice.

  American professors attempting to overcome *the disadvantage of the language barrier* in group work, have experimented with allowing or encouraging students to use their native languages when participating in instructional groups. In these situations, students "spoke quickly and comfortably and focused on the content and process of the task rather than on speaking in English," one professor observed. When students discuss problems or cases in their native language, they may be more verbal, more fluent, more participatory, and more accurate, but the disadvantage of students' using native language is, obviously, that most visiting professors will not easily be able to follow conceptual progress or evaluate the groups' process. This inability may necessitate the use some kind of translator. One American professor reported trying two translation strategies. "First, I taped the group sessions and had a colleague translate the main points. Second, I hired a colleague to come to the sessions and listen to the students and summarize their main points in English for me," he explained. Other professors minimize the language barrier by placing the most proficient English speaker in each group and using that person as a key informant on the process or the product. Another way was to have check points where translation was done, so that steps in the group work were checked—not just final products.

  The second problem area in the use of group work across cultures is *the difficulty of evaluating student performance* in groups. Does it matter if there is or is not equal participation in the groups? Is there a group-only or individual-only or combination grade? If a combination, how does a group product influence an individual grade? Some professors decide to use group activities in classes for instructional purposes only and did not evaluate them, but this choice may impact negatively on the quality and energy of participation. Questions concerning grading group work hint at the larger problem of how to evaluate students across cultures generally and is discussed more broadly in Chapter 11 Evaluating Student Performance.

  A third area of concern in the use of group work is that *individual practice is limited*, and therefore, it may not accomplish your objectives for all individual students. In class group activities, teachers often are unable to control what each student is doing or to see what each is accomplishing. It is, therefore, difficult to ensure that each student gets an adequate measure of individual practice within group work. One professor to Thailand offered an example of this problem:

> *The students were working in groups of five on an assignment in which 4–5 strategies for handling an employee-employer interaction were to be identified. Some students in each group made all or most of the suggestions—some offered none.*

Organizing Individualized Instruction

Individualized work, organized by American professors for their students across cultures, primarily included individual student writing and a few individually contracted projects. Individualizing was time consuming (especially where students were reported not to work well independently). Because most students preferred group work and avoided individualized assignments and work in English was often avoided, individualized work was not very common. One professor in Mexico, who found his students did not do the assigned out-of-class assignments and readings, described an effective method of individualization. He created workbooks that students worked on in class and passed to him for correction. It gave the students experience scanning reading material, researching the facts, and citing sources. It allowed him to vary assignments based on "experience, reading comprehension in English, and some rudimentary notion of aptitude for the subject matter."

A San Diego State teacher of sociology in Mexico argued for individualized "shoulder-to-shoulder" coaching in libraries, classrooms, and labs. He said, "Course requirements are not enough—I had to be a coach!" He realized he had to "give student *tools* not information; e.g. how to access databases; how to use the Social Science Citation Index; and how to access library materials." An American literature professor in China began individualized work when students requested it. She said, "One of the things that never happens in the United States is students asking for more work. Here that happens several times a month."

Individual Accountability in Group Work. You can boost individual practice by holding each student individually accountable for some product or process of the group work. While the group may discuss an assigned theory, model, or case, an individual student may be assigned specific worksheets, answers, or presentations. Higher rates of individual practice are obtained when students confer with partners or group members (but respond with their own product) than when groups work together. Dyads are preferable to larger groups when this individual response is desired.

Instituting Student Presentations. American professors who used student presentations reported that, due to limited or no traditions of this instructional activity in most cross-cultural classrooms, students were not skilled or sophisticated in making them. They reported that students did not use research well in documenting oral reports, strayed from their main points, and did not manage their time well. Deborah Rogers, a TEFL instructor in China, advised leading off this activity by giving a "model" presentation for the class so students can see what the expectations are. Additionally, it was suggested that both minimum and maximum time limits be set for presentations.

Contracting with Students. When a student contracts for work in the American context, it is usually by a written document specifying the exact tasks and performance demands for a certain grade. This contract is usually initiated by the professor and negotiated with him. Contracting was useful to one professor of American literature in Thailand who found some of his students were anxious about getting high marks. Each student signed a contract for the grade the student would work for with the minimum expectation for each letter grade clearly specified. The contract detailed the quantity of reading assignments, minimum test grades, paper standards, and class attendance. While such a contract may require some "negotiation," it is essentially a policy statement that is signed, and differs from a contract that calls for differential assignments.

The second kind of contract, displayed in Figure 8-5, is actually negotiated between the professor and the student. It may involve a student's production of a written or oral product with criteria expected. Contracting works best with U.S. students who are high achievers and who work well independently. With those who need extra direction and support, it may be necessary to be more specific with task expectations. One asset of this contract in a cross-cultural setting is its implicit license to seek the professor's help—which may not be sought otherwise.

One caveat is that students in some cultures and some university settings will have little experience with syllabi or the concept of contractual relationships between students and teachers. An example of this caveat was described by a public health professor to Brazil who wrote "in laborious detail" her "course plans, readings, expectations, procedures for completion of papers and projects, and consequences for incompleteness." She even had the syllabus translated so there would be a minimum of language confusion. "The material was fail safe," she recalled, "except students didn't read it."

TEACHING FOR CRITICAL THINKING

What I would remember Peter most for when he is gone back is he asks us to think for ourselves, to listen to our inner voice. (A graduate student, China)

Professors who teach for critical thinking among their students believe it is an ability that can be developed and improved through guidance and practice. They advance the abilities and attitudes needed for competence in solving problems and making informed decisions in life. They believe that critical thinking

TEACHER-STUDENT CONTRACT

STUDENT NAME   <u>KIDD ISUMU</u>

WHAT OBJECTIVES ARE TO BE ACCOMPLISHED:	HOW ACCOMPLISHMENT IS TO BE DEMONSTRATED:
1. Planning a systematic study of the variety of services available to college students who seek personal or academic counseling on this campus.	Present a study plan detailing resources, 3 reference people and dates for research tasks.
2. Collecting information about the possible need for short-term/long-term intervention with this populaton.	Present an interview protocol, an interviewee list, and on-going reports.
3. Understanding of the major points of view in the literature concerning institutionalization of chronically emotionally-disturbed college students.	Participation in an in-class debate on the appropriateness of levels of intervention.

RESOURCES TO BE USED:

✔ University Health Service information.	✔ Journals of School Counseling.
✔ Counselors in each Faculty.	✔ IIE files at AUA.
✔ Tests: Marley; Sarawak; Laman; Buros.	✔ Interviews with students and reps.

STEPS TOWARD THE OBJECTIVES (S):	CHECKPOINTS AND DEADLINES
1. Obtain list of counselors and relevant student representatives. Identify 10 students.	October 7
2. Review mental health and counseling literature for material on college-student services.	October 1 – 23
3. Set up an interview schedule with counselors, reps and students; Prepare protocols.	October 11
4. Do interviews.	October 14 – 23
5. Summarize interview data; use library material.	October 31
6. Prepare debate topic.	November 7

FINAL DEADLINE FOR PROJECT COMPLETION:

November 11

Kidd Isumu

_____
Student

_____
Instructor

FIGURE 8-5   **Professor-Student Contract Sample**

unites life experiences with academic training. Every year, a number of American professors abroad, dedicated to teaching for critical thinking, are presented with situations which test their conviction. Students they have taught and loved or colleagues with whom they have trained and collaborated are faced with conflicts. Their own or their government's past, present and future values clash and battle in the streets or in the psyches.

Examples of the clash and battle are memorable. I was first in Thailand in 1973 when a student-led "revolution" instituted sweeping political and educational reforms. But in 1976, a severe retaliation led by conservative groups against the students and their reform program left many students dead and some leading intellectuals and influential university educators imprisoned or in exile. A sizeable number of Thai university professors themselves were students during that tumultuous period and the experience shaped their politics and visions of student culture (Morrell, 1981). A letter from an American professor in Thailand confirms that more than a decade later, students still think critically about institutional governance decisions:

> *Students here are still 'shouting up the corridors of power.' They are staging a sit-in to protest a university leadership decision—no student representation in the election of the university rector. . . . A cremation pyre is lighted and the Chair of the Board is burned in effigy. A tent shelters the twenty or so students who appear to be living at the headquarters for the demonstration. Bull horns and a brassy p.a. system own the air for blocks. . . . Even though I cannot understand everything they say, the diatribe sounds familiar. Students are demanding one-third of the votes for the rector—a demand so far the Board has refused to consider. A hunger strike is rumored!*

And again in 1989, few can forget the Chinese student protests and the PRC government's swift and fierce reaction in Tianamen Square in Beijing. As that siege mounted, I was sitting in a Hong Kong video suite editing "Teaching the Chinese Student," which profiled the lives of American professors teaching at major universities across China. I was carefully selecting teaching segments where American professors were encouraging students to stretch their thinking. And I was tearfully framing the faces of critically minded students whose voices might never be heard again. Indeed, some were not. Most of the situations which call for critical thinking or test one's conviction toward it are not such dramatic battles as the Thai and Chinese examples, but rather are situations of simpler problem-solving.

Planning for the Teaching of Critical Thinking

It has been suggested by some advocates of international education and scholarly exchanges that one of the most useful contributions American professors bring to the cross-cultural teaching assignment is a set of techniques for advancing students' higher level thinking processes and critical problem-solving. In this encouragement of critical thinking, American teachers I observed had advantages over host professors who often were wedded to traditional teaching methods. How they capitalized on those advantages needs discussion.

The first step in effective teaching of critical thinking is planning for it. John Chaffe, director of the Critical Thinking and Reasoning Studies Center at CUNY's Laguardia Community College, trains more than 800 students annually in multicultural settings to develop critical thinking skills. His program, activities and materials (which supplement curricula across disciplines) are available and would be useful to the American professor planning to teach in a cross-cultural classroom (Chaffe, 1988). Two essential characteristics Chaffe emphasizes were observed in the work of American professors abroad dedicated to teaching for critical thinking—teaching the fundamentals of critical thinking and having students think for themselves.

Teaching the Fundamentals of Critical Thinking.   The first step in instituting a focus on critical thinking is to teach the fundamentals of thinking, reasoning, and documenting needed for academic success in your discipline. Chaffe argues that professors cannot assume that all students are aware of these fundamentals, and in a cross-cultural situations such an assumption is more fallacious. A Fulbright professor of law in China found that he needed to teach elementary documentation skills to new law students:

> To be good lawyers, and even to be good students, they need to be able to support their viewpoints with reasons and evidence. I had to teach them that when we think critically, we give good reasons to back up our ideas. To support a position only by describing it as 'an example of capitalism or imperialism' was not going to sharpen their ability to think clearly or solve problems.

Other professors instituted simple debates in class to sharpen students' skills for supporting ideas with reasons and evidence. An American literature professor in Bangkok, who had witnessed numerous motorcycle accidents among his students, had them practice providing supporting documentation by writing on whether or not "Motorcycle Helmets Should be Mandatory."

Having Students Think for Themselves.   Some American professors felt very strongly that students in cross-cultural situations could and should examine points of view and decide for themselves their own views, opinions, and beliefs. They encouraged students to avoid blindly accepting or rejecting beliefs because of custom, political persuasion, or tradition.

Students noticed when their American professors respected their independent thinking. The Chinese graduate student remembered a Fulbright professor who "asked us to think for ourselves." This American Fulbright professor gave his graduate classes this exercise to debate: whether he should shave his mustache. Following principles of teaching for critical thinking he heard students give documentation on the reasons he should or shouldn't shave. One student remembered, "He gave me the highest marks, because all of my reasons were that *he* should decide if he should do it . . . with some consideration to his wife's view. But if he wants to, he should. He should think for himself!" The professor shaved his mustache.

Relating Critical Thinking to Students' Lives

Another important component in teaching for critical thinking is relating the process to students' daily lives. Paulo Friere, the internationally known Brazilian educator, teaches critical thinking skills. His teaching is based on activities that stimulate and sustain "critical consciousness," though it is less a pedagogical method or procedure than an educational philosophy. He is famous for his ideas of teaching for political and cognitive emancipation. He believes that many Third World "students" accept social images, customs, myths, and popular culture as realities, and are politically unempowered and psychologically devastated by them. According to Friere (1970), teaching the dominant culture's view (translated to mean the views of Western, capitalist, and heavily industrialized countries and cultures) encourages students in developing countries to acquire behavioral characteristics of self-deprecation, emotional dependence, and fatalism. Friere argues that the primary task of education or of good teaching is to help students overcome these attitudes and replace them with critical thinking and human responsibility.

In the Friere model, professors and students are collaborators and co-investigators, together developing their consciousness of reality and their images of a possible, better reality. This ability to step back from an unconscious acceptance of things as they are and to perceive the world critically, even in the midst of pervasive and powerful forces which distort and oppress, is what Friere means by attaining "critical consciousness." The politicized environment of Latin America made Friere's ideas controversial, but the underpinning educational value of the model may hold validity and utility for students around the world. Friere's model is worthy of consideration by American professors teaching across cultures, because it is predicated on the idea that the "educator" or "teacher" (who usually comes from the dominant culture) has much to learn about the culture and "realities" of the student. A second reason it is worth investigation is that it incorporates activities and strategies intended for use with students in small groups. Finally, it should be considered because it models some of the best values in American education—egalitarian participation, collaboration between students and teachers, respect for peoples no matter how culturally "different," and willingness to address openly and freely contradictions and disagreements.

The procedures of the model are greatly simplified here, but can provide an overview of the general method (Freire, 1970; Shor, 1980). First, a professor or team of professors *collect data on the realities of students lives*. He or she meets with representatives of the students to discuss plans and to secure permission and cooperation for mutual learning. The professor then visits the students' homes, worksites, sacred places, and recreation areas. The teacher studies the language, behaviors, postures, dress, and relationships of the students. The educator looks for anything and everything that indicates how the people perceive "reality" and their situations, so that he or she later can facilitate students' development of critical consciousness using these data.

In the second and third steps, the professor or team *present the findings of their observations* to groups of students. During these meetings, discussions of various ways these data, incidences, contradictions, or observations can be interpreted are discussed. Then the educators and the students *identify the "generative themes."* These themes become the heart of the teaching, teacher training, literacy program, or social science curriculum, etc. The idea, in Friere's model used with adults, is reminiscent of that used by New Zealand educator Sylvia Aston Warner and American Grace Fernald. Their method, developed in the 1940s to teach non-readers to read, used "key-word vocabularies." The idea was that certain words and phrases had a much more significant emotional or cognitive impact for students than others and would, therefore, be remembered and processed more efficiently if they were used to teach reading. Friere expands this into "generative themes."

Fourth, the professors and students *assign each theme to a "thematic investigation circle."* The role of the educator here is to create or elicit specific incidences illustrating the themes upon which students express their views. For example, rather than being encouraged to blindly oppose the distilling of home brew among local youth in the capital city, students are encouraged to investigate often dimly perceived relationships to other social conditions like stresses centered around employment prospects—e.g., few jobs, geographic discrimination, and low wages.

Fifth, the work of "thematic investigation circles" having been completed, *develop relevant learning materials* to be used with student groups. The materials are presented to students for discussion. Materials are always posed as problems, never as answers. Sometimes they are dramatized or told as stories. Students' own lives are reflected back at them in ways that encourage critical awareness. An American professor in Malaysia illustrated the meaningfulness of this final step when she observed:

> *I finally realized that Malaysian students and faculty want* my *observations of their life—much more than they want to learn about my life, workplace, and situation. . . . Most American professors miss this overture and hear their request as 'tell me about the West' or 'teach me the American way.'*

The major pitfall in thinking about adapting some of Friere's ideas for university teaching across cultures is to think of it as a "procedure." Critical thinking is an aim, not a list of procedures. And it is not just an educational aim for illiterate peasant farmers in Brazil where it was first implemented. University students, with a long educational history of passive listening to didactic lectures, deserve help to fine tune their critical thinking as well.

Engaging Students in Controversy

Conflict is the gadfly of thought. It stirs us to observation and memory. It instigates invention. Conflict is a sine qua non *of reflection and ingenuity.* (John Dewey)

The third component of teaching for critical thinking is directly engaging students in active thinking surrounding controversy. When students think actively, they get involved rather than sit on the sides, get started on their own rather than wait to be fed information, and follow through on their ideas. Activities mentioned throughout this chapter were ways American professors tried to activate students to participate in their own learning. Students' active thinking is not always easy to plan for, but there is probably no more certain way to activate them than engaging them in controversy. Johnson and Johnson (1989) found in their research on the use of structured controversy as a teaching tool that students evidenced the following:

1. Greater *mastery and retention of content;*
2. More demonstrated *generalizations of principles* applied to a wider variety of situations;
3. Higher *quality solutions* to more complex problems;
4. More ideas, *more creations of original ideas,* and a wider range of ideas;
5. More solutions, *more novel solutions,* and more variety of solutions.

My experience of introducing the Friere method to a graduate seminar in curriculum theory in Thailand was an example of involving them in a controversy—though an unexpected one. After implementing the program and witnessing more student participation and involvement than I had in any of the previous units we had covered, students petitioned me to omit the Friere material from the final exam. They argued that since Friere was identified with leftist political ideology, they "were interested to know about the ideas, but did not want to put their names on any papers associated with those ideas." Their concerns stemmed from a governing sentiment that involvement with any ideas associated with "communist thought" might jeopardize their careers under less sympathetic regimes. They put forth cogent arguments documented with supporting points and data. Friere was omitted.

Another example of an incident faced by Fulbright professor Benjamin Strickland identifies the importance and the difficulties of using controversy as a teaching tool for critical thinking. His story is told in Figure 8-6. Because of the timeliness of this event and the sensitivity surrounding it, all of the identifying information in Strickland's account has been altered, including his assignment location to 'some Asian country.' After reading the case, consider Ben Strickland's options. Which do you think he chose? Which would you have chosen?

Benjamin Strickland is a well-known and respected professor of Communications at a prestigious West Coast university in the United States. His credits include numerous books and scholarly and popular-press articles on access and freedom of information. During his year as a Fulbright professor at a major university in his host country, he occasionally reported for several American newspapers and periodicals on U.S.-Asian relations, university culture, and consumer issues.

In Strickland's graduate journalism course on advanced reporting (with fifteen students), a major part of the curriculum was "guided practice" in interview techniques in which he invited guests to class and had the students interview them for the purpose of writing an assigned story. Because no one on his Communication Faculty had ever used this teaching method before, and because Strickland worked carefully with his invited guest to assure they demonstrated the "lesson" he was trying to teach in each class, when he began to use the method, students and other professors raved about its utility and creativity.

That Spring on campuses around the country, demonstrations had begun for "more democratic measures." Students wanted more freedoms, more input on governance issues and more university access. Some students opposed government policies which provided university access, quotas, fellowships, or jobs benefitting only some segments of the population. Many issues were raised and many solutions touted. The demonstrations and the student organizations promoting them were typically controversial, but Strickland noticed that faculty members were untypically (from his experiences on U.S. campuses) silent about these events.

A *New York Times* correspondent, Harrison Kiel, was very interested in these student demonstrations which were, even if a potpourri of rather unclear issues, the first tempests on the Asian academic scene he had reported on since his assignment there six months earlier. He was the first to break the stories of student dissent to the American press. He also provided information to the "Voice of America" radio station for its coverage. In the beginning, almost no reporting of the dissent was present in the national or regional press. Kiel had heard rumors that the "powers that be" were not pleased with his "narrow coverage" of some campus incidents. Benjamin Strickland was impressed with Harrison Kiel's perceptive writing about the student unrest and invited him to be one of the interviewees in this graduate seminar on advanced reporting. He planned to have the students interview Kiel and report on the story as was the usual assignment.

On the Tuesday of Strickland's class, all of the students and several faculty members, including the Dean of the Communications Faculty, were present for the Kiel interview. Kiel talked about forty-five minutes on his observations of campuses throughout the country and his research and observations of the conditions which led up to the unrest. Students asked questions as usual for the preparation of their stories. On Thursday morning, students' stories were handed in to Strickland. That afternoon, Strickland received a letter signed by the Dean requiring that all the students' papers, based on the Tuesday class, be handed over to him.

FIGURE 8-6   A Case of Controversy as a Teaching Tool

Concept Map

9

STRUCTURING LANGUAGE SUPPORTS FOR TEACHING

HELP! I was told my students could speak, read and
write in English. They cannot!
—A KENT STATE PROFESSOR, TURKEY

The Fulbright professor who said "My biggest hassle is the difficulty of teaching students who have a lot of trouble with English" shared the views of most American professors teaching abroad. An "enormous and unpredictable variability in English proficiency" is how Fulbright linguist Vincent Linares characterized students and teachers he trained on several academic exchanges. The resulting language difficulties arise not only because of students "trouble with English," but because:

- Most visiting professors do not speak fluently the native language of their host countries;
- These instructors have been asked to teach and train only in English;
- Professors have often been assured by host and sponsoring agencies that the English proficiency among university students and faculties is much higher than it is.

ACKNOWLEDGING THE NATIONAL VERSUS INTERNATIONAL LANGUAGE DEBATE

A debate grows louder around the world, and especially in developing nations, over the use of a national versus an international language in university teaching. Though university faculties sometimes play only a marginal role in the formulation of the language policy, the implications of the debate affect academic life demonstrably. Visiting professors are sometimes viewed as "promoting an international language," so they contribute to, as well as are affected by, this policy development.

Illustrative examples of this debate and its complexities can be heard from the Philippines, Thailand, Malaysia and the former USSR's Republic of Georgia. In these, as well as many other countries, recent government policies have elevated one national language to the official language, though large segments of the populations speak other "mother-tongues." This language becomes the medium of governmental intercourse and of instruction in the schools and universities. Until recently, instruction in these countries had been, as some argued, given in "colonial languages" (e.g., English in Malaysia) or, as others argued, in "international lingua franca." The educational arguments became obviously entwined in political contention, for example, when well-known Georgian linguist Mena Kvavatskhelia became that republic's newest Minister of Education. Some of the arguments of this debate can be summarized as:

1. University students and faculty members without professional fluency in an international language may not have access to the international research literature and professional contacts in leading areas in their fields.

2. If proficiency in an international language is required for university access, then urban students and students with more opportunities to learn a world language will be significantly advantaged in admission.

3. Translation, the frequently canvassed solution, is more easily promulgated than effected, because journal articles, which report the advancements in most fields, often are not translated.

4. Compulsory bilingualism as a goal is quite remote for many students who are already overburdened by their studies in their own language.

5. Using an international language for university instruction encourages a "brain drain" in exporting talent to world hubs of research and scholarship leaving developing countries without needed resources to train advanced students.

Points on both sides of the debate are obvious, but the implications of the choice may not be. In Thailand, for example, where university classes are taught in Thai (with a small number taught by visiting professors in English), there are only a few key Thai or translated texts as main references in a field. The translations of foreign texts into Thai and the writing of Thai texts are being encouraged by small grants programs, but the progress on both is slow. New professional and academic vocabularies are being created in Thai, and such creations are a point of professional pride, but these vocabularies are still largely full of English words. With some recognition that students need access to up-to-date books and international journals (and these are limited in Thai), a modicum of English proficiency is still required to pass a university entrance exam and English is still a required part of the university curriculum.

In Malaysia, where Bahasa Malaysia has been chosen as the medium of instruction over the English instruction of the past, a visiting linguist reported,

"English proficiency is decreasing at an enormous rate . . . and there are progressively fewer faculty members to form the infrastructure to support instruction in English." These changing proficiency levels juxtaposed with the increasing demands for global education and international savvy may be a primary reason for hosts' commonly reporting English proficiencies among students and staffs as higher than they operationally are.

DETERMINING STUDENTS' LEVELS OF ENGLISH PROFICIENCY

My real problem is the language . . . the students' language skills are highly variable . . . some of them clearly understand most of what I say . . . many of them do not. (A University of Minnesota professor, Indonesia)

In cross-cultural teaching situations, many host administrators and faculty colleagues report that students and faculty members have functional skills, if not outright proficiency, in English and that visiting professors will be able to "teach in English with no problem!" These assessments are based on the fact that English language training often has occurred for many years in early schooling and that university entrance exams (with English components) are passed. I am sympathetic to the false hopes of those assessments when I remember, as a young teacher, facing my first cross-cultural classroom in West Germany scared speechless but having straight A's on my college transcript in German. The contradiction between the language proficiency reported or advertised and the skill level needed for sophisticated classroom work can present some awkwardness for the American professor abroad. For example, a Fulbright professor to Bangladesh reported:

I realized a large proportion of the students had difficulty understanding me. I spoke to the chairperson about this who assured me 'no problem—students understood me well enough.' But well enough for what?

Recognizing Proficiency Differences and Difficulties

American professors abroad report three common observations regarding English proficiency among their students. First, the statement *"very modest levels of English proficiency"* best characterizes the observations of many of these professors concerning their students language expression and/or comprehension. The second observation is that *"proficiency levels are wide-ranged, variable, and unpredictable."* And the third common assertion is that *"some discrete skills among all students are stronger than others."*

Observing Limited Proficiency. From Poland, a Fulbright professor reported, "Teaching was often a frustrating experience because many, if not most, of the

students seem inadequately prepared to handle reading and writing in English."
Another to Pakistan remarked, "Students did not have the aural comprehension
necessary to learn from the material I offered." A visiting professor to Japan
estimated that "half had difficulty with my lectures and the other half understood virtually nothing." From Nepal, an American chemistry professor reported,
"There are approximately ninety students in a class and I am suspicious that 30
percent can not comprehend any English whatsoever." Another to Thailand remarked:

> *Despite what was told me, my students didn't speak or understand English. It*
> *took me some time to figure out this contradiction—I kept saying, 'Well, they*
> *are just shy; they are more reticent than I expected.' But actually, they hardly*
> *understood anything spoken to them in English!*

From Turkey an American professor observed, "The official language, English, had not really been mastered by many students." Another to Turkey offered, "Most of my students spoke virtually no English at all; but occasionally I
met a student who was fluent in the language. The result was as might be expected—most of the Turkish professors conducted their courses in Turkish. This,
of course, caused difficulties for the 10% of the students who did not speak
Turkish."

Recognizing Variability in Proficiency.   A visiting instructor to Egypt illustrated the variable span of English skills witnessed by many American professors
abroad:

> *Some students were fully fluent in English and were eager to explore the litera-*
> *ture and history of the U.S., but others were still struggling with the rudiments*
> *of the English greetings!*

A computer science professor in Prague found, "Two-thirds of the students and
all of the faculty and staff have a reasonable knowledge of English. The remaining one third do not seem to understand spoken English at all." One Fulbright
professor to Indonesia, whose students took the Educational Testing Services's
standardized Test of English as a Foreign Language (TOEFL), had numerical data
to describe his students' variability. He said, "Among the twenty students, there
was a wide variety of English ability—on the TOEFL some are beyond the 550
score level and some are as low as 350."

Sometimes the variability was not within classes but between classes. Two
professors of American literature to China described the range they observed.
"Only in one course have I so far been able to teach throughout the whole course
in English with no help in summary or interpretation from my teaching assistant.
And in that course I saw the need to move very slowly," reported one. "My
students receive all the signals that I am broadcasting . . . they even have senses
of humor in English," reported the other in contrast. Two Fulbright professors to

Japan had sharply different experiences with proficiency. One public policy professor described his graduate students as "top drawer in their overall ability and English is only a moderate problem." The other lamented that "students admit to understanding about 50 percent of what I say in an English lecture."

Crediting Skill Strengths. This third set of observations are examples of American professors' awareness of discrete competencies in English which had an impact on their teaching. Some found that students could read English fairly well, but could not speak it. Others described vast *differences between receptive skills and expressive skills*, i.e., differences between listening/reading and speaking/writing. A Fulbright professor to China found that her students were "almost uniformly good with grammar [better than we are]. Their listening and speaking skills need the most work, and they themselves are concerned exclusively with vocabulary expansion." Another remarked, "In Pakistan, written and spoken English is far more limited than receptive English, especially reading." Sharon Hom, a law professor to China, described the divergent competencies in her classes:

> *Language, that is the real problem. Despite what the university told me that their English levels were good, they weren't. Their listening comprehension was terrible. Their reading comprehension was quite good. And their speaking ability was worse than their listening comprehension.*

A Carlton professor of literature to Nepal remarked, "Although instruction at the university is in English, most of the students [and some of the faculty] have trouble with listening comprehension, especially when complex ideas are being discussed." A similar problem in Czechoslovakia was attributed to students having "only a theoretical background in English." One professor observed, "From a practical view, students' English is weak . . . listening and speaking skills are lacking."

Occasionally, it was observed that students had conversation skills in English and "could carry on pleasant hallway chatter," but had limited capacities for sophisticated classroom discourse or limited reading and writing skills. From Tel Aviv, a Fulbright professor remarked:

> *The use of English in the law school is a tricky business. Because most of the faculty are fluent in English, one can get the impression that the students are also fluent. Some are, but not many. There is a big difference between conversation and paper writing—hallway chat and classroom analysis.*

Another American professor in Israel noted, "Most student have some English, but only a few can handle academic work in English." A visiting professor in literature from Valdosta State, whose course plan included extensive written expression, found that Mexican students "could speak and understand spoken English pretty well, but their written English was bad in most cases."

There were two main sources of differences in English competencies observed among student populations—*demographic and programmatic.* English competencies were more predictable among students with the following demographic characteristics: those from urban areas, those in more highly selective universities, those in areas with more "cross-fertilization with the West," and males. Age was a factor, as well, with older students and graduate students usually having more English competencies. But age was a predictable factor relative to the government policies concerning the official language of instruction and/or the number of years of English classes offered in elementary and secondary schooling. In some cases, where a movement toward a national language for instruction has recently occurred, older students and faculty may have superior skills compared to their younger cohorts. An American professor to Malaysia described the age factor:

> *English levels must be seen historically. Considering the situation in the country, English levels are pretty good. Up to twenty years ago the medium of instruction was English, but since independence, English is only one subject. For teachers to expect the English levels to be the same as then is a waste.*

American professors to Eastern Europe noted the interaction of age and limited access to the West. One reported, "Unlike my experience in Czechoslovakia years ago, relatively few of my Czech colleagues know English today. This has resulted in several uncomfortable situations for me during several staff meetings and social events." Class and rank are related to English competencies, as well. A visiting professor to Turkey observed, "Even if all the faculty could speak English [which they can't], I soon realized that the secretaries, technicians, and photocopy workers, do not!"

Programmatic factors surrounding English competencies also were observed. A Fulbright professor reported, "In Pakistan, there seemed to be two 'informal' tracks—English and Urdu, but students from both tracks took my courses. Some of the Urdu track students had real difficulty understanding anything I said and were unable to do any of the written work. Though the English-medium students were generally better, even then there were great differences in English abilities." From Nepal, a law professor concurred, "Law students have some English, but it is usually not at a level at which they can discuss legal matters in a sophisticated way. All courts are conducted in Nepali, so there is not the base of English-language legal material that exists, like in India."

Predictably, students majoring in English, TEFL, English literature or American studies were observed to have more English competencies than other students. American professors to Prague reported major differences between students in the field of English and American studies and all other fields. They suggested in these related fields that the students' command of English was "quite good," "basically pretty good," "good grammar and book knowledge of the language," but outside these fields, they reported, "not adequate for English lectures," "what English skills?" "barely rudimentary levels," etc. A professor of literature in China remarked favorably on his literature graduate students' proficiency levels:

> *I'm essentially talking to them at the same level that I would talk to comparable students in the States; I'm most grateful for that, for language is the medium of literature [like clay is the medium of pottery or stone of sculpture]. If I had to speak at a different level, I think that it would hinder my teaching.*

ASSESSING LEVELS OF ENGLISH PROFICIENCY

In a cross-cultural classroom where the medium of instruction is English, one of the earliest teaching tasks will be to assess students English proficiency. First, you will need to know the *range of proficiency* (the difference between the student with the most competencies and the student with the least). You will want to identify those students whose listening comprehension or oral expression is very limited and there will likely be some. You will want to use this information in planning learning activities and lectures to avoid directly teaching only to those students facile or comfortable with English. Additionally, you will need to know the *variability in proficiency* (about how many students can be characterized as proficient, moderately proficient, or having limited proficiency).

There are several methods of informally gathering data for assessing language levels. These can be used to roughly gauge the average level of English proficiency among your students. Informal assessments work well when you have large classes, when there is limited access to more sophisticated instrumentation and standardized data, or when students have a serious aversion to measurement. The ones discussed here are the student interview, the teacher-initiated conversation, and passage retelling (Larsen-Freeman, 1983).

1. **Student-interview.** Each student in class is asked the same questions in English:

- What is your name?
- What is you home town and province/state?
- How many years have you studied English?
- Tell me about your family.
- Tell me about your future plans.

2. **Teacher-initiated conversation.** You elaborate on the interview questions above with additional questions:

- Is it better to come from a small town or a city?
- Is it better to come from a large or small family?
- Is it better to work in your home town or another town?

3. **Passage Retelling.**   A passage or story is read to each student. The student then retells the tale in her own words. This can be written by the student or told verbally and recorded by you.

One common technique used for analyzing this material is the coding of *T-units*—recording a main clause plus whatever clauses, phrases or words happen to be attached to, or embedded in, the phrase. Analysis of T-units can vary in difficulty from counting them, counting only the error-free ones, counting the number of words in them, or only words in the error-free ones. Whatever method you chose, use exactly the same criteria for every student. While counting T-units gives you a measure of English expression, it does require listening comprehension (reception) to execute the answers, conversation, or passage retelling. T-unit analyses for a whole class will give you a gross indicator of both range and variability of skills for "participating in language exchange" in a classroom.

One professor interviewed used another informal method of English assessment—the "mini-comprehension quiz" method. He gave a mini-lecture of fifteen minutes, then asked ten factual questions from the material, and finally asked students to write the answers in complete sentences. He credited a response that was error-free. While this professor's technique is perhaps a more natural "classroom type" assessment, he may be assessing more nearly his own communication skills than his students' by such a measure.

MODIFYING CLASSROOM INSTRUCTIONAL LANGUAGE

I find it very frustrating that I can't talk as fast as I want to talk. (A University of Alaska professor, Hong Kong)

Limited English proficiency levels among students usually meant that professors had to modify classroom language. Most found they first had to *slow the pace of delivery and presentation*. Everyone had to slow down more than they wanted.

One fast-speaking New Yorker teaching in Israel said, "I learned to speak slowly, but it wasn't easy for me!—I found it easier to learn Hebrew!" Another to China added, "It's frustrating when you get excited about the material to speak about it so slowly." A Fulbright professor to Thailand years later remembered only one phrase in Thai, *cha cha noi—go a little slower!* From Pakistan another remarked, "When I was careful to pace myself very, very slowly, to select my vocabulary, and to keep a constant eye out for furrowed brows, I was somewhat successful."

Others found they had to rework their course plans *to simplify vocabulary and content*. This meant they had to begin earlier in a sequence of materials, teach more limited content and require much longer time frames for coverage than they anticipated. One professor to China found that slowing her speech was necessary, but not sufficient to promote English comprehension. She had to simplify her vocabulary, which she described as "about 50 percent legal" and to try other strategies. She described this shift:

> *After I started speaking slower, then I started thinking of how to break these ideas down. That shifted the focus from 'Why is this student slow and not getting it' to 'What can I do to help this student get it.'*

A journalism professor to Pakistan described his situation. "In all of the classes the difficulty was finding the correct level at which to start. Neither my students nor the journalists I worked with had strong English skills—the starting level was always lower than I expected."

Still others found the need *to structure their classroom methods to accommodate students' limited proficiency.* An ecologist to Indonesia described breakout groups assigned by English proficiency:

> *Because of variability in English, I often divided the class into groups based on elementary, intermediate, and advanced English levels and had them discuss problems I posed with each other. There would be two groups with English discussion [advanced and intermediate] and a couple in Bahasa [elementary]. That worked much better. I then could hear what concepts they were having difficulty with. And they had a lot of difficulties!*

A professor to Bangladesh altered his method of information dissemination, "Since most of the students could read English much better than they could hear or speak it, I agreed to write up five-page summaries of the lessons. These were duplicated and distributed to the students." Figure 9-1 summarizes the points offered here and suggests guidelines for Accommodating Instruction to Students with Limited English Proficiency.

SPEAKING NATIVE AND HOST LANGUAGE IN THE CLASSROOM

Using Native Language as the Medium of Instruction

Some American professors, especially in countries where Spanish, German, French, and Portuguese are spoken, are expected to teach in the host country languages and many who teach there are proficient. However, even professors competent in the host languages are often not prepared for the difficulties of using them as the medium of instruction. Two commonly reported problems are:

1. Underestimating the *amount of time* it takes to prepare lessons in another language; and
2. Laboring with *limited vocabularies* in instructional processes and professional terms.

1. **Recognize the scope and range of proficiency among students.**

   - There are often differences between reception (listening) and expression (speaking).
   - There are often differences in skills between writing, speaking, and reading.

2. **Assess individual proficiency informally.**

   - Use interviews, guided conversations, and passage retelling.
   - Use the "cloze procedure" (which deletes words from a passage and requires a student to fill in the blanks) to assign comprehensible reading material (See Chapter 2).

3. **Assess group proficiency informally by using T-unit analysis.**

4. **Slow the pace of delivery and presentation.**

5. **Simplify and control your vocabulary.**

6. **Become familiar with the features of the native language.**

   - Note how a student miscues in English due to native patterns.
   - Formulate classroom questions using native language tags to facilitate Q/A processes.

7. **Use predictable classroom structures and procedures.**

   - Familiarity with routines, procedures, and language patterns minimizes misunderstandings and errors.

8. **Use advance organizers, scaffolds, and visual aids.**

   - Models, outlines, charts, etc., maximize comprehension and minimize language dependency.

FIGURE 9-1   Guidelines: Accomodating Instruction to Students with Limited English Proficiency

One Fulbrighter who had grown up in Eastern Europe, but had been a professor in America for almost three decades, shared examples of both of these problems:

> My 'thought-to-be fluent' Czech has proven to be inadequate for smooth lecturing. My lecturing in Czech requires that I prepare my lectures very carefully. It takes huge amounts of time! I often need to consult others about the specific social science terminology that I acquired only in English.

His story was repeated by other professors who taught in Latin America with their "rusty Spanish" or "book-learned Portuguese." I am reminded of my first year instructing in a German school. By day, I would teach and by night I would struggle to prepare the next day's lessons—checking vocabulary, searching for

German examples, writing out verbatim explanations, and making more detailed lesson plans than I would ever do again. Giving this struggle some perspective, one professor to Mexico reported, "Blessedly, Mexican students and faculty are forgiving of my less-than-perfect Spanish." But another with several experiences teaching abroad reinforced the value of trying to perfect the language. "My effectiveness here seems in direct proportion to my fluency in Spanish."

Learning Native Language for Managing Daily and University Life

> *As my Norwegian improved, so did my teaching! (A Temple University professor, Norway)*

Debating Language Learning. There is probably no topic more highly debated in international education than the role and expectation of language learning. American participants in academic sojourns have found that because sufficient English is spoken in most places in the world, they can get most of their needs met. Reasons for not learning language usually have two thrusts—"I will only be here in country for three months, six months, one year, etc., which is inadequate time for language learning" or "Most everyone speaks some English, so I don't need the host language." In contrast, advocates of language learning argue that learning the host language is important because it enhances cultural sensitivity and the meaning of "exchange." These quotes illustrate the advocacy position of many American professors abroad:

- *Thai language is the key to the soul of the Thai people.*
- *If I use their language, even in my faulty way, they are thrilled!*
- *Language learning, yes! It's a matter of respect.*
- *It doesn't matter if you become fluent in Bahasa, but if you are going to get any real meaning from your time here, you've got to learn something.*
- *Using Norwegian indicates a level of cultural sensitivity and respect that can be delivered in no other way.*
- *By learning as much language as I can, I can return home knowing that I have truly lived in Turkey!*
- *What one gets out of one's stay here depends on one's fluency in Spanish.*
- *I did not know the language at all when I arrived in Czechoslovakia, but I signed up for a course that met three nights a week. It was time-consuming but worth the effort.*
- *Everything essential is possible in English, but everything important happens in Chinese.*

Additionally, those who advocated giving a priority to language learning in their academic exchanges reported that it enhanced job effectiveness. A biologist to Indonesia, who studied the language every day remarked on its value for professional relations:

I learned Bahasa because what I do here depends on the success of it... on their terms. For centuries there have been foreigners telling them how to do things. What they need is people who can appreciate their problems from their point of view. . . . The way I can do that is by getting as involved with their culture as much as possible . . . language is inseparable from that.

A Fulbright professor to Norway argued, "It is advantageous to learn Norwegian for my teaching and my lecture preparations. Admittedly, so many speak English that it is hard at times to practice it, but I have learned how to manage my classes, deal with the staff, and negotiate most of my campus activities." A nursing professor to Norway offered, "I had not expected that the one thing that would make the exchange work so well was the fact that I studied the language. So many of my colleagues commented on this fact and said that they were surprised an American would bother!" A visiting professor to Brazil knew only a few words of Portuguese and Spanish and frequently felt "isolated and misunderstood." He described his experience as "very frustrating." Another American professor to Mexico added, "Even as a TEFL instructor where most of the instruction is in English, Spanish was essential for daily survival. Shopping, school arrangements for the children, medical treatment, traveling, etc., would have been extremely difficult if I had not known Spanish." Another American medical faculty member to Chile warned, "Yes, many colleagues speak English, but Spanish is necessary for communicating with everyone else [like the secretary], don't forget!"

Arranging for Language Learning. For the last six years, I have worked with a group of colleagues, including some staff from the United States Information Agency (USIA), Institute of International Education (IIE), Council for the International Exchange of Scholars (CIES), and the Southeast Asia Summer Studies Institute (SEASSI) to develop programs and curricula for preparing American professors and scholars for academic exchanges abroad. The consensus based on the experiences of the international educators involved is that language learning should be the centerpiece of such cross-cultural preparation (George, 1990). Figure 9-2, Language Learning as Part of Teaching Across Cultures, provides guidelines for learning a language on the job and as part of your job. Another good resource is *The Whole World Guide to Language Learning* (Marshall, 1992) available from Intercultural Press (see appendix D).

Using Classroom Expressions in the Native Language

The use of *classroom management expressions* in the native language "seems to put students more at ease," argued a visiting professor of political science in Thailand. Often-used phrases incorporated into your classroom speech should be learned early in language training. Some examples of such phrases are given in Figure 9-3, but your own language, content, and style will necessitate a tailored list.

1. **View learning the host language as part of your work.**

   - Build language study into your work day; don't think of it as "extracurricular" activity.

2. **Find a language teacher in your first weeks in the country.**

   - Try to find a trained language teacher (even an English teacher) as a tutor.
   - Negotiate this tutoring with your university host.

3. **Use a systematic book or method to direct your language learning.**

   - Unless you have an experienced, trained language instructor, you will likely have to set the pace and direction of your lessons.

4. **Plan for more intensive language training early in your stay.**

   - For example, have lessons one hour per day for the first semester and two hours per week during the second semester.

5. **Learn phrases to keep others talking and helping you learn.**

   - For example: "Can you repeat that?"
     "I don't understand, please say it again."
     "Can you speak more slowly?"
     "I want to speak (host language) with you."

6. **Pay less attention to reading or grammar than to oral expression.**

   - Try to talk!

7. **Learn "courtesy language" early.**

   - The routines of greeting and other professional courtesies (e.g., greeting speeches) are very important.

8. **Build your vocabulary daily.**

   - Keep a running lists of new words by category or situation.
   - Try to work from your new language to English.
   - Carry your dictionary at all times.

9. **Make yourself a personal "phrasebook."**

   - Shopping, tailoring, barbering, copying, navigating are but a few situations where often-used phrases are essential. For example, have phrases on:
     - *Doing work tasks:* copying, typing, obtaining supplies.
     - *Ordering:* food, tickets, stamps, etc.
     - *Seeking services* from: tailors, barbers, cleaners.
     - *Buying:* clothing, food, photos, bargaining.,
     - *Giving and receiving invitations:* yes, no, R.S.V.P.

FIGURE 9-2   Guidelines: Language Learning as Part of Teaching Across Cultures

Good!	Say it again.
Good answer!	Be quieter, please.
Correct! Right!	Come in. Be welcome.
Not exactly right.	What is (Eng.) for (native)?
Try again.	What is (native) for (Eng.)?
Look at this carefully.	What is this/that called?
Do you have questions?	Think carefully.
Do/can you see/	Take your time.
I do/n't understand.	It's true!
I understand. I see.	It doesn't matter. Never mind.

FIGURE 9-3   Classroom Expressions Worth Learning in the Native Language

Another example of using native language in the classroom is the *localizing of examples and referents.* Effective visiting professors learned about the local, national and regional issues in their disciplines and found examples to illustrate points and draw comparisons. For a continued discussion of "localizing" examples, read the section on Relating Lecture Material to the Cultural Context in Chapter 5. One simple way some professors localized the content and examples in the classroom was to keep a running list of common names and local celebrities, which they used in examples and stories. "It never failed to produce a stir of interest when I used a local hero in one of my examples," a professor to Malaysia said. Another professor used case studies from his work in the United States, but changed all the names and contexts to Mexican names.

A final example of classroom use of native language is the *greeting speech.* As folks say in the American South, "A glad hand smooth an early wrinkle." Similarly, a visiting professor's initial gesture of hospitality can be one of his or her most remembered characteristics in a cross-cultural teaching situation. The greeting speech or polite opening remarks of your first class, lecture, or meeting are not to be overlooked in your enthusiasm to begin. If those opening remarks can be made partially in the native language of the host or students, according to a near-unanimous consensus from academic communities abroad, your cultural sensitivity and job effectiveness may be more appreciated. A simple greeting speech learned in the host language might be general enough to serve many uses and occasions:

Dean/Faculty/Students, I bring greetings to you from <u>(my university)</u>. I am very glad to have the opportunity to <u>meet/speak/be</u> with you. I am learning to speak <u>(the host language)</u>, but today, I will <u>talk/lecture/teach</u> in English. Thank you for inviting me.

EMPLOYING TRANSLATORS AND TRANSLATIONS

Some professors teaching in a cross-cultural situation found it necessary, useful, or preferable to have their lectures and classes translated. Effective translating is a skill many of us appreciate only when we read Japanese haiku or Garcia de Marquis's novels. But talented translators in the university setting are valuable resources. In Japan, it was reported that about half of all visiting professors use translators. In China, about 10–20 percent use translators. In Southeast Asia and Hong Kong, translators were commonly used for large public lectures, but rarely used in classrooms. International relations professor Al Bailey said of his use of translators in China, "I've never worked with interpreters before I came to China and I thought it might be difficult getting used to, but it was not hard at all."

Employing translators is not without its problems and disadvantages, however. One professor to Thailand warned of its deleterious impact on student attention. "When you use a translator, be prepared for students not to listen. They wait for the 'replay.'" A professor to Japan, where translator use is common, did not like the awkwardness of this role. "When I taught through a translator, I felt more like an item on display than a teacher." Another was frustrated by the content and meaning lost in translation, "I shouldn't even waste time preparing the perfect lecture—it comes out so differently anyhow when it is filtered through a translator." Another visiting professor to Japan found "teaching in well-measured two sentence parcels and then pausing for translation" not to his liking and added, "It has taken quite some adjusting on my part."

Choosing a Translator. The logical choice of a translator is a cooperative colleague, such as the professor with whom you team-teach. This colleague/translator will likely know the vocabulary and content of the course. Educational leadership professor Fran Trusty described his arrangement:

> I have asked a Thai faculty to translate in my classes by summarizing my lectures. To help prepare him, I create an outline [which I also share in class with the students]. The translation causes the classes to go at a slow pace, but students appreciate the slow pace. It is a much slower pace than I am used to.

Because of the potential value of this special working relationship, care should be taken to foster it. Relational difficulties may arise if the balance of status is tipped and you become the expert professor with a "sidekick." Guidelines for Using a Translator Effectively are provided in Figure 9-4.

A professor who used two translators described his relationship with them. "I got to know them very well and we also became friends. They became guides to show me and my wife around. They played the role of administrative assistant in the course [dealing with overhead projectors and transparencies, checking on classroom lighting, and telling us of important visitors]. There's a good deal

1. **Plan ahead for the use of translation.**

    *   Prepare lecture and teaching materials ahead of time and spend ample time (at least an hour) discussing your ideas with your translator colleague.

2. **View translation as a "collaborative" teaching arrangement.**

    *   Make it known to your translator that you want her to elaborate on the concepts and add her own ideas.
    *   Ask your translator/colleague what he thinks of ideas, concepts, etc., and incorporate his thoughts into your lectures for him to then expand upon as he translates.

3. **Acknowledge the value of the translation.**

    *   Refer to your communication as a "team effort." You can not do your part effectively without her, so let her know.
    *   Credit a translator with his good job publicly to students, faculties, and audiences.

FIGURE 9-4   Guidelines: Using a Translator Effectively

of liaison-type work which interpreters do. I found both of my interpreters excellent at this as well as at interpretation."

Using students in class to translate key words and concepts is also possible, if there are students in your classes who have English proficiency. The liability of this practice is the potential for elevating a student to a more public role than he feels comfortable with. One American professor to Thailand recommended the method he used of hiring a graduate student with good English skills as a "teaching assistant" to serve as an intermediary in class discussions and evaluation of student material done in Thai. A professor to Czechoslovakia told of "co-opting the *scripta* [class scribe] idea." He contracted with the student who had the best English listening comprehension (and who took good notes) to takes notes in Czech for the entire class, which the professor then copied and distributed.

Organizing the Translation.   Effective use of translators depends on planning and preparing prior to class. One professor who understood the use of timely preparation explained:

> *Generally an hour or two before my classes, my interpreter comes to my apartment and spends an hour going over the material. We review terms which are particularly unfamiliar to the Chinese. . . . At the beginning we spent relatively more time doing this, but as the interpreter gets to know me and how I speak and what I like to emphasize, it is now a shorter procedure.*

During the delivery of information, there are several translation sequences—simultaneous; sentence-by-sentence; passage-by-passage or summary methods. *Simultaneous translation* (usually accomplished with the use of electronic devices and audience headphones), though increasing in usage at international academic meetings, is still not commonly used for classes and lectures. The *Sentence-by-sentence method* and the *passage-by-passage method* are more commonly used where you speak or read a segment, pause to have it translated, then continue. Sentence-by-sentence translation, while good for students taking verbatim notes, is jerky and boring for most American lecturers. International relations professor Al Bailey described the order of his translation:

> *I give the lecture, pausing at what would seem like natural points for interpretation. That seemed very normal; it did not take much in the way of adaptation to get used this. I found it very pleasant, for when I was pausing and the interpreter was translating my words into Chinese, I could then collect my thoughts for my next paragraph of interpretation. That is a luxury one doesn't have in America.*

An alternative is to complete an entire set of expressions or descriptions supporting a main point before pausing for the translation. Coverage of a point or subpoint may take several minutes of presentation, but then the full set can be summarized as it is translated. Regardless of the method you choose or find most comfortable, you will improve over time. If you work well with your translator, you will develop good sequencing.

Using a 'Rapporteur."   Some international organizations, such as the United Nations and others with educational missions and many language barriers, have developed the "rapporteur" role to summarize at the end of a meeting, class, or event the main points, examples, or lessons. This language support idea has the advantages of *restatement* and *translation*—restatement in the native language for those trying to follow a lecture in English, for example, and translation for those with limited English facility. The use of a rapporteur works well when the group has a wide range of English language proficiency, such as a group of faculty members ranging from some with fluency and Ph.Ds from Western universities to some with no experience living or studying abroad and limited English proficiency. An effective rapporteur, like a good translator, will know the content of the topic, be versed in the professional vocabulary, and be briefed well by you before serving in this capacity.

One strategy proved very effective for American professor Tone Carlen in Prague, who experimented with the use of the rapporteur. Countering its typical use of summing up at the end, he asserted, "This service is most effective at the *beginning* of the lecture. The listeners then know the story or main points and can listen to the English." A side benefit, as pointed out by Carlen, is that because the translator is delivering the key points first, he or she shares near equal status with the lecturer.

TEACHING ENGLISH BY DEFAULT

Every American professor [regardless of discipline] is sometimes seen as a TESL instructor. (A Brigham Young professor, Pakistan)

Most American professors at some time during their academic exchanges served as instructors of English language. The role of English or TEFL (Teaching English as a Foreign Language) instructor was sometimes small and included little more than working with students on grammar and vocabulary development in a particular field. However, for some professors, those small roles expanded to include more TEFL work, for example:

- *Making English language recordings used by language classes and language labs (Japan);*
- *Occasional radio tutorials (Turkey);*
- *Establishing an English 'Conversation Club' (Indonesia);*
- *Writing applications and proposals for colleagues and grad students (Thailand);*
- *Editing Law Review articles (Malaysia); and*
- *Setting up 'Coffee Hours' for students where they were required to converse in English (China).*

Occasionally, professors became actual instructors of English (or TEFL or TESL) by default. An Arizona State professor to Indonesia described this latter case:

After spending some time in the program, I realized that I couldn't teach what I had come here to teach [American history]. What they needed was English instruction. Many of the students wish to study abroad. So much of my focus is aimed at comprehension for the TOEFL (Test of English as a Foreign Language).

Another professor to Nepal redefined his entire job description over time. "The aim of my Fulbright, I figured out, was not to teach American literature, but rather to make my students' spoken English more 'communicative' within the constraints of the Nepali context." A professor to Indonesia whose role included much English teaching, reported how he got help to assume this new role:

I've never really taught English before, but USIS has a program in teaching English as a second language and is anxious to help—they've provided books and catalogs and answered questions quickly. Their experts in TEFL have been willing to put on workshops and provide tapes on how to teach English. . . . There is a lot of support here for someone who's never done TEFL.

The TEFL hat did not fit comfortably on every professor, as a Fulbrighter to Israel described. "Being viewed as an English teacher caused me no small amount of frustration—a feeling I shared with other foreign teachers who felt unable to function in that capacity." From Pakistan, another professor lamented his unplanned-for role as a language instructor with "with no audiovisual equipment, large classes, and mixed ability levels!"

From Turkey, a visiting instructor warned that foreign teachers who agree to "help with English teaching" may find themselves required to "teach composition to large classes, to promote practice without a.v. equipment, to design syllabi, and to design exams for nationwide use—all outside their expertise." From Mexico, an American professor with skills in Spanish had extra requests for translations into English and remarked, "I was an easy target for colleagues and administrators seeking advice on refining English writing and translation of documents, bios, professional papers, and correspondence." Knowing the copious requests for English instruction from previous experience, one Fulbright professor in Eastern Europe defended her restraint:

> *There continues to be too many expectations for American lecturers to serve as language teachers. The need grows constantly for native speakers of English to teach, make recordings, do radio work, and help with translations. I began by saying 'yes' to almost every request and found myself overwhelmed with extra work. Now, I have learned to be more selective and, in general, limit myself to helping colleagues and students.*

Teaching English as a Foreign or Second Language instruction across cultures has been a discipline for many years with extensive literature, professional organizations, and instructional models. A discussion of the methods of that profession is beyond the scope of this text, but a good overview is available in Patricia Byrd's *Teaching Across Cultures in the University ESL Program* (1986).

Concept Map

10

ENHANCING LEARNING WITH TECHNOLOGIES

*Students need the additional stimulus of my main
points beamed large upon the wall!*
—A CARLTON COLLEGE PROFESSOR, JAPAN

American professors in cross-cultural classrooms reported that they needed to use many more visual aids when they taught and lectured than they normally did in their home classrooms. While existence of audio-visual equipment is increasing at universities everywhere, existence of equipment in cross-cultural situations did not guarantee access and was never assured. As a forewarning, whether you have adequate equipment will depend on the general availability of the equipment in your country, the specific availability in your placement, and your own equipment needs. But, as a general rule, equipment is not as readily available or as commonly used as it is in most U.S. universities. For example, the only situation which we examined where American professors did not complain about availability and access to audio-visual equipment was in New Zealand. A professor to Nepal explained this accessibility problem:

> *Cassette players lie unused in locked cases, even batteries are locked away. Overhead projectors available here are not used. Even though campuses have pieces of equipment, they are without funds for maintenance, training, and simple supplies.*

A professor to Turkey concurred with this availability problem. "There is a TV and VCR, but because there is no cart and no elevator, it is difficult to move from room to room and must be used in the library—a real zoo, because it is so small and not free during class hours."

A professor to Ireland warned against reliance on availability of audio-visual equipment. "Lack of familiarity with the uses of the equipment or Americans' fondness for it means you can't expect there will be any." From Pakistan, another maintained, "In many cases a-v equipment is simply not available and can't be obtained for your use." An American physics professor to Thailand related the story of a spectrograph machine he was told before his arrival was "available" in the physics department. However, when he requested its use, he was told by his department head it was "too valuable for use in teaching." He was disappointed in his thwarted access to the technologies he needed.

American professors often reported that they "scrounged around for equipment" and sometimes found it in English, medical, or communications faculties when they were not available at their own. A two-time Fulbright professor of Law to Nepal and Sri Lanka remarked, "I learned from Sri Lanka that somewhere there is a cache of equipment and I just have to find it. At this university (in Nepal), the *English* department has excellent a-v equipment."

RELYING ON LOW-TECH AUDIO-VISUAL EQUIPMENT

I rue the day I came here without my collection of every slide I have ever made. Here a good picture is worth a million words. (A professor who forgot his slides, Indonesia)

Many visiting professors in cross-cultural situations found the use of *overhead projectors with transparencies* supplemented their lectures well. A foreign professor in Japan who used overhead projectors with reported frequency and success said, "My using overheads with basic notes typed out was much more interesting and engaging for students than the way most of their Japanese professors taught. It likely kept students coming back."

Despite its utility, overhead projector equipment was rarely as accessible, as functional, or as commonly used as in the U.S. classroom. Therefore, dependency on it was sometimes problematic. Overhead equipment and supplies are expensive in many countries and projector copy film (the kind for overhead reproductions from a typewritten sheet) are sometimes prohibitively dear or unavailable. One professor to Pakistan conveyed, "There are no ways to make overheads from photocopies, so these need to be prepared ahead of time, but the real problem here is availability of supplies, not equipment." Others advised "bringing transparencies and marking pens from the United States" for those who plan to use this equipment extensively.

The most beneficial use of overhead transparencies in a cross-cultural situation is presenting material visually in *digestible portions* as you proceed through a lecture. In this way you can control the amount of information and protect students from "overload" (a high risk in classes where the content and the language are difficult). Guidelines for Optimizing the Usefulness of Overhead Projections in the cross-cultural classroom are offered in Figure 10-1.

1. **Project your advance organizers.**

    • Models, outlines, time lines, diagrams are good use of overheads. These might replicate the handout material or reinforce it.
    • Allow students to copy these organizers in preparation for the lecture to come, especially in the absence of handout materials.

2. **Present one point at a time on the screen.**

    • While this is an obvious function of overhead equipment, students may need you to provide the extra supports of highlighting the discussed point in order to maintain focus.

3. **Use the "highlight-and-mask" technique.**

    • Highlight the discussed point and cover all the points but the point you are discussing.

4. **Use overheads as a "write-on" surface.**

    • Use the overhead to present an outline, map, or model which you then fill in with additional material as you proceed.
    • Project the transparency onto a chalkboard or whiteboard and fill in material with chalk or marker at the board as you proceed.

5. **Overlay one transparency upon another.**

    • Overlays allow you to present small segments of material at a time.
    • Register a position dot or marker on the outline, map, or model as the presentation proceeds and each overlay is added.

FIGURE 10-1   Guidelines: Optimizing the Usefulness of Overhead Projections

        While the utility and novelty of projected visual material for enhancement may be obvious, the drawbacks to dependency on overheads may not be. First, in some areas with marked resources limitations, electricity is not altogether dependable and universities have outages periodically. At least some part of every week at the major university in Thailand's second largest city where I taught, there was no electricity to run computers, air-conditioners, lights, or teaching equipment. Another instructor in Nepal remarked, "Electricity supplies are still so sporadic, planning for the use of a-v equipment seems pointless." Another drawback of overhead use is the noise the equipment makes in an atmosphere where language comprehension is already difficult.
        Another piece of low-tech audio-visual equipment which professors found useful for teaching was the *cassette tape player*. Tapes players were plentiful, versatile, and owned by almost every student. Batteries and adaptors were readily available and inexpensive and the vagaries of electricity were not a hindrance. Professors recorded stories, plays, television shows, assignments, lectures,

readings, and summaries of classroom materials in English and native languages. Students checked out copies of these recorded materials for repetition and review.

TEACHING WITH FILM AND VIDEO

American professors are expanding and improving their use of video equipment in cross-cultural teaching situations. Some of the professors we observed found that, as an English professor to Nepal said, "Videocassettes are my most useful teaching tool." A history professor in Indonesia remarked, "I incorporate as much film as I can into the class." A sociologist to Japan reported, "Every class employs at least one full-length feature film . . . classic films that expand my students' horizons." An American literature professor to China described his video use, "I am fortunate to have a lot of videos of American films here—often films of the plays that I am teaching in my drama course. In the poetry course I am able to show the PBS television series on American poets. I have a complete set of those videos and I am structuring the course around them."

A sociology professor to China found many "micro-teaching" uses of videos in class. He found he could prompt "systematic observation and discussion" when he used everyday situations in the United States portrayed incidentally in films (e.g., store clerks and customers, telephone conversations, casual meetings on the street, etc.) and in China when he or his students recorded similar situations themselves. Some other uses of video equipment reported by visiting professors included:

1. Taping their lectures to improve delivery (pace, volume, vocabulary, etc.);
2. Taping students involved in debates, presentations, role-playing, and discussions for their review of their own and each others' performance;
3. Taping U.S. examples of situations or techniques for comparison and demonstration in class, e.g., interviews, counseling sessions, classroom interactions, teaching techniques, etc.;
4. Setting up self-teaching sessions for students, e.g., students can view an assigned drama or historical documentary outside of class time.

The strength of video material is its motivational quality, especially in settings where host professors do not often use the equipment instructionally. Some reported that the novelty served to captivate the interest of students, but others remarked that American films, video, and television programs employ language that is too difficult for students to understand. One professor to Japan described this difficulty, "I expected that videos would be highly motivating to students, however, less than a quarter watched the videotapes. They would say how difficult the videos were to understand [even with my notes]."

For visiting professors who use video material satisfactorily, language supports are usually necessary. One Fulbright professor described how he modified his video use for his work in Japan. "I asked an interpreter to render a one-page summary of my videos in Japanese and to translate a list of a dozen or so key phrases culled from the video for special attention in class as part of the teaching . . . the effort paid off." Another American literature professor who used video successfully as a teaching tool in Norway described modifications for cross-cultural situations:

> *Here it is impossible for students to view a whole video and have anything to say about it. The dialogue is so fast and complicated. But what I do is, after the students view the complete video, I record five or ten minutes segments, bring them to class, making sure they know the vocabulary and then discuss only these segments. That works beautifully.*

Robert Drexler, a Fulbright professor of American literature, trained Thai professors in effective use of film and video in the classroom. He explained:

> *One of the things I do in staff development is to show how to use video in the classroom. The way teachers have been using video is to get students in a room and show the entire video and bring them back to the classroom and make them discuss it. But it doesn't work well. So what I train them to do is have students look at the film, then record about ten minutes that show something important about the film. Because these segments are illustrative of the film as a whole, they can get discussion of the bigger picture going in class. My problem is convincing the Thai faculty that they have to go through that second step of dividing the film up, taking clips, and teaching the segments.*

Considering Availability and Access. Just as with other audio-visual equipment, video equipment can be "available but not accessible." System compatibility and unfamiliarity with equipment are two of the hurdles in cross-cultural situations. Additionally, the equipment at the universities is sometimes not portable, making it cumbersome for use in distant classrooms or lecture halls. In some cases, as one professor to Pakistan remarked, "Video equipment is simply not available to me." Despite these hurdles, some Western professors have found video equipment, as in situations with other teaching equipment, in distant units within their university such as an English department, a medical school, or an educational technology program.

In some countries, China being the best known example, movies and videotapes used in the classroom are required to be previewed by officials for determining their "acceptability." For example, in some Chinese universities there are procedures to be followed for requesting viewing rooms, securing equipment, and obtaining the signature of an official who vouches for the film or video's suitability. Though these procedures were considered "only a formality" by most visiting professors, the process can be time-consuming and tedious. One Fulbright professor in Beijing reported that his university took months to review his video library of films to accompany his course in American studies. When the tapes were returned to him they had obviously been badly copied. "I wouldn't have minded that they copied my videos," he vented, remembering the long hours of tape preparation he had done, "but they gave me the damn copies!"

Considering System Compatibility. The biggest difficulty with accessible video, however, is system compatibility. The video systems in some countries are not compatible with the American system. Besides the NTSC system (used commonly in the United States and North America), there are two other international standards—PAL (used in Europe, Asia, and many African countries) and SECAM (world-wide, but less commonly used). Videotapes purchased in the U.S. or made on NTSC equipment will not play on any of the other formats. If you have videotapes from the United States you wish to use abroad, where the NTSC system is not the standard, you have several options:

1.   Seek out a *Multi-system VCR and monitor.* This equipment is available at most universities abroad, but because of its expense, it is not in every unit and may be parsimoniously safeguarded.

2.   Have a *standards conversion* on key pieces of video (dubs made from your tapes to a new tape, e.g., into PAL format). This process varies in expense. In large cities, conversions can be done commercially for about $25–30 an hour. Some U.S. university language labs have this capability as well.

3.   If your needs are not specific, plan to use *lending libraries,* e.g., United States Information Service (USIS), British Council, American University Alumni Association (AUA), etc., as sources of video materials.

PLANNING FOR COMPUTER USE

Few American professors can imagine living a year without a computer, but many of these who participate in academic exchanges must do so. Customs regulations, voltage variations, climatic conditions, and security are all good reasons to reconsider the absolute necessity of having a personal computer abroad. There is so much "conventional wisdom" about traveling with computers, so many weekly regulatory changes, and so much variation in local availability of alternatives, that a full discussion of computer use abroad is beyond the scope of this text. However, because possession, acquisition, and safeguarding of this equipment causes so much concern and anxiety among American professors, it deserves mention.

Considering Voltage Transformers.   Voltage transformers are often necessary when planning to use a computer abroad. Because each computer and system is different, consulting the retailer or the manufacturer on requirements for running your computer equipment using these transformers will be necessary (Ward, 1993). Four types of transformers are commonly used and mentioned here:

1.   *Fixed voltage converter.* This simple and inexpensive transformer is readily available in electronic equipment stores in the United States. There are two

varieties—*solid-state converters* (designated for certain wattage capacities) and *low capacity transformers* (usually for up to 50-watt equipment). These cost less than $10, weigh less than a pound, and are commonly used with small travel equipment, tape players, and battery rechargers. They work with some, but not all, electronic equipment.

2. *Manual voltage regulator.* This unit is used to adjust for voltage that is steadily at a too high or too low level. For example it reduces a voltage of 220 to 110, which is the standard for your American-purchased equipment. This piece of equipment runs about 10 pounds and costs $100–$300. A brand name sometimes used to describe this generic equipment abroad is VARIAC.

3. *Automated voltage regular.* This transformer holds voltage that may vary to a set standard level. For example, if the voltage varies between 186–260, the unit will automatically adjusts it to maintain 110. Be sure to purchase a unit where the standard is switchable from 220 to 110. This unit is comparable in weight and price to the manual regulator.

4. *Uninterruptable Power System (UPS).* UPS offers the most versatility and protection. With costs from $120–$620 and a weight of 12–75 pounds, this unit protects equipment and data from most kinds of voltage problems—brown-out, black-out, and surges. Some systems have a safety mechanism of a built-in battery pack to allow the user to shut off equipment with no data loss in case of power outages.

While some professors reported no problems using the inexpensive fixed-voltage converter with their computer equipment, not everyone was so lucky. A professor to Ireland recently reported, "My own bad experience taught me to find out how each individual computer will react to variable current and adaptors. My computer should have been used only with an isolation transformer or automated voltage regulator. It burned out using an ordinary transformer!"

Troubleshooting Other Computer Problems. In my years of international work as a researcher and professor, the utility of computers has been invaluable and the technical problems have been many. One of my laptop computers was fatally damaged en route, another's CPU developed a malfunction that took a year and hundreds of dollars in long-distance service calls to Australia to repair. Once, I typed an entire book manuscript abroad on a computer with no reparable capitalization capability.

But not all the problems of computer use abroad are technical ones. A University of Montana professor told a story about getting his computer through Hungarian customs easily. But what he didn't expect was "having to take it out every time I went out of the country!" Another professor purchased a computer for her work in Prague. She encountered so much navigation of customs, permits, stamps, and regulations as she entered, exited, transferred, and traveled that it led her to say, "Unlike American where you *can* until a rule says you *cannot*, in Eastern Europe, you *cannot* until a rule says you *can!*"

Despite the enormity of hassles, many visiting professors are managing to take or obtain personal computers for their work. From Pakistan one related, "I brought a personal computer for my own research. I had trouble getting it through customs with some time and cost. But bringing my computer with me was worth all the hassle." Another to Japan reported, "Remember, I didn't have secretarial support, so my most important professional tool was a laptop computer. It was my portable work station. It was my memory, my notebook, my research instrument, and my typewriter for class materials. I also used it for notes, diary, handouts, correspondence, articles, lectures, book manuscripts and reports." Another professor hooked up his laptop computer to a television monitor and projected maps and outlines for class "overhead style."

MANAGING TECHNICAL PROBLEMS

For professors in fields where work required technical equipment, teaching across cultures, especially in developing countries, presented special challenges. Depending on the availability of technical equipment that is "state-of-the art" and in good repair produced many frustrations among American professors abroad. An ecologist to Indonesia advised visiting professors:

> *Don't be technically dependent because it is very likely you won't find the equipment you need. If the equipment exists, it is not in good repair or is not used for fear it will breakdown and they simply don't have the funds for repairs.*

A physics professor to Thailand similarly remarked, "Because money for equipment [especially the maintenance of equipment] is very hard to come by, it is best not to have too high an expectation. If something is absolutely necessary, you have to bring it with you. It is good to have a back-up plan or a budget to spend yourself."

Availability of essential technical equipment for teaching and research may not be easily determined by a simple letter of inquiry. A University of Minnesota biologist told of his first request for equipment in Indonesia:

> *When I first came I needed a dissecting microscope. It is a fairly simple scope used in zoology for dissections and in biology for looking at flowers. I asked my counterparts if there was a microscope I could borrow and they said, 'Oh yes, we'll see about getting one for you.' A week went by and nothing was said about it, so I mentioned the microscope again, 'It would be nice if I could have a microscope; could I borrow the one you use?' They answered, 'Yes, yes, we'll see to that.' Nothing happened for another week, then a third time, I suggested, 'Well maybe I could I go to the students' plant taxonomy lab and look at my samples.' There was this embarrassed silence. Then it dawned on me that the reason I'm not getting a microscope is because they don't have such a microscope. So I asked my colleague who teaches plant taxonomy, 'Do you have student microscopes?' 'No.' 'How do you teach taxonomy, if the students cannot see the fine details of*

these flowers. How do you teach plant identification?' And he said, 'We only use big flowers.'

Even when the equipment is available, repairs and maintenance present difficulties. From Nepal, an American biologist reported, "The microscopes they have are research quality but are dirty and need professional cleaning. Because there are no facilities in-country that can clean them here, they need to be sent to Germany. This would cost hundreds of dollars and they don't have the funds!" Film professor Robert Hooper in Malaysia told of other problems with maintenance of technical equipment:

The first day I arrived on campus, smoke was billowing out of the television studio...I was told the whole studio was burning to the ground. In that fire, we lost all of our microphones and most of the sound equipment. But we didn't lose our cameras. . . . The second thing that happened was, when the studio door opened, a waft of warm moist air, I would estimate at about 95 degrees, came rolling out of the room. . . . That air smelled just like the film equipment that was decomposing.

Another professor of film making found the major problem was not just lack of equipment or maintenance, but problems in the infrastructure to support technical work. He described such a problem:

To do classroom work in film or television requires a vast amount of out-of-classroom work. In the United States, the United Kingdom and some other European countries, this work is done by technicians, grad assistants, secretaries, and people to order the thousands of little things you need. Here, none of that exists. Everything that would be done by five or six people [even in a small program] here I do myself.

He lamented the lack of technical support because of its impact on students and programs. "If we don't get film, the students don't get to learn what they need to learn—they don't get to make their films. Then you realize the enormous potential of your position has been compromised and you are not sure you can pull it off right!"

Difficulties with availability, maintenance, and technical support for teaching in fields requiring technical equipment were surmounted best by the professors who were willing and able to handle much of the equipment preparation and maintenance work themselves and those who reembraced the values of teaching using simpler and less technically dependent methods. A professor of veterinary medicine in Nepal explained the latter:

I had to become competent in most of the essential as well as the non-essential procedures in conducting laboratory research. While many of the research and lab methods are considered 'outdated' by Western standards, I found them still reliable and easier to explain than the more modern techniques.

TEACHING ABOUT THE UNITED STATES THROUGH MEDIA

American professors abroad, regardless of their disciplines, often taught about the United States using American film, video, and television. A professor to Japan remarked, "Students come to class to 'experience' an American teacher! I had to think carefully about being a cultural communicator and about the needs and interests of my students. I think videos of really good films and television were the key."

Film evenings and festivals were customary social, as well as cultural, features of academic exchanges. Arizona State history professor Dick Burg described his film *soirees* in Indonesia:

> *I get an American film every week from the USIS. We talk about the film and I give historical information. We have seen* 'Gone with the Wind,' *not only touching on the Civil War but on the romantic notion of Southern life. We talk about costume, the history of the book, the history of the film, and a little bit about Clark Gable so they'll know why this is such an enduring film. Tonight, the movie is the* Wizard of Oz . . . *a classic . . . a landmark movie in the history of American film making. Other films were the Marx Brothers and* Romancing the Stone, *and the Indiana Jones movies. They tend to be more interested in action films, because their language comprehension is not as good as I'd like it to be.*

Many of the films American professors taught were available through USIS libraries in NTSC and PAL formats, but others professors brought from the United States. Some of the films, videos and topics American professors reported effectively using are shown in Figure 10-2.

For some, the major reason for teaching about American life through media was, as an instructor in Mexico reported, "Because students ask me about the 'sit-com' life they see on exported U.S. television all the time." A senior Fulbright Professor to Turkey depicted his students as "sincerely interested in Western life beyond the 'B-movie version.'" He related:

> *Even as they subscribed to the older laws of Islam, they wanted to know about the Empire State Building, Space Shuttle launches, and the American film industry. Nothing pleased my students more than when I arranged for them to see an American film in the air-conditioned and comfortable screening room of the United States Information Service building.*

A geography professor to Norway reported his reasons for organizing American media events was primarily "to overcome their prejudices." He explained:

> *The stereotypes of the United States are quite rampant among Norwegian students with little or no direct experiences in the United States. It is not surprising considering the very selective media exposure they are given. I sometimes try*

American agrarian life and culture:

Gone with the Wind
Wizard of Oz
Heartland
Country
The Road to Bountiful
Places of the Heart

American urban life and culture:

Koyaanisqatsi
Midnight Cowboy
Crocodile Dundee II (New York segment of this Australian film)

American youth culture:

Breaking Away
American Graffiti
"DeGrassi Junior High" (PBS television series)
Stand and Deliver

American pluralistic culture:

Brother from Another Planet
Do the Right Thing
A Singing Stream (PBS documentary on gospel music)

FIGURE 10-2   Sample of Films and Videos Used in Teaching About Life in the U.S.A.

to imagine what my impressions of America would be after a steady diet of 'Dallas,' 'Falcon Crest,' Rambo *and American music videos!*

Another professor to Norway recalled feedback after his "American Film Festival" from students whose impressions of the United States were broadened. "After the semester, students and staff celebrated at a local restaurant. At the end of the evening, a student shyly approached and thanked me. 'Now I understand how very little I knew about your country. For the first time I would like to go there and see for myself.' " Similarly, another visiting professor remarked, "I used carefully chosen American films to counteract the Pakistani vision of the United States as a totally materialistic, sexually licentious, and valueless society. The contradiction was, at the same time, that Pakistanis envy and admire the United State's riches and power."

Another use of the media is for vivid teaching examples which both teachers and students share across culture and age. A professor to Poland illustrated:

In one class I was laboring to clarify the differences between 'Yankee' humor and 'Frontier' humor. I had emphasized the quiet, understated craftiness of the Yankee comic type as opposed to the flamboyant physical exploits of the backwoodsman. Unfortunately, the examples I offered (Jack Downing and Davy Crockett) fell flat. At this point, one helpful student offered, as an alternative example, a comic character who had become well known in Poland because of a popular U.S. television series—'Columbo.' The detective with his bedraggled raincoat, sad basset hound, and dilapidated automobile, had much in common with the Yankee comic figure. Another student suggested the cartoon character 'RoadRunner' [again a television import] and 'Popeye' were latter-day embodiments of frontier superheroes.

An excellent resource for those professors who wish to teach about America using film is Ellen Summerfield's guide, "Crossing Cultures Through Film" (1993). This guide focuses on film use for teachers in diverse fields and addresses needs of professors providing advisement for host students' planning to study in the United States. This guide is available from Intercultural Press (see appendix D).

Concept Map

11

EVALUATING
STUDENTS PERFORMANCE

*I praised one of my Korean students in class today
and said his paper was very good. The student bowed
his head, shied away with humility and modesty and
tried to deny the compliment. He said, 'No, not all
good.' In the United States, a student would have
said, 'Thank you very much.'*
—A UNIVERSITY OF HAWAII PROFESSOR, KOREA

American professors' evaluating students in cross-cultural settings experienced all the ambivalence, contradiction, and uncertainty that evaluation provokes in conscientious teachers in their home institutions—only more so. Many concurred with the Fulbright professor to Israel who said, "Academic requirements about grading, examinations, and papers were inadequately explained to me." Several evaluation issues which had an impact on American professors' teaching and their students' accountability were consistently observed to be woven into the evaluation conundrum in cross-cultural settings: the national testing programs, the role of attendance, the effects of assessment on student behavior, and the bias of language proficiency.

CONSIDERING EVALUATION
IN A CROSS-CULTURAL SETTING

The first evaluation issue to perplex American professors in cross-cultural contexts was the presence of *national testing programs* which served as gate keepers to determine university admissions, advancements, completions, and certifications in many countries. Exams were the ubiquitous and traditional means of evaluation at universities where often little value was assigned other forms of assessment frequently used in the United States, such as papers, cases, projects, or class participation. These tests often drove curricula and affected student motivation. Finding ways to honor both the students' examination mandates and their own knowledge of what were important skills and content became one of many American professors' major challenges.

The second evaluation issue which puzzled American instructors was the *role of attendance* in the over-all scheme of student performance. In many instances, attendance was reported as sporadic, low, unpredictable, or uncontrollable. Where attendance and participation in classwork and activities were not required of students (and examination scores provided the sole measurement), visiting professors were often perplexed about their role in student evaluation. From Japan, a visiting professor of American history remarked, "My problem with grading students was that they were not required to attend class [there was not even a class roster]." From New Zealand, a professor of American studies was "never clear about the rules of attendance" and he remarked:

> *At the outset, my assistant, who was delegated to inform me about the routine matters of the department, indicated that attendance was voluntary, because most of these student were 'mature in their outlook and attitudes.' Toward the end, I was informed that I should have taken attendance, 'because some students were so immature that they never showed up'.*

Another American professor to Australia commented, "Student attendance made evaluation difficult—some never came after mid-term." A Fulbright professor to Japan related that he wished he had argued for mandatory attendance. "If I were repeating this, I would require attendance and promise As and Bs to all regular attendees." Another to Japan reported he had implemented such a plan. "I put an attendance requirement in the second semester—more than two absences and only a B was possible. I wish I had started it the first semester." A broader discussion of this attendance issue is found in the chapter 6 section on Anticipating Potential Conflicts.

The third evaluation issue with which most American professors grappled was the *effect of assessment on student behaviors.* In many cultural traditions, frank and direct praise or criticism is avoided. Even mild public criticism might cause a student to "lose face." One Fulbright professor of American literature found symbolism to explain his students' behavior:

> *There are ancient Chinese wisdoms that suggest that the tallest tree in the forest gets struck by lightening or the stone farthest from the shore gets washed away by the river. The moral of these sayings is that you don't want to do anything that would draw attention to yourself.*

Evaluating students in the Western academic tradition sometimes involves frank and direct criticism. American professors ask students to rework faulty assignments—and maybe even to redo them a second or third time. What American professor has never admonished an American class for a misdirected assignment or neglecting required reading? Some have resorted to anonymous, computer-scored, proctored exams to avoid the potential animosity of students in the evaluation process. In recent years in the United States, the sales of "malpractice insurance" against the eventuality of a student's litigious complaint that he or she was evaluated unfairly have burgeoned.

Evaluating students in cultural traditions where frank and direct criticism is rare, can cause, as was said in Thailand, *cai hai* (a student's heart to disappear) as a result of shock or embarrassment. Host professors in this tradition often avoid strong criticism and usually do not require students to redo work. For American professors abroad, finding meaningful, effective, and face-saving ways to assess student performance fairly and accurately, to have work done or redone correctly, and to give honest criticism frankly but politely become the summons.

The *bias of English proficiency* was the final issue woven throughout the evaluation perplexity. American professors were more often not teachers of English. But students' English proficiency affected their ability to comprehend lectures, to produce written text for tests and papers, and to participate in class discussions. An American law professor remarked on the relationship between the type of assessment he chose and his students' performance:

> *Israeli students, because of their difficulties with written English, write far superior papers [with time, resources, and coaching] than they perform on written examinations. But it took me an entire semester to figure this out.*

Instructors were distressed that their evaluation procedures rewarded students' language over their ideas, preparation, or effort. This issue is a major theme in the following discussions on assessing in-class and out-of-class work and assigning student grades.

ASSESSING IN-CLASS ACHIEVEMENT AND PERFORMANCE

Two common evaluation practices college teachers use in the United States are probing to assess comprehension (e.g., questioning and quizzing) and giving oral feedback (e.g., praising) on student responses, solutions, and in-class work. Both may require some modification in the cross-cultural setting.

Probing to Determine Comprehension. Before final or summative evaluations of student achievement and performance are done at the end of a course or a project, small, daily, objective-by-objective assessments need to be accomplished. Teaching in the United States, you may omit these "spot checks" on comprehension and achievement and justify their omission by saying they are burdensome, unnecessary, or an "infantilizing" of the university teaching process. Instructors who use them may do so informally. When used, routine ways of informally assessing comprehension and achievement typically included:

1. Picking up facial and classroom discussion cues of comprehension;
2. Listening to students' questions or responses;
3. Observing students' patterns of attention; and
4. Watching the degree of involvement in class discussions.

In the cross-cultural university classroom, where the subtleties of language and culture are unfamiliar, these informal checks are necessary, but may not be sufficient. In this case, more systematic or periodic checks on student comprehension and achievement are essential formative evaluation measures. A professor to Hungary reported, "Students take notes as rapidly as they can write, but when I examine their notebooks and find the notes bear no resemblance to what I have been lecturing about, I know I have to make some changes!" Optimally, every class you teach will have objectives and every lecture will have main points of content you wish students to master. Techniques to determine whether students have accomplished these objectives by the end of the class become more important when circumstances make it harder to know if they have. Guidelines for Checking on Student Comprehension in the Cross-Cultural Classroom are provided in Figure 11-1.

Evaluating class discussions, cases, debates, and other class presentations using traditional methods of assessment are difficult in cross-cultural contexts. If students do these activities in their native language and you are not proficient in their language, you will not be able to monitor their work and will need go-betweens to translate and summarize. The question then becomes whether evaluation is of the student's performance or the translation of the performance? A Fulbright professor to Thailand videotaped the student sessions and hired a colleague to summarize the main points from each presentation. He was confounded, however, by whether the presentations represented more than just the few ideas his colleague translated.

Providing Feedback and Giving Praise. Immediate oral feedback on student performance is a common teaching technique in the American classroom. In an intercultural context, using public, direct observations and comments on a student's responses, actions or work can mean that a professor risks causing a student discomfort or "loss of face," even when the feedback is positive. When students are working with new material or processes in class or practicing new skills, positive feedback is important—both to reinforce their efforts and to demonstrate to them which actions will be rewarded. However, clear, descriptive and systematic praise, such as "You identified your main idea well and supported it with a sound argument" is more effective than "You did a good job." Other suggestions for providing feedback and giving praise can be seen in Figure 11-2, Using Positive Feedback Effectively in the Cross-Cultural Classroom.

1.   **Review student notebooks.**

     • Class notes provide you with clues on conceptual organization and language comprehension.

2.   **Administer self-graded mini-quizzes.**

     • Ask two or three factual questions at the end of each lecture to encourage retention of essential data from the presentation.
     • Ask at least one inferential question to promote listening for relationships.

3.   **Ask follow-up questions on the content of the class or presentation.**

     • Use the exact vocabulary of the presentation to assess comprehension on what was just presented.

4.   **Fine-tune verbal questioning strategies.**

     • Students' oral responses, when they are forthcoming, provide one of the best aids for determining comprehension.
     • Refer to questioning techniques discussed in the Chapter 8 section on Encouraging Student Participation.

5.   **Use rhetorical listening checks.**

     • Ask the listener "Do you understand?" "Are you with me?" "Do I make sense?" Am I clear?" to serve as a check. One American professor warned, however, that his Thai students *always* say "yes."

FIGURE 11-1   Guidelines: Checking Student Comprehension in a Cross-Cultural Classroom

Some professors, unsure of the appropriate uses of oral feedback in class, used the alternative of having students evaluate their peers. This method was discouraged by two American professors to Southeast Asia. One said, "Students rate everyone's performance very high and give only laudatory comments." An American psychology professor in Thailand, who used role-play and videotaped training sessions in class, reported, "Students who use a more analytical evaluation style are quickly censored by the others."

EVALUATING OUT-OF-CLASS WORK

Many American professors complained that, in their cross-cultural teaching situations, there was no custom of out-of-class assignments. Though there were exceptions, this common pattern of students' not doing homework and assigned readings presented difficulties when the course objectives were predicated on out-of-class work. An American professor to New Zealand complained, "For

1. **Give praise judiciously and honestly.**

   • When students work with difficult materials, processes or language, positive feedback may serve as an incentive.
   • Praise (public or private) in some contexts may cause a student discomfort or "loss of face."
   • Avoid singling out a student to be made "a positive example of" or whose work you wish others to imitate.
   • Avoid falsely praising with the intent to balance criticism.

2. **Give praise descriptively and specifically.**

   • Your new students may need more description of praise worthy behavior, e.g., "Correct! You identified the key point that the author made."
   • Specify the sought behavior, e.g., "You brought your dictionary to class. Good!" rather than, "I like it when you are prepared."

3. **Find out what kinds of feedback or rewards are preferred by students.**

   • Don't assume that students in your host country seek the same kinds of feedback or rewards as U.S. students. Find out.
   • Talk to host colleagues about feedback and rewards.
   • Experiment with a variety of praises and rewards (e.g., public praise, high marks, notes on papers, exemption from assignments or tests, extra credit, opportunities to work collaboratively, student conferences, etc.).

FIGURE 11-2   Guidelines: Giving Positive Feedback in a Cross-Cultural Classroom

my students, there are few serious penalties for failure to do or complete work. They can easily retake a course almost free of charge." A Fulbright professor of American literature to Japan bemoaned the fact, "The more you emphasize papers and reading, the less likely you will have a full class by the end of the semester." "Remember in Japan we are talking about students doing very few outside classroom assignments," explained another. A Fulbright professor of history to Poland tried to turn around this low expectation:

Formerly no outside class-work was required of students studying with foreign professors in Poland, but I deemed this academically useless. Now I require reading assignments and short papers. No work, no signature in the index book, which students must have in order to receive credit for the course.

In Norway, an American professor observed, "Students can be asked to read only short materials. Since they are graded solely on one exam, this setup is not optimally designed to motivate completion of assignments." From Turkey, another professor concurred. "In general, students are not used to doing homework and Turkish teachers don't expect much out-of-class preparation from them."

Another to Czechoslovakia remarked, "Students have a somewhat lackadaisical attitude toward assignments and do not seem to strive for top grades." Another professor to Japan was more angry at his students' refusal to do out-of-class assignments, "I have a sense, because so few students attend university, that they think their mere presence is worthy of reward."

Another problem recounted was when students' out-of-class work was not accurately done. One explanation for this inaccuracy was the pattern of students' not seeking help to direct their out-of-class work. Sometimes American professors demanded that incorrect work be redone—a practice unfamiliar to many students. Opting for students to redo work (which has the appeal of giving them another chance to rework the material and to meet with success) might get the work redone, but emotional strain may be present. One U.S. Fulbright professor to Malaysia illustrated such a demand and its reaction by relating the story of finding that most of her students had done a homework assignment incorrectly. She asked them subsequently to review the readings and class notes and redo the work. She reported:

> *During most of the remaining class, students were clearly bothered by the demand and talked constantly among themselves, as if to get support or seek advice. All redid the work, but again no one asked me for assistance. And all did it wrong the second time!*

The "homework cartel" (named by an American physics professor in Southeast Asia but identified by many others) was the practice of students working together and handing in collaborative or copied work as their own. Perhaps the best advice on how to deal with such a cartel comes from the professor who "co-opted" it and assigned collaborative work initially and extensively. The section in chapter 4 on Setting-Up Cooperative Learning Systems gives suggestions on how to organize learning environments for students' cooperative and collaborative work. One American literature professor to China warned visiting professors to note that in such collaborations, "There is a bigger burden on the students more proficient in English to help others."

To motivate out-of-class reading, a law professor to Japan required students to write a paragraph summary of each outside reading for the week. He remarked, "That way I was sure they had been doing the reading and I had a chance to check over their comprehension." An American professor in Thailand reported a similar technique to both motivate and evaluate students' out-of-class reading. She required a short abstract of each assigned reading to be handed in before class began. On pre-prepared photocopied sheets, seen in Figure 11-3, each student was required to give the essential information and list the main points from each reading in less than eighty words.

Two other professors administered short quizzes to motivate out-of-class reading. One gave a one-question "readings quiz" at the beginning of each class and the other gave a "Minute Paper" (requiring a mini-summary of the reading), both of which a student could answer only if he or she had read the assigned article.

ASSIGNED READING # ___8___

Bibliographic reference:

    Mathews, P.W. and Werner S. K. (1993). The operation and management of small newspapers:

New findings for old problems. Canadian Journal of Mass Communication, 42, 99-117.

Main subject area of reading:

    Print Journalism Management

Sub topics:

    Financial Management, Staff Management, and Community Issues

Thesis or main idea:

    Survival of small newspapers is predicated on the management strategies aimed at small

businesses and a diversified, multi-talented staff.

Main points of the Reading:

    1) The financial viability of small newspapers today depends on their usefulness to a

      utilization of advertising of small businesses. In studies of towns (of less than 100,000

      people) where small newspapers did or did not do well, small investments critical.

    2) Staff diversification, as in large papers, seldom works well with small papers. "Business

      editors," for example' were examined for flexibility of rules – the "one room school

      house" again!

    3) Community "ownership" facilitates survival of small newspapers. Multi state or city or

      regionals not as sucessful as in the 1970's or as originally expected.

STUDENT NAME ___Siurlai___

FIGURE 11-3   Sample Readings Abstract

Both the abstract and the reading quizzes reportedly encouraged students to do the assigned reading and gave professors simple measures of whether students were doing and comprehending this out-of-class work.

EVALUATING STUDENT WRITING

I decided not to use grammar, syntax or spelling in English as a criteria for correctness . . . otherwise no one would ever complete or pass an assignment! (A George Washington University professor, Pakistan)

Despite the risks and difficulties of motivating and evaluating students' written work, many American professors believed that it was a necessary part of the academic process (especially for graduate students) and built it into their required coursework. *Determining evaluation criteria that are understood and supported by the students* was their first challenge. The professor to Pakistan who reported his decision "not to use grammar, syntax, or spelling in English as a criteria for correctness" evidenced such a predicament. A history professor to China described his plan:

> *I always grade papers by basing four-fifths of my evaluation on historical substance and one-fifth on English. Students came up with this formula and said this approach was an opportunity to improve their writing. Many worked hard to do so.*

Two criteria which proved difficult for students were "succinctness" and "documentation." A commonly discussed problem in the area of written assignments was what one English professor in China called the "tendency toward circumlocution." She remarked, "Chinese students are never succinct—they are very flowery." Another professor of American literature remarked, "What in China has been regarded as the mark of tact, good breeding and education occasionally presents a problem in student writing. It can be difficult to get some students to compose essays that have a clearly stated thesis at the beginning, followed by evidence and arguments."

The second practice in evaluating writing that proved effective was *requiring rewrites of assignments*. A professor of international studies in Mexico contended:

> *One of the methods that I've introduced is the 'reworking' method. They hand in papers which I correct, but do not accept until they had been reworked with less than eight errors per page! With some pain, this has produced the greatest improvement I have seen in student performance over a semester.*

However, a professor to Norway who required rewriting was frustrated by its effectiveness. "There is no recognition that thinking and writing are two parts of one process. Typically, students' written works here receive no marks and students are not required to revise and resubmit them. When I take special care to give lots of useful feedback, students might not even pick their papers up. To them, teacher responses are irrelevant! But ironically, to pass the exam, students must not only write, but write well." With ample guidance, some professors observed that their students' writing markedly improved. A public health professor to Brazil found, "My students needed very descriptive and specific evaluation comments on their papers and written work. If the comments were specific, descriptive and personal, they were received well and seemed to be heeded."

Establishing time-frames for assignment completion was one of the most troublesome evaluation areas for written work. "The paper system is bizarre, with students expecting to be able to hand in their papers up until about twenty years after the end of the course," a psychology professor in Israel protested. Another visiting professor observed, "The custom of New Zealand students to request innumerable extensions for written work was problematic. The experience taught me that I should have ascribed penalties for such lateness." Pakistani students irritated their professors because they were so "relaxed about completing assignments." An American professor of Pakistani graduate students remarked, "Three weeks into the second semester, six of sixteen papers from last semester have yet to be handed in." From Hungary, another observed similar tardiness and changed her requirements. "The first paper was handed in very late because I did not make it absolutely clear late papers would be downgraded. I pitched a fit and laid down the law. After this was clear, there were no late papers," she explained.

American professors who required papers using research materials found *addressing the meaning and practice of plagiarism* with their students was necessary. A geography professor to Turkey described his problem with plagiarism:

> *Midway through the second semester, several of my first-year graduate students were found to have plagiarized papers. Even though the university has a 'code of conduct' about plagiarizing, much of it is ignored by the faculty. When I discussed this situation with colleagues, their response was one of both chagrin and leniency.*

South Carolina literature professor Bernie Dunlop described his dilemma surrounding this issue in Thailand:

> *Plagiarism isn't really understood here. If a paper contains material from a book from the library, unacknowledged but quoted directly, it is considered research. Because I didn't want anyone to lose face, I had to be considerate in dealing with this. My way was to design assignments that make plagiarism irrelevant by requiring a certain amount of imaginative effort. That discomforts the students, because it is not usual here.*

It was advised by a law professor in China who required extensive writing of legal cases and briefs that "Students need to know specifically what is expected of them. We can not assume that they share our expectations about criteria, independent work, or documentation."

GRADING STUDENT PERFORMANCE AND ALTERNATIVES

> *If it is not going to be on the exam, we don't need to study, read, or learn it!* (Student, Norway)

Three areas of consideration were important in the assignment of final or summative grades to students—the role of standardized course-end or program-end tests, the role of teacher-made tests, and the method of grade assignment.

Considering Standardized Testing of Student Achievement

Many American professors abroad face, for the first time, an examination system that minimizes their individual classroom assessments and their role in the evaluation of students. For example, one Fulbright professor to Ireland remarked, "Degrees hinge completely on marks on these third-year exams! What's the purpose of my grading them?" Standardized course-end or program-end exams, which form the exit criteria for many universities outside the United States, are often dismissed by American professors teaching abroad who either have no familiarity with these exams or a bona fide disdain for them. Coming out of an educational tradition in which professors are "horses for single harnesses," American academics enjoy autonomy and control over the content of what is taught in their classrooms. In the systems where single standardized test scores determine whether students matriculate or receive degrees, tests rather than teachers drive what is taught. Sometimes *the influence of standardized testing precipitates professional conflicts* for visiting professors. An American literature professor in Norway shared a common reaction to this type of testing:

> *I am very dissatisfied with the way the examination system controls the educational process. Because all the instruction is pointed toward the exam, which in turn is limited to a very restricted group of works, there is virtually no opportunity in this system to explore broad connections or to study a specific theme, author, or text in depth. This kind of education rarely, if ever, challenges the students to develop clearly articulated theoretical perspectives or to think for themselves.*

Another disgruntled American professor to Turkey agreed, "Here externally decided syllabi and final examinations dictate what the students want to learn and deprive the faculty of any means of compelling them to attend classes and do the reading assignments." An American professor who taught in China identified other conflicts provoked by the testing influence (Porter, 1983):

> *The Chinese feel that testing is the ultimate measure of a person's command of a foreign language, a position many foreigners do not agree with. In addition, some foreigners feel that tests are used at times indiscriminately and unfairly in China. In part, this is because those compiling and grading the tests, especially if they are foreigners, have little or no say in how those tests are used in deciding a person's future.*

Some American professors reacted to standardized exam systems with different points of view. Albert Gilgen did not find the Irish testing system harmful to his objectives. "Because students were tested only at the end of the year, I was stimulated to focus more on truly important concepts, theoretical formulations, and finding ways to present the material more systematically" (Gilgen, 1987). A Fulbright professor to Malaysia whose students had an examination mandate described another position:

I didn't come 10,000 miles to duplicate what their teachers did, but I respect their way. Because they will be tested, I taught the syllabus religiously. But I followed my methods.

The implication of such importance and emphasis being placed on exams meant that *some content and some courses were viewed as ancillary and expendable curricula.* One Fulbrighter to Prague observed, "Classwork not related to exams is not taken seriously by many, and most of the classes the foreign teachers teach are not part of the final examining process." A language instructor in Malaysia reported:

Language learning, beyond vocabulary memorization, was not tested, so there was reluctance to participate in the beginning. But by the end of the first semester, I had convinced them that I was committed to helping them pass their exam as well. Then students began to discuss and do group work. In order to be fair to them, I made sure the curriculum that they needed to know was taught well.

Entrance exams, exit exams, and final exams in some countries have been elevated to such a sanctified position that the *exam-driven systems evoke "test reverence."* This role is not altogether unfamiliar—in the U.S. education system, we have increasingly elevated standardized tests to the lofty role of "gatekeeper and soothsayer." But American academics have never held tests in as much esteem as academics do in other parts of the world. For example, professors in Thailand get extra pay for preparing, proctoring, and grading exams. A Thai dean once asked if an American professor would like to "type his host professor's exam," because the task was considered a "sacred charge." It was reported that greater efforts were often taken to secure tests during preparation and grading times than is typical on American campuses. Additionally, it was observed by American professors abroad that their students often "accepted test marks as measures of their performance without protest."

Additionally, these *exam systems encourage enormous student anxiety.* An American professor to Turkey reported his experience with anxious students:

About a half hour before the examination, a delegation of about ten students suddenly entered my office to announce that, because of the arrest of some other students the previous day, they were not prepared to take the examination. I suspected that long, unsettled, and irregular academic conditions in Turkey had sapped them of their academic interest. I told the student delegation I would confer with my colleagues. They all advised me to give the examination, and pointed out that two other professors in the department had done so that very day. Then began the examination to which nobody came. I sat alone in a large lecture hall, while outside the student leaders haggled with two or three Turkish professors who had been sent to help me as proctors. Finally, after almost an hour, all seventy-two students quietly and politely entered the room and took their seats.

Considering Teacher-Made Tests

The lessons of "test reverence" and test-driven curricula do not apply only to national standardized exams in some cultures, but to the classroom competency exams and teacher-made tests as well. A professor of American literature in China illustrated these lessons with his students' responses to class discussions:

> *I often give several interpretations of an issue without indicating which I believe is the best one. Students often asked, 'If you won't tell us which is correct, how will we know what to put on the exam?' I try to convince the students that the myriad answers they offer in class discussion are equally appropriate for the exams. But they insist that their ideas are only for class discussion, and that on the exam they must know the view which the professor considers correct.*

Good teacher-made tests are harder to construct in cross-cultural settings than in your home setting where you can easily identify items that match your objectives, choose well-written items from pre-prepared tests, and write good items yourself. A sociology professor to Czechoslovakia introduced the American-style multiple-choice examinations in her department. "They horrified students who were used to oral and essay exams," she said, adding, "Scores on the first exam were terrible. But after the first exam, I spent hours pointing out the strong and weak areas in the students' performance and how to study for the next exam. That worked miracles! The finals were outstanding." Another professor to Japan who administered essay exams coached students on the essay process with success. "I copied a couple of the best exam papers with student names removed and posted these on the American Studies bulletin board to give students an idea of what two different top-rated papers looked like. This 'modeling' helped."

In test construction in the cross-cultural context, language becomes the unpredictable variable. The best advise for the creation of test items is to write them using straightforward language with controlled vocabulary (i.e., exact vocabulary and constructions from the lecture material or text). Even then, the bias of language proficiency is evident. As a Fulbright professor of educational psychology, I was chagrined to see that my first test scores in a research class were perfectly correlated with my informal assessments of the language proficiency of my students. That is, the ones who spoke English the best also identified research models the best, though I had worked to make the test very readable. Even if you try hard to create tests in straightforward language and to use the exact vocabulary of the text or class notes, it is hard to eliminate the language proficiency bias.

Because of their students' difficulties with English, some professors attempted examining in the students' language. Some professors were proficient in the host languages and others used translators. One professor in Indonesia who spoke Bahasa Indonesia discussed some of the difficulties with that process:

Whew! What a job grading those exams in Bahasa Indonesia was! I always sweat and groan when reading exams. . . . Here the difficulty was magnified a hundred-fold by my own language weaknesses. Though, most of the questions were short-answer [two or three sentences], I discovered how much I rely on key words in context to puzzle out meaning. When key words are unfamiliar or handwriting unreadable, it becomes nearly impossible.

A sociology professor to Japan used translated exams and reported, "Translation creates a problem for the non-Japanese speaking lecturer—he or she has no idea whether students' incorrect answers in testing situations are due to inaccurate translations or to inadequacies in student learning."

Assigning Grades in the Cross-Cultural Context

American professors teaching abroad experienced the full spectrum of expectations on the assignment of grades, from teaching in nongraded situations to having major responsibilities for developing the national examinations which served as the credentialing agent for thousands—and everything in between. Even with all the variation in expectations, five options were commonly exercised by these instructors regarding assignment of final grades. They were the "norm-referenced" system, the "uniform grade" standard, the "multiple marks" approach, the "process-not-product" method, and the "no-grades" approach.

Normative" Grading Systems. The routine grading system of U.S. university classrooms which is normative and based on comparison of student scores to a norm or average was implemented by some American professors abroad. With norm-referenced grading systems, instructors usually gave teacher-made exams and graded them "on a curve." In New Zealand, a Fulbright professor reported, "Evaluation may be handled either internally by the faculty member or through a set examination administered by the university. I chose to develop my own exams, quantify the scores and assign grades accordingly—like I do in the United States."

Norm-referenced grading differs from criterion-referenced (or competency-based) grading in that a set number of correct responses is considered necessary to obtain a certain grade (or to have "mastered" the content). Norm-referenced grading requires creating a statistical distribution of scores and using some cut score (usually the standard deviation) to draw lines of demarcation between grades. Depending on the experience of students and faculty with psychometrics and statistics, the use of the "normal curve" to describe the distribution of test scores or grades in your classes may or may not be understood or appreciated. But the use of criterion-referenced systems, which are more intuitive and better understood, present problems in the cross-cultural context as well.

An American professor to Indonesia described the *problem of low scores* using his traditional methods of test scoring in the cross-cultural context:

I scored with the same standard that I apply to an undergraduate class at the University of Minnesota. At Minnesota I might have expected a range of grades from about 90 percent to 40 percent with a median [near the mean] of around 75 percent. The exam scores here were low. Here it was 67 percent to 90 percent and the median and mean were 43 percent.

Some American professors and/or their colleagues chose different ways to deal with large numbers of low test scores. One professor of medicine to Thailand related the story of his department's choice to modify normative grading:

The number of failing grades was so high on the first exam, it was politically unacceptable—so they went to another statistical scheme, but the failures were still too high. Then they just 'eye-balled' the scores and drew a line.

From Malaysia, a University of Georgia professor found a similar solution. "Grade cut-off points are just set very low. Out of 144 students, only two failed and three got Ds."

Just as in the U.S., student performance on exams raised *the problem of validity*—did the test measure what it was intended to measure? One professor in Indonesia observed variable performances with different types of questions. He found that questions which elicited answers that come directly from the lecture notes or readings were generally answered well, though often with a kind of formulaic response. But on the questions "which required the students to put together and reason from two or more items of information, or that were presented in slightly different contexts, or were taken from separate parts of the course outline," students answered them very poorly. A professor to Japan noted, "His students often missed multiple-choice questions containing the same answer they recalled correctly in another 'fill-in-the-blank' question." A University of Oregon law professor to Japan concurred. "The multiple choice portions of my exams were generally disappointing." But in attempting alternatives, she found:

I was hoping failure on multiple choice tests reflected students' problems understanding the questions in English. But the essay answers were an education for me in how Japanese students think about problems. The answers ranged from unintelligible to fascinating but incorrect.

A suggestion offered by a Fulbright professor in Thailand, who used norm-referenced exams to assign grades, addressed this validity problem. "I toss out assignments or questions on which a large majority (80 percent) of the students do incorrectly or very poorly—I figure the error is probably my own."

Another problem with test scoring was the "more than occasional" *problem of cheating*. A geology professor to Pakistan reported, "Universities in Pakistan are much troubled by student unrest at present, and this manifests academically in uncontrolled cheating. This problem is most severe at lower academic levels."

Professors who used normative grading methods found they had another test scoring difficulty: *the problem of test repeaters*. The oddity was described by a Fulbright professor to Japan as "phantom students." Another called them "rogue retakers." One explained, "When failures count as 'no credit,' I get the phenomenon of students showing up to take the exams in my course they never attended . . . nothing ventured, nothing lost!" Another geography instructor in Japan observed, "As is typical, a large number of students showed up to take the final exams who had only rarely [or never] come to class, since a failing grade means that the student receives no credit, it does not appear on their transcript." From Nepal, a professor described a situation of students retaking exams they previously failed with no time limit imposed on how many attempts they could make. "It meant some students from the early l970s would show up to class on exam days demanding exams which followed their syllabus from another decade." An American biology professor in Indonesia shared a similar situation:

> *In class I never saw more than thirty-five students at any one time, and there were at least eight total strangers at the exam. Apparently that's not unusual. My counterpart told me that students can repeat a course as many times as they please, and the best grade stands. Those poor students who showed up just for the exam hadn't counted on running into me!*

The final problem of *bargaining for different cut scores* was described by an American instructor in Turkey. "A passing grade is only 50 percent and students who fail the final exam are given multiple make-up exams. Bargaining for cut scores seems to be very common among students and can become quite annoying to the teacher not used to it."

The "Uniform Grade" Standard. Some visiting professors decided to assign all the students in their classes a single grade (e.g., As), with the justification that language barriers made assignment of grades entirely dependent on English proficiency. This practice was common among professors whose appointments were for only one term. The automatic assignment of grades was usually not discussed with students beforehand, and sometimes, as one professor described, "A 'figleaf' of performance-criteria was accepted by all." One visiting professor to Japan wanted to "avoid being a stickler" so he "assigned mostly As or an I-type grade instead of failures."

"Multiple Marks" Method. The next approach was the "multiple marks" type, in which professors put many criteria and variables into the evaluation equation. Included were grades on daily assignments, class questions, quizzes, tests, attendance, papers, cases, debates, reading abstracts, etc. The defense of this method was that it allowed the greatest number of students with the widest range of variability in language, energy, aptitude, interest, hard work, etc., to score high on one or more variables. As a Fulbright professor of American literature first to Sri Lanka then to Nepal declared, "I am trying hard this time to find other ways to evaluate students rather than end-of-semester exams which deaden intellectual life!" One advocate of this method was a Fulbright professor to Japan who argued, "Students need more grades rather than fewer and more information about their progress, because they are so concerned about their limited language." Another to Japan who used this method felt his grading was "generous," but students felt it was too "tough."

One professor of American history to New Zealand using multiple criteria "prepared an explicit statement of terms for completion of the course and contracted with each student for the award of a grade." Another professor to New Zealand spoke to the need for using multiple grades, rather than the program-end exam score, to motivate students. He explained, "I try to deemphasize the final exam by emphasizing papers, therefore I do have some control over evaluation as motivation for students in my class."

"Process-Not Product" Method. In the "process-not-product" method, professors graded on measures of participation and effort. There were criteria spelled out for making each grade, but the criteria dealt with process. Among the criteria: attending so many classes, asking so many questions, debating for so many minutes, or working on so many cases. It was not test accuracy, but being there and participating actively that earned a student high marks. One process a professor of American literature to Nepal included was translation work. He offered, "One category for consideration in a scheme of grading should be 'helping others in the group with English translation.' Students with good language skills in English will be used by other students often so should be rewarded as well." Another remarked, "When the contributions of questions and discussion are rewarded, we will get them. Otherwise they will not come easily."

The "No-Grades" Approach. Assigning no grades was the choice and the expectation of some American professors abroad. This approach sometimes was used because the class was supplemental or no-credit. Other times, standardized course-end or program-end exams provided the only evaluation, so grades were irrelevant. A professor to Pakistan described this situation, "I examined students on my subject matter, but it was only for informal feedback—the scores played no part in their final grade." A history professor to Indonesia reported, "It is difficult to tell how much effect my work is having on them, because we do not examine them regularly and there are no grades. The 'final exam' is scoring high enough on the TOEFL to get a grant to go abroad to study in a foreign country."

Occasionally, external decision-makers (administrators, team teachers or other host colleagues) assigned grades to students. An American professor of international relations in China reported:

> *My grading is done with more difficulty than at home. I don't keep records on them, nor can I, due to the structure of the Chinese university. I am not concerned with attendance here, nor do I think it my function to check daily on that.*

Their final end-of-course examination [which I do not grade or administer] is the only grade. My evaluation is much more distant here in China.

For some, external graders may be in the form of "second readers" or "second graders," like those used in countries with Bristish-style university traditions. Fulbright professor of library science to Jamaica, Desretta McAllister, found the use of the "second grader" useful when solutions or language are culture-specific, but the practice added some pressure of accountability on her for her standards and evaluation methods to be very systematic and defensible.

Getting Feedback for Improvement from Students

Soliciting feedback and suggestions from students on how to improve your teaching or how to make assignments, readings, or evaluations more appropriate or relevant is common practice in our "market-place culture" where consumer research is customary. However, student evaluations of courses and professors will likely be unfamiliar in the cross-cultural context. Some professors reported that they attempted to gather data from students in an effort to change their courses for the next semester. Individual conferences with students at the end of the semester provided some with useful information.

To solicit students' suggestions and evaluations of the effectiveness of her methods, Sharon Hom, a law and legal education professor to China, developed an End of Semester Feedback Form, displayed in Figure 11-4. She found this form was particularly useful if she reviewed the concepts and discussed each item with the class first. She got suggestions about pace, difficulty, and scope of her assigned materials and presentation. She received support for careful planning and appreciation for eliciting student opinions. She learned how best to use small group work. And she heard students emphasize the importance of employing a variety of approaches to communicate with and teach them in the cross-cultural classroom.

Name (Optional):   Class:

Date: Teacher:

1. **In terms of CLASS TEACHING METHODS, what did you find most interesting? Why? What suggestions do you have for improvement?**

   a. *Lecture*
   b. *Use of summary charts*
   c. *Case briefing*
   d. *Problem analysis*
   e. *Role-play exercises*
   f. *Small group work*

2. **Please comment on the pacing, the sequence, the level, and the choice of reading MATERIALS.**

3. **Please comment on the following aspects of our TEACHING:**

   a. *Planning and organization of the class*
   b. *Preparation for class*
   c. *Relationships with students*
   d. *Openness to feedback and suggestions*
   e. *Technical grasp of the materials*
   f. *Ability to convey information clearly and effectively*
   g. *Other*

4. **What was the most significant aspect of YOUR LEARNING EXPERIENCE this semester? Why? Please use the back of this form for your answer.**

FIGURE 11-4   End of Semester Feedback Form

Source: Sharon K. Hom (1989), *American Legal Education Methodology in China,* p. 105. New York: City University of New York Law School. Used with permission of the author.

CONCLUSION

In the Southern hemisphere, currents and seasons move in reverse. That's why I came here, to be dis-located, cracked open, forced out of my shell of preconceptions about how the world spins. That's why I came to teach in New Zealand . . . a choice most of my colleagues found quixotic. I wanted to learn to see again.—GERNES, 1987

American professors abroad who are effective in the cross-cultural context learn to observe the cultures of their classrooms and the behavioral complexities of their students and colleagues. They experiment with structuring new learning environments which stretch students and themselves beyond the "comfort zones of tradition." They modify and reform their old familiar teaching methods to fit the new instructional demands. And they transcend the limited horizons of their own American culture. An old Georgian fable from the Black Sea region tells of the journey they take and the choice they make:

Once there were three women who had heard of the tangy, sweet, juicy fruit, but had never seen oranges. Filled with splendid stories about the succulent fruits, they resolved to have some. The first woman set out on her quest full of mission and adventure. She traveled for many days and began to worry that she was lost. The farther she went, the more she worried. Finally, she sat under a tree to think. "No silly fruit is this important," she decided. Then she turned and went home.

The second woman who dreamed of oranges set out and after many days she ended up underneath the same tree where orange, round fruits were all over the ground. Thrilled, she picked one up and bit into it. It was rotten and bitter and the orange skin burned her mouth. She spit it out and left disappointed.

The third woman set out on her journey for the oranges. She talked with the first traveler who had made the journey but who returned emptyhanded. She talked to the second sojourner who had made the trip but had been disappointed. She asked questions of those along the way. After many days she too ended up under the same tree. She patiently looked at the oranges on the ground and the oranges on the branches. She mindfully felt the skins and smelled the flesh. She chose one that was neither too soft nor too hard. She carefully opened it to the middle and let its sweet, tangy juice drip on her tongue. Then she took an orange home to share its seeds with the others who dreamed of oranges.

The experiences of the American professors whose voices are shared here illustrate that observing classroom cultures, experimenting with learning structures, modifying familiar methods, and transcending cultural myopia are possible. An epilogue to this chronicle of the experiences of American professors abroad is that many returned with "fresh eyes" on their own life's work. Like the professor to New Zealand who went to the Southern Hemisphere to be "dislocated, cracked open, forced out of preconceptions," some "learned to see" their practice, their language, and their conceptualizations as a university professor in new ways. The lessons they learned and shared promise that a richer understanding of university teaching, both across cultures and at home, can be the reward.

REFERENCES

Alexander, C. (1991). Personal history : An ideal state. *New Yorker,* (December 16), 53–88.

Ausubel, D. (1960). The use of advance organizers in the learning and retention of meaningful material. *Journal of Educational Psychology, 51,* 267–272.

Bailey, J.A. (1993). Personal communication of August 29, 1993.

Bailey, K.M., Pialorsi, F., & Zukowski/Faust, J. (1984). *Foreign teaching assistants in U.S. Universities.* Washington, D.C.: National Association of Foreign Student Affairs.

Bean, M. (1981). English material in China and for China. *Teaching English Internationally,* 2(2). n.p.

Blatchford, C.H. (1983). Teaching in China: EFL teacher training, *Asian Survey,* 23(11), 1199–1203.

Board of Foreign Scholarships. (1987). *Forty years: The Fulbright Program 1946–1986.* Washington, DC: U.S. Information Agency.

Buescher, J.B. (1992). Putting Asia in the core curriculum. *The NEA Higher Education Journal,* 67-76.

Burton, J. (1991). *International exchange locator.* New York: Liaison Group for International Educational Exchange. [This guide to U.S. organizations active in international educational exchange is available from the Institute of International Education, 809 United Nations Plaza, NY 10017-3580.]

Byrd, P. (Ed.)(1986). *Teaching across cultures in the university ESL program.* Washington, DC: National Association for Foreign Student Affairs (Available from NAFSA, 1875 Connecticut Ave., N.W. Washington, DC 20009).

Chaffe, J. (1988). *Thinking Critically.* Boston: Houghton Mifflin.

Chamberlin, L.J. (1970). *Team-teaching—Organization and administration.* Columbus, Ohio: Merrill.

Chickering, A. & Gamson, Z. (1987). Seven principles for good practice in undergraduate education. *Wingspread, 9,* 1–8.

Council for the International Exchange of Scholars. (1993). *A survey of returned Fulbright scholars 1985–1992.* Washington, DC: CIES (Available from CIES, 3007 Tilden St.,NW, Suite 5M, Washington, DC, 20008-3009.)

Council for the International Exchange of Scholars. (1994). *Annual report, 1993.* Washington, DC: CIES (For availability, see citation above.)

Cushner, K., McClelland A., & Safford, P. (1992). *Human diversity in education.* New York: McGraw-Hill.

Druett, J. (1988). *Fulbright in New Zealand.* New Zealand-United States Educational Foundation: Wellington, NZ.

Fieg, J.P. (1989). *A Common core: Thais and Americans.* Yarmouth, ME: Intercultural Press.

Fieg, J.P. (1989, June). Examining the Thai university workplace. Paper delivered at the Southeast Asian Summer Studies Institute, University of Hawaii-Manoa.

Fieg, J.P. (1980). *Thais and North Americans.* Yarmouth, ME: Intercultural Press.

Frier, P. (1970). *Pedagogy of the oppressed.* New York: Seabury Press.

Furey, P. (1986). A framework for cross-cultural analysis of teaching methods. In P.Byrd (Ed.). *Teaching across cultures in the university ESL program.* Washington, DC: National Association for Foreign Student Affairs.

Gage, N.L. & Berliner, D.C. (1991). *Educational psychology* (5th ed.). Boston: Houghton Mifflin.

George, P.G. (1994, Winter). Cooperative learning and the multicultural university classroom *Journal of Excellence in College Teaching,* 5(1).

George, P.G. (1992, March). University teaching in Thailand: Hurdles and hopes in the ursuits of educational excellence in Southeast Asia. Paper delivered at the Comparative and International Education Society Annual Conference, Annapolis, MD.

George, P.G. (1987). *University teaching across cultures.* Bangkok, Thailand: United States Information Service.

George, P.G. and Ward, R.Q. (1989). *Teaching the Chinese Student—A documentary.* Washington, D.C.: United State Information Agency.

Gernes, S. (1987). The other side of sunrise. *Notre Dame Magazine,* 15, 73–74.

Gilgen, A.R. (1987). A year in Galway. *The Fulbright experience 1946–86.* New Brunswick, NJ: Transaction Books, 177–179.

Gold, J.J. (1993, May 19). Cobbling together sabbaticals, leaves and visiting appointments. *The Chronicle of Higher Education,* B3.

Goodwin, C. & Nacht, M. (1986). *Decline and Renewal.* New York: Institute of International Education. (Available from IIE, 809 United Nations Plaza, New York, NY 0017.)

Gunn, V.P. & Elkins, J. (1979). Clozing the reading gap. *Australian Journal of Reading,* 56, 144–151.

Gunter, M.M. (1987). On Turkish students. *The Fulbright experience 1946–86.* New Brunswick, NJ: Transaction Books, 281–292.

Hom, S.K.(1989). *American legal education methodology in China.* New York: The City University of New York Law School.

Hull, C.L., (1920). Quantitative aspects of the evolutions of concepts. *Psychological monographs,* No.123, Washington, DC: American Psychological Association, 40–41.

Iizawa, S. (1991). *Review of past grantees' experiences experiences in Japan 1987–1991.* Washington, DC: Council for the International Exchange of Scholars.

Johnson, D.W., Johnson, R. & Holubec, E.(1990). *Circles of Learning: Cooperation in the classroom.* Edina, MN: Interaction Book Company.

Johnson, D.W., Johnson R.T. & Smith, K.A. (1991). *Active Learning: Cooperation in the College Classroom.* Edina, MN: Interaction Book Company.

Kagan, S. (1988) *Cooperative Learning.* San Juan Capistrano, CA: Resources for Teachers.

Leonard, D. (1986). A walking footnote: Teaching American and English literature to Chinese students. *Occasional Papers in Intercultural Learning,* 11, 3–19. (Published by the AFS International Programs, Inc. 313 E 43rd St., NY, NY 10017, USA).

Levine,R. (1985, December). It wasn't the time of my life. *Discovery,* 66–71.

Lyman, F. (1991). Personal communication to L.W. Sherman, reported in Sherman, L.W. *Cooperative Learning in Post Secondary Education: Implication from Social psychology for active learning experiences:* ERIC Doc. # Ed 330 262, HE 024 349.

Marshall, T. (1990). *The whole world guide to language learning.* Yarmouth, ME: Intercultural Press.

McKeachie, W.J., Pintrich, P., Yi-Guang, L., & Smith, D. (1986). *Teaching and learning in the college classroom: A review of the research literature.* Ann Arbor, MI: The Regents of the University of Michigan.

McKeachie, W.J. & Julik, J.A. (1975). Effective college teaching. In F.N. Kerlinger (Ed.) *Research in Education, 3,* Tiasca, IL: Peacock Press.

McLeish, J. (1976). The lecture method. In N.L. Gage (Ed.) *The psychology of teaching methods.* Chicago: University of Chicago Press.

Mestenhauser, J.A., Marty, G. & Steglitz, I. (1988) *Culture, learning and the disciplines: Theory and practice in cross-cultural orienta-*

tion. Washington, D.C.: National Association for Foreign Student Affairs.

Miller, M. (1990). Reflections on reentry after teaching in China. *Occasional Papers in Intercultural Learning, 14,* 3–25. (Published by the AFS International Programs, Inc. 313 E43rd St., NY, NY 10017, USA).

Moffet, O.E. (1983). State of the art of foreign language education in the PRC, *Foreign Language Annuals, 16*(1), 13–16.

Moore, K.D. (1992). *Classroom teaching skills.* New York: McGraw-Hill.

Moore, W.E., McCann, H. & McCann, J. (1985). *Creative and critical thinking.* Boston: Houghton Mifflin.

Morrell, D. (1981). *Politics in Thailand: Reform, reaction and revolution.* Cambridge, MA: Delgeschlager, Gunn and Hain.

Muehl, L. and Muehl, S. (1993). *Trading cultures in the classroom: Two American teachers in China.* Honolulu: University of Hawaii Press.

National Education Association, (1993). *NEA Almanac 1993.* Washington, D.C.: National Education Association.

Oberschall, A. (1986). Teaching sociology in China, *China Exchange News, 14(3),* 5–8.

Porter, E. (1983) A conference summary. *Language learning and communication, 2*(1), 79–82.

Purisinit, V. & Pitackwong, J. (1986). *Aspiration and success in career : A study of female university instructors.* ChiangMai, Thailand: Women Studies Project of ChiangMai University.

Putnam, J. & Burke, J.B. (1992). *Organizing and managing classroom learning communities.* New York: McGraw-Hill.

Ronda, B. (1986). American studies in China: Experiences and reflections, *China Exchange News, 14*(3), 10–12.

Sagaria, M.A. (1993). Personal communication on September 25, 1993.

Shaughnessy, M.R. (1986). A year at Nanjing University, *China Exchange News, 14*(3), 8–9.

Shive, G.L., Gopinathan, S., and Cummings, W.K. (Eds.). (1988). *North—South Scholarly Exchange: Access, Equity and Collaboration.* London and New York: Mansell Publishing Limited.

Shor, I. (1980). *Critical teaching and everyday life.* Boston: South End Press.

Spaulding, C.L. (1992). *Motivation in the classroom.* New York: McGraw-Hill.

Stave, B. (1986). Teaching and learning in the PRC, *China Exchange News, 14*(3), 5–8.

Swierczek, F. (1989). *International academic affiliations—Final report.* Bangkok: Thailand-United States Education Foundation.

Swierczek, F. (1987). *International academic affiliations survey.* Bangkok: Thailand-United States Education Foundation.

Thorson, J.L. (1987). The Fulbright as beginning. *The Fulbright experience 1946–86.* New Brunswick, NJ: Transaction Books, 167–172.

Ward, R.Q. (1993). Personal communications from North State Public Video Corporation, Durham, NC, in August 1993.

Watkins, B.T. (September 29, 1993). Council urges colleges to make better use of returning Fulbright Scholars. *Chronicle of Higher Education,* A43–44.

Whitehead, A.N. (1929). *Aims of education.* New York: MacMillan.

Wilhelm, A.E. (1987). The shortest way home. *The Fulbright experience 1946–1986.* New Brunswick, NJ: Transaction Books, 119–121.

Woolfolk, A.E. (1993). *Educational psychology,* (5th ed.), Boston: Allyn and Bacon.

APPENDIX A

RESOURCES FOR HIGHER EDUCATION
FACULTY EXCHANGES

Sources of Fellowships, Scholarships, Professional Development Training and Travel or Research Grants

Academy for Educational Development
1255 23rd St., NW
Washington, DC 20037
Tel. 202/862-1900
Fax. 202/862-1904
(AED administers post-secondary faculty exchanges in a variety of fields including arts/culture, business and professional fields.)

African-American Institute
833 United Nations Plaza
New York, NY 10017
Tel. 212/949-5666
Fax. 212/286-9493
(Offers scholarships/fellowships for post-secondary faculty and working professionals; Primary focus is African development.)

American-Mideast Educational and Training Services
1100 17th St.,
NW, Suite 300
Washington, DC 20036-4601
Tel. 202/785-0022
Fax. 202/822-6563
(Administers post-secondary faculty exchanges in cooperation with other agencies focused on the Arab world.)

American-Scandinavian Foundation
725 Park Avenue
New York, NY 10021
Tel. 212/879-9779
Fax. 212/249-3444

(ASF administers exchange programs for post-secondary faculty and supports exchanges in the arts/culture, business, and professional areas. Additionally, it has some short-term programs; Grants to individuals and institutions.)

Asian Cultural Council
280 Madison Ave.
New York, NY 10016
Tel. 212/684-5450
Fax. 212/684-8075
(Offers scholarships/fellowships for academic and research to post-secondary faculty and artists; Provides some travel grants.)

Association of Professional Schools of International Affairs
2400 N Street, NW
Washington, DC 20037
Tel. 202/862-7989
Fax. 202/862-3750
(Though APSIA does not offer fellowship/ scholarships directly, it represents a consortia of American graduate schools with many international faculty exchange efforts.)

American Historical Association
400 A Street, SE
Washington, DC 20003
(The AHA publishes periodic listings of grants and fellowships for international teaching and research of interest to historians.)

American Philosophical Association
University of Delaware
Newark, DE 19711
(This association provides information and
    some small grants and travel stipends
    for international exchanges and re-
    search.)

Center for International Education
U.S. Department of Education
400 Maryland Ave., SW
Washington, DC 20202
Tel. 202/708-7283
(Faculty research, group projects, seminars
    overseas and bilateral activities are
    supported; some emphasis on non-
    Western languages and areas.)

**Committee on Scholarly
Communication with China (CSCC)**
1055 Thomas Jefferson St., NW
Suite 2013
Washington, DC 20007
Tel. 202/337-1250
(Resources in the social sciences and
    humanities for graduate students and
    scholars for exchanges with the PRC.)

**Community Colleges for
International Development**
1519 Clearlake Rd.
Cocoa, FL 32922
Tel. 407/3784
Fax. 407/639-0078
(Affiliated with technical colleges and
    universities in Hungary, Slovakia, the
    Czech Republic, Romania and Bulgaria.)

**Council for the International
Exchange of Scholars (CIES)**
3007 Tilden Street, NW, Suite 5M
Washington, DC 20008-3009
Tel. 202/686-4000
Fax. 202/362-3442
(CIES administers the following programs:
    Fulbright Scholars, Indo-American
    Fellows, NATO Research Fellows,
    Occasional Lecturers, Alexander

Hamilton and John Marshall Fellowships,
    East European Initiatives Lectureships,
    and Fulbright Scholars-in-Residence.)

**Council for International Educational
Exchange (CIEE)**
205 East 42nd Street
New York, NY 10017
Tel. 212/661-1414
Fax. 212/972-3231
(While most of CIEE's work is aimed at
    study abroad, it does sponsor profes-
    sional faculty development programs.
    Major overseas centers include London,
    Paris, and Bonn.)

**Educational Commission for Foreign
Medical Graduates**
3642 Market Street
Philadelphia, PA 19104-2685
Tel. 215/386-5900
Fax. 215/387-9963
(While most of ECFMG's efforts are aimed
    at foreign doctors, it is a resource for
    other medical exchange information. It
    offers scholarship/fellowships to visiting
    medical faculty through its Foreign
    Faculty Fellowship and International
    Medical Scholars Programs; linkages
    possible.)

Eurocentres
101 N. Union St., Suite 3000
Alexandria, VA 22314
Tel. 703/684-1494
Fax. 703/684-1495
(With geographic focus in France, Spain,
    Italy, Germany, Switzerland, the United
    Kingdom, and Japan, Eurocentres offers
    scholarships and fellowships for three
    month programs.)

Faculty Exchange Center
952 Virginia Avenue
Lancaster, PA 17603

Tel. 717/393-1130
or 1/800/572-0760
(The FEC provides a registry of American and international academics and institutions who wish to participate in exchanges in many disciplines and countries. Additionally, it provides a housing exchange registry for academics who already have international appointments.)

Fulbright-Hays Teacher Exchange Programs
Center for International Education
Office of Post-Secondary Education
U.S. Department of Education
Washington, DC 20202
Tel. 202/245-2794
(The DOE programs include annual faculty exchanges, summer exchanges, and summer seminars abroad.)

The Independent Colleges Office
1730 Rhode Island Avenue, NW
Suite 1205
Washington, DC 20036
Tel. 202/232-1300
Fax. 202/331-1283
(This organization is a group of three consortia of independent, liberal arts colleges in the Midwest, Great Lakes and Pennsylvania areas which all have international programs. There are exchange opportunities for affiliated faculty.)

Institute of International Education (IIE)
809 United Nations Plaza
New York,
NY 10017-3580
Tel. 212/883-8200
Fax. 212/984-5452
(One of the largest academic exchange organizations, IIE sponsors the "Junior

Fulbright" program and is the source of much information on other exchange opportunities.)

International Research and Exchanges Board
126 Alexander St.
Princeton, NJ 08540-7102
Tel. 609/683-9500
Fax. 609/683-1511
(Administers exchange programs and offers scholarships and travel grants in the social sciences and humanities. Affiliated with other programs sponsored by the American Council of Learned Societies and the Social Science Research Council; Has field offices in Romania, Russia and Prague; sponsors a few "developmental fellowships" to prepare for academic exchanges.)

International Student Exchange Program (ISEP)
1242 35th St., NW
Washington, DC 20057
Tel. 202/687-6956
Fax. 202/687-7041
(ISEP provides a structure to facilitate regular exchanges of junior faculty on a one-to-one basis between its 200 participating member institutions worldwide. Check to see if you college is a member.)

Latin American Scholarship Program of American Universities, Inc.
25 Mt. Auburn St.
Cambridge, MA 02138
Tel. 617/495-5255
Fax. 617/495-8990
(Based at Harvard, this consortium administers some faculty development programs; focused on the Caribbean, Central America, Mexico and South America.)

**The Liaison Group for International
Educational Exchange**
1825 Eye Street (#475)
Washington, DC 20006
Tel. 202/659-0151
Fax. 202/828-4724
(Publishes the *International Exchange Locator*,
   a guide to activities and support for
   international exchanges.)

**National Committee on U.S.–China
Relations**
777 United Nations Plaza
New York, NY 10017
Tel. 212/922-1385
Fax. 212/557-8258
(Administers exchange programs for
   faculty and professional areas; focused
   on the PRC.)

**National Registration Center
for Study Abroad**
823 N. 2nd Street
Milwaukee, WI 53203
Tel. 414/278-0631
Fax. 414/271-8884
(Eighty-six member institutions in sixteen
   countries seek exchange faculty periodi-
   cally; programming includes teacher
   workshops; areas include Asia, Central
   America, Western Europe, North
   America, and South America.)

National Science Foundation
1800 G Street, NW
Washington, DC 20550
Tel. 202/653-5862
(NSF has programs which cooperate with
   foreign governments and institutions and
   support international research. Write for
   the *Guide to Programs* for the current year
   and to be put on the mailing list.)

Partners of the Americas
1424 K St., NW

Suite 700
Washington, DC 20005
Tel. 202/628-3300
Fax. 202/628-3306
(Partners, provides fellowships, seed
   grants, and travel grants; focus is on
   Caribbean and Central, South and North
   America.)

The Phelps-Stokes Fund
10 East 87th St.
New York, NY 10128
Tel. 212/427-8100
Fax. 212/876-6278
(The Fund administers a small academic
   exchange program with sub-Saharan
   Africa and South Africa.)

Social Science Research Council
605 Third Avenue
New York, NY 10016
(SSRC sponsors several foreign area
   fellowship and grant programs in
   cooperation with the American Council
   of Learned Societies.)

**United States Information Agency
Teacher Exchange Branch**
Office of Academic Programs
301 4th Street, SW
Washington, DC 20547
Tel. 202/619-4555
(USIA sponsors the U.S. Fulbright pro-
   grams, some visiting scholars programs
   and other academic speciality, profes-
   sional and cultural exchanges.)

United States Peace Corps
1990 K Street, NW
Washington, DC 20526
Tel. 212/876-6278
(Peace Corps places American professors in
   universities, teacher-training colleges,
   and in other exchange programs in
   developing countries.)

Guides and Additional Resources for University and College Teaching Exchanges

Intercultural Press
P.O. Box 700
Yarmouth, ME 04096
Tel. 207/846-5168
Fax. 207/846-5181
(The Intercultural Press quarterly catalogue offers the largest collection available of material on cross-cultural exchanges and international living.)

International Exchange Locator.
A guide to more than 600 organizations and government agencies responsible for exchanges involving more than 100,000 U.S. and foreign nationals annually. Order from: Institute for International Education or the Liaison Group for International Educational Exchange (see previous addresses), $25.

Midwest Universities Consortium for International Activities (MUCIA)
134 Derby Hall
154 North Oval Mall
Columbus, Ohio 43210
614/292-2755
(The consortium of Universities of Minnesota, Wisconsin, Iowa, Indiana, Illinois, Michigan State, Ohio State, and Purdue has participated in university development and training programs in Indonesia, Malaysia, Bangladesh, Burma, Nepal, Ethiopia, Somalia, Peru, and Thailand and provides many exchange opportunities for affiliated faculties.)

University of Maryland's University College
University Boulevard at Adelphi Road College Park, MD 20742-1642
(Maryland provides one-year renewable appointments in the Department of Defense and undergraduate college

programs overseas in *Europe*: Azores, Belgium, Greece, Iceland, Italy, the Netherlands, Portugal, Spain, Turkey, United Kingdom, Germany, and *Asia*: Australia, Diego Garcia, Guam, Japan, Kwajalein, the Philippines, and South Korea in more than twenty disciplines.)

Guides to work, study and academic travel abroad.
Guides are available from the Council for International Educational Exchange (see CIEE's address).

Money for International Exchange in the Arts.
A 1992 resource guide for U.S. artists and arts specialists. Order from the American Council for the Arts or the Institute for International Education (see previous address), $14.95.

Financial Resources for International Study.
This guide provides information on grants, fellowships, and sources of research support for academics and professionals planning academic sojourns abroad. Order from: Institute for International Education (see previous address), $36.95.

Education International Congress
This 1993-born organization sponsored by the National Education Association has plans for higher education exchanges. Stay posted through: NEA, 1201 Sixteenth St., NW Washington, DC 20036-3290.

Grants and Awards Available to American Writers.
This comprehensive list includes grants for international work. Available from PEN, American Center Publication, 47 Fifth Avenue, New York, NY 10003.

Language learning and international studies resources.

Coalition for the Advancement of Foreign Languages and International Studies (CAFLIS)
1 Dupont Circle, Suite 710
Washington, D.C. 20036
202/778-0819
(CAFLIS can put you in touch with organizations sponsoring language and areas studies, summer institutes, intensive immersion programs, etc.)

International House Exchange Program
Faculty Exchange Center
952 Virginia Avenue
Lancaster, PA 17603
717/393-1130 or 1/800/572-0760
(Provides a directory of international program participants seeking to exchange housing.)

Survival guides for living abroad.
There are many guides for managing daily and university life overseas with all degrees of usefulness and datedness. Three good general ones include the classic *Survival Kit for Overseas Living* (Kohl, 1994), *Women's Guide to Overseas Living* (Piet-Pelon and Hornby, 1992), and *Moving Your Family Overseas* (Kalb and Welch, 1992). They deal with culture shock, managing food and shelter, making friends, working effectively with the hosts and reentry. Available from Intercultural Press (see previous address).

The Experiment in International Living
P.O. Box 676
Kipling Rd.
Brattleboro, VT 05302-0676
Tel. 802/257-7751
Fax. 802/254-6674

APPENDIX B

RESOURCES FOR FACULTY EXCHANGES
BY REGION

AFRICA

African-American Institute
833 United Nations Plaza
New York, NY 10017
Tel. 212/949-5666
Fax. 212/286-9493
(Offers scholarships/fellowships for post-
    secondary faculty and working profes-
    sionals; primary focus in African devel-
    opment.)

The Phelps-Stokes Fund
10 East 87th St.
New York, NY 10128
Tel. 212/427-8100
Fax. 212/876-6278
(The fund administers a small academic
    exchange program with sub-Saharan
    Africa and South Africa.)

The African Studies Association
255 Kinsey Hall
University of California at Los Angeles
Los Angeles, CA 90024
(Awards available for academics in a
    variety of disciplines to research African
    issues are announced in its *Directory of
    Financial Aid in Higher Education*.)

John Gay's books on West Africa
Red Dust on Green Leaves and *The Brighten-
    ing Shadow* are good resources for the
    sojourner to West Africa. The story of the
    Kpelle of Liberia is told from the perspec-
    tives of two brothers—one traditional way,
    one Western way. Available from Intercul-
    tural Press (see appendix A).

MIDDLE EAST

**American-Mideast Educational and
Training Services (AMIDEAST)**
1100 17th St., NW
Suite 300
Washington, DC 20036-4601
Tel. 202/785-0022
Fax. 202/822-6563
(AMIDEAST is a clearinghouse for infor-
    mation and resources on the Arab world,
    including North Africa and the Middle
    East. They administer the Cyprus-
    America and Royal Palace of Jordan
    Scholarship Programs.)

Intercultural Press's Interact Series,
on *Understanding Arabs* (Nydell, 1987) is a
    good examination of Arab beliefs,
    values, and social practices, and pro-
    vides background information on each of
    the twenty Arab countries. From IP (see
    appendix A), $15.95.

EAST ASIA AND THE PACIFIC

Asian Cultural Council
280 Madison Ave.
New York, NY 10016
Tel. 212/684-5450
Fax. 212/684-8075
(Offers scholarships/fellowships for
    academic exchange and research to post-
    secondary faculty and artists; provides
    some travel grants.)

Council for International Eductional Exchange (CIEE)—Asia
205 East 42nd Street
New York, NY 10017
Tel. 212/661-1414
Fax. 212/972-3231
(CIEE has a small professional and faculty development program; Asian centers include Hong Kong, Kyoto, and Tokyo.)

Grants for University Research in Australia
Prepared by the Graduate Careers Council of Australia and available from the Australian Studies Association of North America (see appendix D for address).

Southeast Asia Summer Studies Institute (SEASSI)
% Southeast Asia Program
120 Uris Hall
Cornell University
Ithaca, New York, 14853
607/255-2378
(A consortium of universities which trains scholars in Southeast Asian languages in the summer sponsored by the United States Information Agency. The institute rotates biannually between Michigan, Cornell, Hawaii, Northern Illinois, and Washington; languages usually include Thai, Tagalog, Indonesian, Vietnamese, etc.)

International Research and Exchanges Board—Mongolian Program
126 Alexander St.
Princeton, NJ 08540-9500
Tel. 609/683-9500
Fax. 609/683-1511
(Offers scholarships and travel grants. Has a specific Mongolian program.)

National Committee on U.S.–China Relations
777 United Nations Plaza
New York, NY 10017
Tel. 212/922-1385

Fax. 212/557-8258
(Administers exchange programs for faculty and professionals; focused on the PRC; the Committee publishes, *China Exchange News,* one of the best newsletters on exchanges.)

National Science Foundation's Japan Program
1800 G St., NW
Washington, DC 20550
202/653-5862
(NSF seeks applications for international research in the sciences and engineering.)

Council for the International Exchange of Scholars (CIES)
Indo-American Fellowships (see CIES address in appendix A); Tel. 202/202-686-7877 and Fax. 202/362-3442.

Intercultural Press' Interacts are a series of guides for working successfully abroad. Some of the series include:
- *Encountering the Chinese* (Wenzhong & Grove, 1991)
- *With Respect to the Japanese* (Condon, 1984)
- *A Fair Go for All: Australia* (Renwick, Smart & Henderson, 1991)
- *A Common Core: Thais and Americans* (Fieg, 1989)
- *Considering Filipinos* (Gochenour, 1990)
- *Subject: India* (Ladd, 1990)

WESTERN AND EASTERN EUROPE

Fellowship guide for Western Europe
Description of resources available for post-doctoral work and research in Western Europe. Available from the Council for European Studies (see appendix A).

American-Scandinavian Foundation (ASF)
725 Park Avenue
New York, NY 10021
Tel. 212/879-9779

Fax. 212/249-3444
(Grants to individuals and institutions;
some short-term programs; source for
Scandinavian Review and *Scan
Newsletter.*)

An Authoritative Guide to European Language Learning

Information about 600 organizations
offering European language courses in
twenty-five nations. Order from IIE (see
appendix A), $22.95.

European Studies Newsletter provides
announcements of fellowships related to
European study and research. Available
from the Council for European Studies,
1404 International Affairs Bldg., Columbia University, New York, NY 10101.

Community Colleges for International Development

1519 Clearlake Rd.
Cocoa, FL 32922
Tel. 407/3784
Fax. 407/639-0078
(Affiliated witha technical colleges and
universities in Hungary, Slovakia, the
Czech Republic, Romania, and Bulgaria.)

Professional Development Fellowships to East Central Europe

Fellowships for U.S. researchers in profes-
sional, policy, and public administration
related fields are available to Bulgaria,
Slovakia, the Czech Republic, Hungary,
Poland, Romania, Hungary, Poland, and
Romania from the Institute of International
Education (see address in appendix A).

Where Walls Once Stood

A guide to more than 300-U.S.-East Central
Europe programs and linkages. Orders
from the Institute of International
Education (see appendix A).

Council for International Educational Exchange (CIEE)—Europe

205 East 42nd Street

New York, NY 10017
Tel. 212/661-1414
Fax. 212/972-3231
(CIEE has a small professional and faculty
development program; major overseas
centers include London, Paris, Rome,
Madrid, and Bonn.)

International Research and Exchanges Board–Eastern European Program

126 Alexander St.
Princeton, NJ 08540-7102
Tel. 609/683-9500
Fax. 609/683-1511
(Offers scholarships and travel grants;
has field offices in Romania and
Moscow.)

**Council for the International Exchange of
Scholars (CIES)** for East European
Initiatives Lectureships (see CIES
address in appendix A); Tel. 202/686-
7877. Fax. 202/362-3442

The Underground Guide to University Study in Britain and Ireland

This guide, though not aimed at professors,
contains relevant academic information,
i.e., on university life, academic procedures, housing, etc. Available from
Intercultural Press (see appendix A),
1992, $14.95.

Intercultural Press's Interacts Series on Europe

This series includes *From Nyet to Da:
Understanding Russians* (Richmond,
1992), *Spain is Different* (Ames, 1992);
and *Understanding Cultural Difference:
Germans, French and Americans* (Hall &
Hall, 1989). These texts examine topics of
European cultural characteristics and
techniques for Europeans effectively on a
professional and personal level. Available from Intercultural Press (see appendix A).

LATIN AMERICA AND THE CARIBBEAN

Partners of the Americas

1424 K St., NW
Suite 700
Washington, DC 20005
Tel. 202/628-3300
Fax. 202/628-3306
(Partners provides fellowships, seed grants, and travel grants; focus is on Caribbean and Central, South and North Americas.)

Center for Latin American Studies at the University of Pittsburgh

This center is a fount of information on resources for U.S. faculty who want to teach in Latin America. For their free *Guide to Financial Aid*, write to the Center, % 4E04 Forbes Quad, University of Pittsburgh, Pittsburgh, PA 15260.

Intercultural Press's Interacts Series on latin American

This series provides a guide for Americans, *Living in Colombia* (Hutchison, 1987), and two guides for working in Mexico, *Good Neighbors: Communicating with Mexicans* (Condon, 1985) and *Management in Two Cultures: Bridging the Gap between U.S. and Mexico* (Kras, 1989). Available from IP (see appendix A).

APPENDIX C

RESOURCES FOR ADVISING FOREIGN STUDENTS ON STUDY IN THE UNITED STATES

A Selected List of Fellowship Opportunities and Aids to Advanced Education for United States Citizens and Foreign Nationals.
National Science Foundation
1800 G St., NW
Washington, DC 20550
202/653-5862

Financial Planning for Study in the United States: A Guide for Students from Other Countries.
The College Board
Box 886
New York, NY 10101
(Detailed information on the costs of U.S. post-secondary education with sections on financial aid, applying for financial assistance, and the problems of currency restrictions and transfer of funds.)

List of Organizations that Accept Applications for Financial Support from Foreign Citizens Who Are Already in the United States.
National Association for Foreign Student Affairs
1860 19th Street
Washington D.C., NW 20090

Film and Video Resources for International Educational Exchange (Zeigler, 1992).
(A list of documentaries and films that describe the United States; good source of media for advising foreign students; available from NAFSA; see previous address.)

U.S. Taxation of International Students and Scholars: A Manual for Advisers and Administrators
(NAFSA, 1993)
(A guide to new taxation issues for international students and scholars; $95). Other foreign student finances papers from NAFSA include *The Risks and Realities of Health Insurance* (free) and *Administration of Foreign Student Finances* ($6); see previous address.)

Guide to Graduate Study in Economics and Agriculture Economics in the United States of America and Canada
(Owen & Cross, 1989)
Economics Institute
University of Colorado
Boulder, CO
(Describes individual graduate programs and specifies whether financial assistance is available to foreign students. A separate section provides general information for foreign students entering U.S. graduate school.)

Costs at U.S. Educational Institutions
Institute of International Education
809 United Nations Plaza
New York, NY 10017
(Contains living costs, tuition and fees, and school calendars at U.S. institutions of higher education to assist in the financial planning for foreign students in the United States.)

English Language and Orientation Programs in the U.S.
(Describes 1,100 accredited intensive ESL programs and courses in U.S.; order from IIE; see previous address.)

Funding for U.S. Study: A Guide for Foreign Nationals (IIE, 1989)
(Grants and fellowships offered by U.S. and foreign governments, foundations, and associations; does not include awards given by U.S. universities and colleges. Order from IIE, see previous address.)

The Handbook of Foreign Student Advising (Alten, 1993) and **Guide to International Education in the U.S.**
(Hoopes & Hoopes, 1990)
Intercultural Press
PO Box 700
Yarmouth, ME 04096
Tel. 207/846-5168
Fax. 207/846-5181

APPENDIX D

RESOURCES FOR AFFILIATIONS AND LINKAGES
UPON REENTRY TO THE UNITED STATES

Resources for Affiliation with Academic Communities Interested in International Exchanges and Issues

(Many of these organizations can be joined as single members or institutions. Most provide newsletters, publications, and sources of continued affiliation with your host country or region.)

African-American Institute
833 United Nations Plaza
New York, NY 10017
Tel. 212/949-5666
Fax. 212/286-9493

The African Studies Association
255 Kinsey Hall
University of California at Los Angeles
Los Angeles, CA 90024

American Association for the Advancement of Slavic Studies
% History Department
Stanford University
Stanford, CA 94305

Association of Asian Studies
One Lane Hall
University of Michigan
Ann Arbor, MI 48109
313/665-2490

Association of Caribbean Studies
PO Box 22202
Lexington, KY 40522

Australian Studies Association of North America (ASANA)
1601 Massachusetts Avenue NW
Washington, DC 20036-2273
Tel. 202/797-3253
Fax. 202/797-3049

Caribbean Association of Professionals and Scholars
617 Kennedy St., NW
Washington, D.C. 20011

Council for European Studies
1404 International Affairs Bldg., Columbia University
New York, NY 10101
(Source of the *European Studies Newsletter.*)

Committee on Scholarly Communication with China (CSCC)
1055 Thomas Jefferson St., NW
Suite 2013
Washington, DC 20007
202/337-1250

Comparative and International Education Society
% Center for International Studies
Oxley Hall
1712 Neil Avenue
Columbus, Ohio 43210
(The Society's conferences and publication, *Comparative Education Review,* are good sources of information on exchange and higher education issues world-wide.)

Council for the International Exchange of Scholars (CIES)
3007 Tilden Street, NW, Suite 5M
Washington, DC 20008-3009
Tel. 202/686-4000
Fax. 202/362-3442
(Write to be put on a mailing list for information on international opportunities; share these with colleagues university-wide.)

East-West Center
University of Hawaii–Manoa
1777 East-West Road
Honolulu, HI 96848
Tel. 808/944-7610
Fax. 808/944-7670
(The East-West Center supports many short-term symposia, courses, and conferences on internationalization, as well as Asia and the Pacific-focused meetings across disciplines.)

European Community Studies Association
Department of History
East Hall
Tufts University
Medford, MA 02155
Tel. 617/627-3979
Fax. 617/627-3478

Fulbright Alumni Association
1307 New Hampshire Ave., NW
Washington, DC 20036
(The FAA holds annual conferences on international issues and publishes a directory of former U.S. Fulbrighters.)

Intercultural Press
PO Box 700
Yarmouth, ME 04096
Tel. 207/846-5168
Fax. 207/846-5181
(IP is an excellent source of materials on culture and area studies; write to be put on the mailing list for quarterly catalogues.)

Intercultural Communication Institute
8835 SW Canyon Lane, Suite 238
Portland, OR 97225
Tel. 503/297-4622
Fax. 503/297-4695
(To keep current with intercultural skills, write for the Institute's summer institute catalogue.)

Latin American Scholarship Program of American Universities, Inc.
25 Mt. Auburn St.
Cambridge, MA 02138
Tel. 617/495-5255
Fax. 617/495-8990
(This consortium administers some faculty development programs focused on the Caribbean, Central America, Mexico, and South America.)

Latin American Studies Association
William Pitt Union, 9th Floor
University of Pittsburgh, PA 15260
412/648-7929

Middle East Studies Association of Department of Oriental Studies
University of Arizona
Tucson, AZ 85721

National Association for Foreign Student Affairs
1860 19th Street
(If your institution is already a member of NAFSA, you may be able to receive their materials and publications.)

National Committee on U.S.–China Relations
777 United Nations Plaza
New York, NY 10017
Tel. 212/922-1385
Fax. 212/557-8258

National Council of Returned Peace Corps Volunteers
1900 K Street, NW
Washington, DC 20526
Tel. 212/876-6278

(For alumni of Peace Corps, there are RPCV organizations for every country and region and an active alumni group in almost every state.)

National Council for Soviet and East European Research
1755 Massachusetts Ave., NW
Suite 304
Washington, DC 20036
202/387-0168

Partners of the Americas
1424 K St., NW
Suite 700
Washington, DC 20005
Tel. 202/628-3300
Fax. 202/628-3306

Society for the Advancement of Scandinavian Study
Department of Germanic Languages
University of Texas
Austin, TX 78712-1190
Fax. 512/471-4025

Resources for Building Institutional Linkages

Some U.S. Professional Organizations Which Suppport Foreign National Scholars to the United States

The American Mathematical Society
PO Box 1571, Annex Station
Providence, RI 02904

American Library Association
4 50 E. Huron St.
Chicago, IL 60611

Association for Computing Machinery
PO Box 64145
Baltimore, MD 21264
(Has a good guide to graduate assistantships in computer science.)

**Amazon Basin Scholarship Program.
Latin American Scholarship Program of**

American Universities
25 Mount Auburn Street
Cambridge, MA 02138
Tel. (617) 495-5255
(Brings scholars from universities in six Amazonian countries to the United States each year to study environmental issues. Specialists in public policy and in the natural and social sciences, the scholars work on multidisciplinary approaches to development in the Amazon region.)

Central American Program of Undergraduate Scholarship (CAMPUS)
Latin American Scholarship Program of American Universities
25 Mount Auburn Street
Cambridge, MA 02138: (617) 495-5255.
(Brings promising students from Central American to U.S. colleges and universities. The program was designed to provide educational opportunities to students with limited financial means and to help them develop the professional expertise needed in Central American countries.)

Edmund S. Muskie Fellowship Program
(formerly known as the Benjamin Franklin Program)
European Programs Branch
Office of Academic Programs
U.S. Information Agency
301 Fourth Street, S.W.
Washington 20547
Tel. (202) 205-0525
(Brings about 150 graduate students from the republics of the former Soviet Union to the United States to study business administration, economics, law, and public administration.)

Foreign Student Program for the Middle East and North Africa
American-Mideast Educational and Train-

ing Services Inc.
100 17th Street, N.W.
Washington 20036
Tel. (202) 785-0022.
(Brings about 100 graduate students from ten Middle Eastern and North African countries to U.S. institutions each year for advanced-degree programs and research.)

Fulbright-LASPAU Faculty Development Program.
Latin American Scholarship Program of American Universities
25 Mount Auburn Street
Cambridge, MA 02138
Tel. (617) 495-5255
(Brings about 150 junior faculty members from nine Latin American countries to the United States each year to study, mostly for master's degrees.)

Graduate Student Program
Institute of International Education,
809 United Nations Plaza
New York, NY 10017
Tel. (212) 205-0525.
(Provides fellowships for nearly 600 U.S. graduate students, young professionals, and artists to study and conduct research in about 100 countries. Each year about 1,200 foreign students come to the United States under the program.)

Hubert H. Humphrey Fellowship Program
Institute of International Education
1400 K Street, N.W.
Washington, DC 20005
Tel. (202) 898-0600
(Brings 140 mid-career professionals in public service from seventy-five developing countries to the United States for a year of university study and work experience in agriculture, public health, public administration, planning, and resource management.)

President's University Student Exchange.
European Programs Branch
Office of Academic Programs
U.S. Information Agency
301 Fourth Street, S.W.
Washington, DC 20547
Tel. (202) 205-0525.
(This program brings about 1,000 undergraduate and graduate students [mostly agriculture majors] from the republics of the former Soviet Union to the United States and will send 1,000 American students to the republics by the academic year 1995–96. Grants are made to U.S. institutions.)

Samantha Smith Memorial Exchange
European Programs Branch
Office of Academic Programs
U.S. Information Agency
301 Fourth Street, S.W.
Washington, DC 20547
Tel. (202) 205-0525
(Makes grants to higher-education institutions that have agreements for undergraduate-student exchanges with universities in Eastern Europe and the republics of the former Soviet Union.)

Teacher Exchange Program.
Teacher Exchange Branch
U.S. Information Agency
301 Fourth Street, S.W.
Washington, DC 20547
Tel. (202) 619-4556
(Provides opportunities for about 250 American school personnel to exchange positions for a year with their counterparts in about thirty-five foreign countries.)

University Affiliations Program
Advising, Teaching and Specialized Programs Division
U.S. Information Agency
301 Fourth Street, S.W.

Washington, DC 20547
Tel. (202) 619-5289.
(Make three-year grants to partnerships
  formed by higher-education institutions
  in the United States and abroad to
  conduct exchanges for faculty members
  in the humanities, social sciences,
  communications, and education.)

Some Foreign National Foundations and
Organizations Which Support U.S. and
Foreign Institutional Linkages

The Japan Foundation
600 New Hampshire Ave., NW
Suite 570
Washington, DC 20037

Goethe Institute and the **German Marshall**
Foundation
1607 New Hampshire, NW
4th Floor
Washington, D.C.
Tel. 202/319-0702

Netherlands Universities Foundation for
International Cooperation
Badhuisweg 251
PO Box 90734
The Netherlands

Swedish Institute
PO Box 7434
S-103 91 Stockholm, Sweden

American-Scandinavian Foundation
725 Park Avenue
New York, NY 10021
Tel. 212/879-9779
Fax. 212/249-3444

Center for Hong Kong American Educa-
cational Exchange
Chinese University of Hong Kong
Library Annex
Shatin, N.T., Hong Kong

Taiwan Foundation for Scholarly
Hsing North Road No. 365

2nd Floor
Taipei 105, Taiwan

Inter-American Foundation Fellowship
Program
Department 555, 10th Floor
901 North Stuart St.
Arlington, VA 22203
(Source of support for academic linkages
  with and scholars from Latin America
  and Caribbean areas.)

Linkage and Scholarship Resources for
Commonwealth Faculty and Postgraduate
Students.

British Council
10 Spring Gardens
London SW1A 28N, England

Association of Commonwealth
Universities
John Foster House
36 Gordon Square
London WC1H OPF, England

The Graduate Careers Council of Australia
PO Box 28
Parkville, Victoria 3052
Australia
Fax. 82-2-794-2889

Other U.S. Programs Which Support
Institutional Linkages

American-Mideast Educational and
Training Services (AMIDEAST)
1100 17th St., NW
Suite 300
Washington, DC 20036-4601
Tel. 202/785-0022
Fax. 202/822-6563
(AMIDEAST brings about one-hundred
  Middle Eastern and North African post-
  graduates to the U.S. for advanced
  degrees.)

Educational Commission for Foreign Medical Graduates
3642 Market Street
Philadelphia, PA 19104-2685
Tel. 215/386-5900
Fax. 215/387-9963
(Sources of sponsorship and support for linkages involving foreign professors and graduate students in medical studies.)

Center for International Education
Office of Post Secondary Education
U.S. Dept. of Post Secondary Education
Washington, DC 20202
202/708-7283
(Source of support for institutional linkages and summer institutes with former hosts and current colleagues.)

Institute of International Education (IIE)
809 United Nations Plaza
New York, NY 10017-3580
Tel. 212/883-8200
Fax. 212/984-5452 or 5358
(IIE's Fulbright Junior Scholars program is a source of support for graduate students to do international research.)

Hubert Humphrey Fellowship Program
1400 K St., NW
Suite 650
202/898-0600
(This program provides support to more than one-hundred foreign mid-career professionals in business, economics, law and public administration for year-long professional development in the U.S. While more an individual than institutional affiliation, internship placements attached to the program offer some flexibility.)

University Affiliations Program
United States Information Agency
301 4th St. SW
Washington, DC 20547
Tel. 202/619-5289

(A resource for linkages is in the form of one-time, three-year institutional seed-grants for faculty exchanges in the humanities, communications, social sciences, and education between U.S. and foreign colleges.)

Scholar-In-Residence Program
Council for the International Exchange of Scholars
3007 Tilden Street, NW, Suite 5M
Washington, DC 20008-3009
Tel. 202/686-4000
Fax. 202/362-3442
(Linkages to U.S. colleges [or groups of institutions] to host a visiting lecturer from abroad are available. The purpose of the program is to develop international programs by internationalizing the curriculum, promoting global or area studies or otherwise expanding contacts of students and faculty with other cultures.)

United States Coalition for Education for All (USCEFA)
1616 N. Fort Myer Drive, Suite 1100
Arlington, VA 22209
(Newly chartered in 1993 and affiliated with the National Education Association [NEA], USCEFA provides access to international referral services, institutional linkages, and international exchange programs.)

Miscellaneous Linkage Resources

International Student Exchange Program (ISEP)
1242 35th St., NW
Washington, DC 20057
Tel. 202/687-6956
Fax. 202/687-7041
(ISEP and its member institutions help build direct person-to-person exchanges; check to see if your institution is a member.)

The Experiment in International Living
P.O. Box 676
Kipling Rd.
Brattleboro, VT 05302-0676
Tel. 802/257-7751
Fax. 802/254-6674
(The Experiment focuses on study abroad
exchanges, but has some short-term
professional opportunities.)

Intercultural Resource Corporation
78 Greylock Road
Newton, MA 02160
Tel. 617/965-8651
Fax. 617/969-7347
(IRC produces videos which explore issues
of the intercultural classroom especially
in the United States. Professors wishing
to build capacities in themselves and
their students to deal with diversity and
multiculturalism will find these resources useful.)

INDEX